Antique Brass Wind Instruments

Identification and Value Guide

Peter H. Adams

4880 Lower Valley Road, Atglen, PA 19310 USA

ACKNOWLEDGMENT

I wish to thank the following people for helping me put together this book. Prof. Lloyd Farrar, co-editor of the *New Langwill Index*, provided copies of the Martin Brothers' catalog, the Distin fragments, the Pepper catalog, a Lehnert fragment, information about makers that did not appear in *The New Langwill Index*, and the artwork that appears on the cover of this book. Dr. Al Rice, head of the Fiske Collection of Musical Instruments, provided a copy of the D.C. Hall catalog, and other information that proved invaluable. He also read the manuscript of this book. Steve Dillon (dealer in antique brass instruments) provided many of the prices in Appendix C, and deserves a special thanks for doing this. Robb Stewart (repairer of antique brass instruments) answered some of the more technical questions about instruments and their construction. Sandy Craig (dealer in used and old musical instruments) provided insight into collecting instruments for use by musicians, read the manuscript of this book, and generally held my hand while this book was prepared. Peter Schiffer of Schiffer Publishing Ltd. was willing to publish this book. Were it not for his insight and the patience of his staff, this book would not have been possible.

I most wish to thank the Library of Congress, Music Division, and its overworked staff. The Library owns copies of the musical instrument trade catalogs that appear in this book: the Boston catalog of 1874, the Foote catalog, the Lyon & Healy catalog, the Slater catalog, and the Stratton catalog.

Special thanks go to the following staff people at the Library of Congress, Music Division. Elizabeth Auman, head of Special Collections, let me index the Library's holdings of musical instrument trade catalogs, both on the general shelves and in the Dayton C. Miller Flute Collection. William Parsons, music reference librarian, assisted in locating valuable related material. Robert Sheldon, curator of the D.C. Miller Collection, allowed me to run around under foot, examining Miller's countless files.

I also very much wish to thank The Winterthur Library for providing a photocopy of the Boston Musical Instrument Manufactory catalog of 1869, and the Fiske catalog of 1868. Catalogs this early are exceedingly rare, and are some of the earliest catalogs in this book.

Finally, thank you to everyone who has in some way or another helped me to complete this book, especially the members of the American Musical Instrument Society for additional help over the years. I hope that, with the help of friends, any errors in this book will be minor ones. All such errors are purely unintentional, but inevitable.

Published by Schiffer Publishing Ltd.
4880 Lower Valley Road
Atglen, PA 19310
Phone: (610) 593-1777
FAX: (610) 593-2002
E-mail: Schifferbk@aol.com
Please write for a free catalog.
This book may be purchased from the publisher.
Please include $3.95 postage.
Try your bookstore first.

Contents

Preface

The purpose of this book is to assist people not familiar with brass-wind instruments in identifying most of the common instrument types constructed before 1921 (and a few unusual types), designed for the American market (both U.S. and Canada). To that end, this book contains illustrations of brass instruments taken mainly from the following musical instrument trade catalogs: The Boston Musical Instrument Manufactory Company's *Catalog of 1869*; the Boston Musical Manufactory Company's *Catalog of 1874*; an undated fragment from a Boston Musical Instrument Manufactory Company's catalog; Isaac Fiske's *Illustrated Catalog of Musical Instruments* of 1868; Isaac Fiske's *Illustrated Catalog of Musical Instruments* of 1881; J. Howard Foote's *Catalog of 1893*; Martin Brothers' *Catalog* of 1879; M. Slater's *Catalog* of 1874; Stratton's *Catalog* of circa 1889; fragmentary catalogs of uncertain years featuring Henry Distin's instruments; and a fragment of a J.W. Pepper catalog from circa 1904. All these illustrations form the body of this book, and in most cases are clearer than photographs of musical instruments. Sadly, many prominent U.S. manufacturers could not be included in this book, most notably C.G. Conn.

About twenty years ago, the interest in collecting brass wind instruments (or simply brass instruments) increased, along with prices. At the time, one could find an adequate keyed bugle for about $150, dating from before ca. 1860. Today, that same instrument might sell for $1,500. The early instruments, however, are becoming harder to find. Collectors are now turning to acquiring instruments made quite recently. So, collecting brass instruments will no doubt continue to evolve. As with all collectibles, the unusual item will command the most interest.

As not every brass instrument of the time appeared in trade catalogs, some instruments will not appear in this book. To assist in identifying some of the more unusual instruments, a few pages of rare instruments have been included to illustrate the fact that manufacturers were always experimenting to either solve a problem of physics, or create a novelty instrument that would hopefully sell well. Many of these novelty instruments were offered for only a short while, are exceptionally difficult to fully document, and are usually the rarest and most valuable of recent brass instruments.

Trade catalogs, as will be discussed below, provide a wealth of information. Yet, they are also fraught with problems. They were never uniform with regards to names of instruments. Today, we might expect a bass horn to be described as a tuba. However, the term tuba was not used by many makers of the time. Others used it for instruments pitched in only a certain key. To overcome this minor problem, instruments are described in this book as Bass horn in B flat, E flat, etc. Instruments identified as Bass horn in BB flat are contra bass horns.

This book is also designed for the instrument collector. The musician's intent upon buying an antique brass instrument to play will have different needs than a collector who might be interested in a research question that does not require that the instrument be in playing condition. In fact, the earliest of the valved brass instruments are rarely well made by today's standards, are usually in poor condition today, and are often quite rare. Even so, an instrument that requires little repairs will tend to sell for more than the same instrument in poor condition. Furthermore, an instrument with a missing valve cluster will often sell for very little.

This book is limited to brass wind instruments constructed between 1869 and 1920. 1869 is the date of the earliest trade catalog that could be located for a U.S. manufacturer of brass musical instruments. Earlier catalogs surely existed (especially for European companies) and await discovery. Instruments constructed prior to 1860 exist that clearly show that this date has absolutely no significance to brass instrument history. The date of circa 1830 is more important. This is the era when valves were invented and began to appear on brass instruments. With their invention, numerous brass instrument types came into existence. However, documenting the first thirty years of the use of valves on brass instruments is quite beyond the scope of this book, and such instruments are exceptionally rare.

The date of 1920 is more significant for collecting brass instruments. As is discussed in Chapter 1, standardization of musical pitch at this time made many musical instruments obsolete. This fact helps to date instruments, and is therefore used as a terminus for this book.

Prices found throughout this book are in U.S. dollars, for instruments needing no significant repairs, unless otherwise stated. Some trade catalogs did not include prices. Instead, a sheet was probably inserted in the catalog, eliminating the need to republish catalogs when prices changed. Such lists rarely survive. One suspects that a separate sheet was inserted for the foreign markets.

Brass wind instruments have existed for at least 2,500 years. Yet, only brass instruments constructed within the last 150 years are likely to be encountered in the U.S. For this reason, and others, musical instrument trade catalogs have been used as the basis of this book. Through this relatively rare resource, musical instruments can be identified, and valued (relatively). Musical instrument trade catalogs even have value in their own right, especially those catalogs printed before 1900, even if they exist only as a fragment.

Musical instrument trade catalogs, however, are not a totally reliable source of information. Often, these catalogs contain misleading information that today would be construed as fraudulent advertising. Litigation resulting from these fraudulent activities still govern current retail practices. Thus, the gross mistakes in the musical instrument trade has non-musical benefits we still enjoy.

Musical instrument trade catalogs often included catalog numbers. These numbers should never be confused with model numbers (or names), or serial numbers. Catalog numbers surely do not appear on musical instruments. Serial numbers did not come into popular use until the end of the 19th century, possibly with the invention of assembly-line construction techniques, and the increasing use of subcontractors (often called jobbers). The beginning date for the use of model numbers and names is equally uncertain. Sadly, almost every specialist agrees today that comprehensive lists of model numbers for companies will be quite impossible. The needed information was not kept. Creating such lists is an on-going effort of many musical instrument researchers. Currently, some lists do exist, but for pre-1900 instruments, such lists are thought too flawed to either date or value instruments. Some of these lists can be had from musical instrument museums, and a few lists have appeared on the Internet.

Most trade catalogs were printed on high-acid paper, and have since disintegrated. Therefore, only photocopies exist for many important catalogs. Because of this sad fact, some of the illustrations found in this book will be less clear than others, especially the J. Howard Foote catalog. Every effort has been made to correct, or otherwise clean up the artwork by digitizing and manually editing the images using computer software. Yet, some artwork was just too faint to even redraw. Subjective lines have been cautiously included with broken lines, such as in the illustration of the Foote instrument number 5023, where the valve cluster simply did not exist in the photocopy. Without the actual instruments in hand, omission, and errors will surely appear here. Fine details found here must be viewed with care. Also, some engravings simply were more complete or precise than other engravings. The illustrations found in the Lyon & Healy catalog required almost no retouching, and are a marvel of engraving.

Musical instrument trade catalogs provide a wealth of information. However, they rarely provide information about how popular, or how well all instruments sold. Many catalogs contain information directing potential buyers to instruments in the catalog. Often, these enticements failed to sell instruments. E flat cornets are such an example. These instruments are often sought by some collectors today, and despised by others. E flat cornets are more difficult to play than B flat cornets, and were therefore not as popular as the B flat model. Large instruments also sold poorly, as a band would often need more cornets than basses. Rarely is such sales information found in trade catalogs. Though some manufacturers did include this information in their catalogs. See Chapters 2 and 3 for more information about rarity, and value. When found, such information was transcribed from the catalogs.

Prices of instruments in the trade catalogs were not always accurate. Trade catalogs also retained instruments that had since fallen out of favor, often at substantially reduced prices. Over the shoulder instruments (OTS) are the most notable example. After they fell out of favor, they were offered for as much as 50 per cent less than while they were popular. A final annoying fact about trade catalog prices, as repeatedly mentioned in *The Musical Courier*, is that published prices were often as much as twenty percent above the actual sales price of instruments.

As trade catalogs were often quite expensive to print, information (especially engraved artwork) was repeatedly reused between editions, and even within a catalog. Printing companies also provided engravings of stock instrument types. These engravings were then offered to a wide number of companies. What differences actually existed between these instruments cannot be determined from the trade catalogs.

The Musical Courier (and its ancillary publication *The American Musician and Art Journal*, which seems to have been devoted mainly to trade news for band instruments) is certainly an important resource for studying the history of music in the U.S. Other similar trade publications also existed. Of these, *The Music Trade Review* is mentioned as an important competitor to *The Musical Courier. Freund's Weekly* also reported trade developments. These, and some short-run serials contain a wealth of information for researchers, which has been little examined. Many of these serials are available on microfilm. Sadly, no indexes presently exist for these publications, though efforts are underway to generate such indices.

The structure of this book is straight forward. Chapter 1 provides some basic background information about the brass musical instrument manufacturing industry in the U.S. Chapter 2 discusses identifying brass instruments, using this book and other resources as guides. Chapter 3 discusses valuing brass instruments.

A few pages are provided following the chapters which depict common valve types, instrument types, and names of body parts. Next appear several pages showing some cornet body designs found throughout this book. These pages should be examined to learn the various designs, especially for cornets, and the terms that can be used to describe them. Next are several pages depicting some rare brass instrument types.

The book continues with artwork and relevant information taken from trade catalogs organized by catalog. These pages will help one learn to identify instrument types, and pitch if possible, and the valve design (or system). Identifying the instrument's pitch is sometimes difficult even for specialists. Identifying the maker is left for Chapter 2. All this information is essential when discussing any brass instrument.

The book contains several appendices. The first appendix is a list of addresses for museums and other resources that may provide information about instruments. These addresses should not change over time. Staff people are always greatly overworked. Reference librarians are always valuable in locating additional addresses.

The second appendix lists some important makers, manufacturers, and importers of brass instruments. This list contains a brief synopsis from The *New Langwill Index* (hereafter referred to as *NLI*). Each reference ends with information that will help determine the importance (and therefore approximate value) of an instrument.

The third appendix includes prices of antique brass instruments gathered from retail lists provided by dealers in old and antique instruments. Some books that discuss a wide range of collectibles include current market values (CMV's) for the most common brass instruments. Such books, for the most part, are completely ignored by brass collectors. Also, for rare antique musical instruments, no consensus about prices exists. Knowing that fact, this book cautiously offers prices, hoping that the prices are a fair approximation. Throughout this book, this fact will be repeated.

As an example of a pricing problem, one antique instrument might sell for the equivalent of $100 in London, $500 in New York, and $1,000 in California. The exact opposite is also possible. The reader should examine this book to see if the instrument in question is described as valuable or not. Currently, any antique brass wind instrument valued over $2,000, of an unusual type, containing an odd feature, or made before 1800 should be shown to an expert to determine a fair CMV. Experts can be located by writing to the museums found in Appendix A, and requesting a current list of experts in the reader's area (Please be advised that Museum staff are greatly overworked, so do not expect a quick response to letters). The Addendum also lists some appraisers. The American Society of Appraisers is another reasonable means for finding an appraiser of instruments. However, most of the experts in brass wind instruments are not members of this society. Most of them are members of The American Musical Instrument Society.

The majority of brass wind instruments constructed before 1920 available from general antique dealers rarely are worth more than several hundred dollars in excellent condition. Most sell for less than one hundred dollars. Instruments from companies such as C. G. Conn, Holton, York, and Olds are quite common, and with some significant exceptions, are seldom worth collecting. Even so, instruments bearing these names should be examined as potentially worth more than one hundred dollars. Some instruments sell for over one thousand dollars. Documenting these exceptions is still an ongoing process.

Instruments with special features often sell for more than ordinary instruments. Some of these special features include having been owned by an important person; having been used in an important event; having been engraved with special artistic work or information; or having been constructed with some special device. None of these features are reflected in the values found in this book. If an instrument does possess one or more of these features, consult an expert.

This book includes a glossary of terms. Readers not conversant with terms for brass instruments should examine the glossary. Without doing so, the reader will be at a distinct disadvantage in discussing brass instruments. The reader is also advised to examine the illustration of parts in this book, following the pages illustrating valve types.

Throughout the body of this book bell directions (and body designs) are given as either OTS, BF, BU, or HD. Some instruments require no designation of bell direction. OTS means over-the-shoulder, as the bell of the instrument rests upon the performer's shoulder, and the bell points backwards. BF means the bell points forward. Though virtually all cornets have bells pointing forward, some cornets are made in a circular shape, suggestive of a helicon pattern (HD). Other cornets have bells pointing backwards (OTS). So, the determination is needed here. BU means the bell points up, as occurs with most, but not all lower pitched brass instruments. HD (helicon model) means that the tubing forming the body outlines a circle, and the bell points up and away from the side of the musician. French horns, and ballad horns require no designation of bell direction, as they always point downwards and to the right side of the musician. Trombones in this book always have bells that point forward. However, trombones have been made with bells pointing in other directions, even OTS. No designation for valve types or bell direction are given for bugles, post horns, and the like.

This book concludes with a bibliography of reference books. Citations for this bibliography were taken from a number of sources, including the Library of Congress' on-line computer catalog, and the OCLC on-line catalog. Because of the different formats used in these data bases, the citations in the bibliography will not always be complete. Citations for books found at the Library of Congress conclude with the Library of Congress call number, needed to retrieve a book. OCLC citations end with an OCLC record number, which can be used to quickly recall this record to locate holdings, assuming that the number has not been changed. For those who have never used OCLC, an experienced reference librarian will prove essential.

As the structure of this book is straight forward, no index is provided. One might wish to have an index if only to find all examples of B flat cornets. However, such an index would be all but pointless, as virtually every company issued the same types of instruments. Rare instrument types are therefore left for the reader to discover throughout this book.

A number of reference books will also be of assistance in identifying instruments, and providing other valuable information. The *NLI*, and *The New Grove Dictionary of Music and Musicians* (NGDMM) are standard reference books in the field. The *New Grove Dictionary of Musical Instruments* is also recommended. These two works are useful in explaining the various shapes, sizes, and names of brass instruments from a European perspective. A third dictionary is also suggested here, being the *New Grove Dictionary of American Music*. Anthony Baines' *Brass Instruments, Their History and Development* is also of great value in concisely discussing some of the truly rare and early brass instrument types without having to hunt through a multi-volume dictionary. Instruments found in his book are almost all museum pieces. Spelling of instruments' names used in this book are largely taken from Baines' book. Spellings for place names are taken from the language in use for the respective location, in compliance with organological dictates.

Items associated with brass instruments also have value, but are outside the scope of this book. Even so, for the general reader, instrument cases should never be discarded unless absolutely necessary. These cases can sometimes help to identify an instrument's maker. Yet, cases are more important as a means of protecting an instrument. Finding a replacement case for antique brass instruments might simply not be possible. At present, no collector of just instrument cases has been identified. Quite often, cases even contain mouthpieces, instruction books, music, etc. that also have value.

Mouthpieces are of special importance. Without such, a brass instrument is quite unplayable. Some people only collect mouthpieces, favoring a maker, patent variants, or unusual construction material, such as gold, silver, glass, rubber, etc. The more unusual the mouthpiece, the more value it is likely to have. Condition is important, but not imperative to the collector. The performer clearly needs mouthpieces, yet will favor ones that are usable.

Finally, some devices, such as Firemens' horns, and Bull horns are not included here. Though possibly produced by the same companies discussed here, only brass instruments used for musical purposes found in trade catalogs are discussed in this book. Non-musical instruments are simply out of the limited scope of this book. A few musical instruments have been included here that are not brass wind instruments, despite looking like they might be. These instruments are found after the illustrations of valve types.

The editor hopes that after reading this book, the reader will not only be able to traverse the difficulties of identification, and pricing, but will also be able to understand the mind set of most collectors, dealers, and curators of antique musical instruments. With this information in hand, surely more significant instruments and trade literature will come forward, and those instruments that deserve obscurity will receive their rewards.

1

A Brief History of the Musical Instrument Industry in the United States

Though the native people of the world were the first to make instruments, precious little credible information presently exists to discuss this subject. These instruments are outside the scope of this book. When colonization began in earnest, immigrants often brought their musical instruments. Some instruments were eventually made by craftspersons, such as furniture makers, or iron workers. One of the most important of the early U.S. instrument makers was Abraham Prescott. He began making bowed stringed instruments, such as violins, violas, cellos, and double basses. He also made an instrument unique to New England called a "Church bass." This instrument has no standard size, ranging from a small cello to a small double bass in size. Church basses were made by many other makers, with varying sophistication. Most church basses look like folk cellos. Prescott (whose instruments are generally of a very high quality) was fulfilling the restrictive dictates of churches in New England that often forbade musical instruments in church, but relented when a firm bass line was found to help guide the choir. Eventually, Prescott brought his sons, and others into the business, and began making small reed organs that rested in one's lap. Still later, the company made full-sized reed organs, and other keyboard instruments, discontinuing the production of bowed stringed instruments.

In 1812, the U.S. and England went to war. The supply of musical instruments from England all but stopped. One company formed to fill that void, being Firth, Hall, and Pond of New York City. The company made many types of wind instruments, especially flutes, and clarinets. The company changed names and addresses with some frequency, which can help in dating an instrument. The company is not reported in *NLI* as having made brass wind instruments.

During the early years of this country, instrument makers emigrated here. Philadelphia was known for having a few piano makers prior to 1800. Generally, these instruments were small square pianos, based upon German models. Immigrants also brought instruments. Some of these instruments are very important, being of early construction. The Moravian Trom-

bone Choir (of Bethlehem, Pennsylvania) is such a case, where historic sackbuts were discovered still in use in the 20th century.

In 1843, Jonas Chickering invented what has been called "the American piano." It is characterized not by shape, but by the all-metal frame. Prior to that, pianos warped because of the strain placed on the body of the piano by the taut strings. The all-metal frame eliminated that problem. It also allowed for an increased number of strings, and an increased string length. A second invention, called overstringing, whereby the strings are canted in such a way that bass strings might run below the treble strings, also heralded the invention of the modern piano.

After the Civil War ended, factories that had produced munitions of war switched over to domestic production, including musical instruments. Piano, reed organ, and band instrument production increased at dramatic levels. Instrument makers who provided instruments for the war, found that tastes had changed, and either developed new styles, or ended instrument production. The years 1860 to 1920 are often described as the "Golden age of bands."

Tragically, many factories during that period regularly burned down, taking company records with them. During that time, many factories were switching to steam engines for power. These engines often exploded, or otherwise caused fires. Only later did factories install fire sprinklers. The destruction of information has greatly interfered with documenting band instruments made during that time. This is why trade literature is so valuable in reassembling the history of a company.

Only within the late nineteenth century was a concerted effort made to standardize musical pitch, beginning first in Europe. This meant that instruments constructed in one pitch (where A often = 440 Hertz) could not play in tune with instruments in another pitch (high pitch, where A often = 457 Hertz) unless the instrument was specially constructed or adapted for that purpose. An apocryphal story states that during the First World War, U.S. bands could not play with European bands, because they were pitched differently. The issue was slowly resolved during the 1920s when 440 Hertz was adopted in both Europe and North America.

As stated above, musical pitch was not standardized until the 1920s. This lack of standardization had a subtle but important impact on instrument construction in Europe and the Americas. In Europe prior to 1800, makers produced wind instruments to comply with the standard pitch of a given city. Some woodwind makers included interchangeable joints that could be substituted when a different pitch was needed, as when a musician traveled to a different city. Brass instruments only partly overcame this problem with crooks and shanks. Crooks and shanks, however, were applied to brass instruments mostly to change an instrument's pitch by a semitone. Many Cornets pitched in B flat were sold with shanks that allowed the instrument to be played in A. Some makers even equipped B flat cornets with a valve-like device (usually placed within the body of the instrument, and activated by turning a knob or dial) that could allow the instrument to play in either key.

The piano and reed organ industry, prior to 1900, also suffered from this lack of standard pitch. However, piano production before the introduction of modern construction techniques was quite limited, as a maker had to produce virtually every part of the piano. Transportation of the instrument between cities was another limiting factor. With new tools, jigs, and the power to operate these devices that allowed for mass production of interchangeable parts, mass piano manufacturing began, and soon exceeded local demands. Thus, piano producers needed to expand their market nationally, and even world wide, or else curtail production. The various pitches, however, hampered sales.

In March of 1887, *The Musical Courier*, printed a list of pitches described as "the new pitch" where A=435 Hertz, as instigated by piano manufacturers, and following European efforts at standard pitch. The Music Teachers' National Association (U.S.) also adopted this new tuning scheme. However, the new scheme was not fully accepted in the U.S.

In 1891, Levi K. Fuller, who was associated with piano manufacturers, documented that no standard pitch existed in the U.S. In an April article of *The Musical Courier*, pitches in Europe and the U.S. were printed, showing that musicians were playing not just in high or low pitch, but many pitches. Fuller requested that European and American musicians accept a standard pitch, whatever that pitch might eventually become. The article documented the fact that keyboard manufacturers used their own pitches, and even changed them over time. To accommodate this multiplicity of pitches, squares and uprights were tuned at high pitch and concert pianos were tuned at low pitch. This meant that, for recitals and chamber concerts, two pianos were often needed to accommodate an orchestra, and a solo voice. The article also points out that Chicago used a pitch a half step higher than in New England to the vexation of vocalists.

As efforts to standardize pitch progressed, wind instrument makers, especially woodwind instrument makers, began stamping instruments either HP or LP. When this concept began and ended is uncertain, but in the U.S. one could safely assume that the dates are circa 1887 to 1930. Thus, all wind instruments stamped either HP or LP were most likely made before 1930. However, companies probably continued to sell previously-made, obsolete instruments. After the new pitch came into common use after 1920, a great many older wind instruments were discarded, as they could not play in the modern pitch. At the same time, new instruments were invented. As an aside, brass instruments made during the U.S. Civil War period have even been found to be pitched very high, possibly as high as A=457 Hertz instead of the current A=440 Hertz.

Brass instruments existed without valves until about the 1830s, when people with metal working skills turned to creating and later improving valve systems. Germany, France, England, and even the U.S. had inventors who developed a number of valve types. (For a fuller discussion of valves and their history, consult Baines *Brass instruments* and Philip Bate's "Valve" in *NGDMM*, vol. 19, p. 510-515.) Granted, Heinrich Stölzel invented a valve system (believed to be piston shaped) around 1814 that used two valves. According to Bate (p. 514), the firm of Griessling & Schlott made instruments equipped with this system. Stölzel and Blühmel replaced this system with another system around 1818, which is described by scholars as a square shaped valve. Many other valve systems were invented by John Shaw (England), Wilhelm Wieprecht (Austria), J.G. Moritz (Austria), Nathan Adams (U.S.A.), Josef Riedl (Austria), and Paine (U.S.A.).

Before the invention of valve systems, various people tried to create a brass instrument that could play a chromatic scale, that was in tune. One idea that had limited success was applying finger holes to brass instruments. Something of an off-shoot of this idea was the keyed bugle, and the ophicleide. The keyed bugle (which was commonly produced in B flat, and occasionally in E flat) is easily identified as it has keys and levers, suggestive of early woodwind instruments, applied to a bugle body. The bell of bugles flares at a very slow rate, giving it a rather fat look. Often, these instruments have a metal bell garland, which strengthens the bell, and provides an additional location for engravings or other elaborate ornamentation. Early keyed bugles are often made of copper. Later keyed bugles are occasionally made with the highest level of artistry the maker could produce. Many of these presentation instruments are heavily engraved, usually dated, and are sometimes made of solid silver or even solid gold. E.G. Wright was the most famous U.S. maker of such instruments. Yet, only 13 of his presentation keyed bugles are currently known, and a solid silver instrument sold some years ago for $2,000.00, quite below CMV.

The ophicleide is a family of bass instruments, ranging in size. (The alto ophicleide was occasionally called the quinticlave, and is quite rare today.) Like keyed bugles, ophicleides have keys and levers instead of valves. For this reason, the two instrument families are often associated, and were jointly used in early brass bands. Both instruments were basically out of favor by the mid-1800s, with keyed bugles disappearing first. Bass ophicleides persisted for some time, as low bass instruments fitted with valves were initially not as reliable as the ophicleide.

About the same time valve systems were being invented, brass manufacturers began patenting all sorts of instruments that the producer hoped would become popular. Only Adolphe Sax succeeded in that regard with his Saxophone (a woodwind instrument). He did patent his Saxhorn (a brasswind instrument), which looks much like the B flat tenor horn offered by Isaac Fiske (Number 10) found in this book. Note how the tubing has a squarer look than other bell up instruments. The rare push rod rotary valve system, found on the Fiske instrument, was not a feature on Sax's instruments.

Manufacturers, who devised new instruments, often invented names for their instruments or models, partly in imitation of Sax's Saxophone. Thus, names like Antoniophones, and Königs horn can be found. Other manufacturers named cornet models after famous performers. The differences are so subtle that specialists often do not make note of the model. In an interesting twist, M. Slater offered "Distin model" cornets, having worked with him. Other manufacturers also copied Distin's designs, at a time when U.S. copyright laws were in their infancy. The usurpation of his designs so angered Distin that he stated in his catalogs that only instruments bearing his trade mark were genuine Distin instruments.

Still other manufacturers followed a different track in naming instruments, resulting in altophones, melody horns, ballad horns, etc. All these trade names result in considerable confusion that still vexes specialists, as they often connote instruments with very subtle "improvements." The rarity of most of these instrument types adds to the confusion. This situation is especially true for alto horn variants.

Regarding valve systems in the U.S., Robert Eliason in *Early American Brass Makers* discusses four makers who are of special significance, being Thomas D. Paine, J. Lathrop Allen, E.G. Wright, and Isaac Fiske. This small book contains very valuable information, but is currently not in print. As such, Eliason documents the development of brass instrument production prior to 1860, in the U.S.

According to Eliason (p. 5-14), Thomas D. Paine popularized brass instruments made with rotary valves, having received a patent for such an invention. Rotary valves had been known in Europe. However, Paine's valves were long and thin, and made with a string linkage. This invention produced a valve that was easier to make, and quieter in use than the European valve. He also made instruments with rotary valves that appear to be more like those still in use today, and continued to experiment with valves for some time.

Until about the Civil War, U.S. brass instruments did not have standardized valve or tubing systems. Eventually, such systems standardized, resulting in standardized fingering systems. Currently, the first valve has tubing that enables the musician to lower the pitch by a whole step. The second valve has tubing that enables the musician to lower the pitch by a half step. The third valve enables the musician to lower the pitch by a step and a half. The fourth (and other) valve has tubing of various lengths, depending upon the manufacturer. The fourth valve can even have a special function, such as transposing an instrument from one key into another, or to activate a different bell. However, before valve tubing lengths standardized, instruments show variations that help to date them. Instruments with such features are especially sought out by collectors.

All instruments that never gained popularity, are quite collectible. This drive to innovate and hopefully increase sales spawned an amazing array of curious instruments, and minor improvements that have kept people scrambling for years trying to make sense of the profusion of ideas. Also, by patenting a variation on an earlier device, the owner of the new patent was not required to pay patent royalties to anyone. Put another way, an instrument with features not found in this book will require additional research. The better researched an instrument is, the more likely the instrument will sell for a high price. The chapter discussing values will provide more information about this topic.

The U.S. musical instrument manufacturers maintained a very close contact with their European counterparts, often having factories in both places. Though Europe was a major development site for musical instruments, the U.S. saw important developments. Many collectors actively seek instruments that document these differences and developments. However, European tastes dominated U.S. artistic and technical developments. Consider the following quote from the Boston Musical Instrument Manufactory of 1869 (p. 6):

The "Distin" Cornet, (English) and the "Courtois," (French), are both excellent instruments and very popular in Europe, but America cannot afford to permit England or France to take the lead in Cornet making any more than in cornet playing.

Dating musical instruments is problematic. Names and business addresses can help. Also, in 1891 the McKinley Act mandated that all instruments must bear the name of the country where the imported instrument was made. The name had to be in English. Al Rice believes that "Made in" was mandated in 1923 by a subsequent law.

The musical instrument industry in Europe and the U.S. saw some important developments, which can not be fully discussed in this book. Even so, the history of the musical instrument industry reflects the growth of the industrialized countries. Specifically, the industry saw the first important patent infringement lawsuits, resulting in changes in the entire patent granting process. Countries were compelled to not just acknowledge other countries' patents, but even collect foreign patents to assist in the patent granting process thereby limiting protracted patent lawsuits. Fraudulent business activities became so egregious that Federal laws were passed in the U.S. governing business activities (often involving the U.S. post office) to censure such illegal actions as false advertising, and theft of mailed checks. Tied up in this morass were trade marks, which did not suffer as much from forgery. With the advent of modern construction techniques and materials, such as steam engines, electricity, aluminum smelting, and the increasing rarity of some materials, the musical instrument industry reflects not just musical taste, but the industrialization of Europe and the Americas. The musical instrument industry also introduced or helped introduce a number of business activities, such as five day work weeks, the installment plan for payment, workers' strikes, and unionization of factories.

Deception in advertising was a major problem during this time. As a result, many laws were passed. This fact is offered here because musical instrument trade literature contained many statements that caused people to be imprisoned for libel. As one might therefore expect, researching musical instruments can not only be educational, but at times quite humorous.

The most infamous person in this matter was Daniel F. Beatty of New Jersey. Mr. Beatty was a manufacturer of medium and low-grade pianos, and reed organs working between about 1870 and 1890. He advertised instruments described as being of a medium-grade but offered for the price of a low-grade instrument. When the instrument arrived, it often did not match the description. Mr. Beatty was finally forced out of business by the Post Office, and several state courts for repeated deception involving the U.S. mail, which today might be described as "bait and switch." In short, he grossly overstated the quality of his instruments.

In conclusion, the history of the U.S. musical instrument making industry parallels the history of this country. When the country began to prosper, instruments were made in larger numbers. When enough money became available, instrument production again increased. When the idea of mass production developed, musical instrument production increased again. When music became fashionable, musical instruments became more elaborate. Currently, because of the extremely high production output of today's musical instrument factories, one wonders when prices for instruments made after 1920 will increase.

2

How to Identify an Instrument

When identifying an instrument, and discussing it with an expert, have answers to the following questions. What type of instrument is it (E flat cornet, trumpet, etc.)? Who produced the instrument? What is the serial number on the instrument (if one exists)? What metal or other material is used to construct it? Which way does the bell point (i.e., what is the body design)? What type and number of valves does the instrument have? Does the instrument have any unusual features, such as multiple bells, additional valves, significant history, etc.? This chapter will assist in answering these questions.

WHAT TYPE OF INSTRUMENT IS IT?

To begin with, almost all brasswind instruments are made of metal. On very rare occasions, these instruments are made of other materials. For the most part, such instruments are curiosities, and often are welcome additions to collections. Instruments made of ceramics are quite collectible, though not necessarily by instrument collectors. Natural horns made of Meissen porcelain are known.

To determine the type of instrument, examine the illustrations in this book for similarities with the instrument in question. Look at the way that the tubes pass through the instrument. Compare the instrument at hand with the illustrations in this book. At this point, one should try to determine if the instrument is a cornet, trumpet, alto horn, tenor horn, baritone horn, bass horn, French horn, trombone, or a less common type.

A very great limitation of this book is that the original trade catalogs almost never included measurements of instruments. So, an alto might look like an E flat bass. The difference here can be measured in feet. Also, tenors, baritones and B flat basses all look very similar in the trade catalogs. A musician who can play the instruments can help differentiate the various types. Cornets were often made in either E flat, C, or B flat. Altos were usually made in E flat; tenors, baritones, and some basses were made in B flat. Some basses,

especially the largest ones, were made in E flat. If all else fails, measure the body length (see Glossary), and provide that to an expert.

In addition to providing illustrations of the above-mentioned instruments, this book includes illustrations of some exceedingly rare brass instrument types. If the instrument in question is not found in this book, consult either Baines or *NGDMM*. Countless rare brass instruments exist, some of which are still not documented. Such rarities (or oddities) can only be identified and valued by an expert.

A second group of instruments have been included here that are in no way to be considered brass instruments, even though they look as though they might be. The instruments depicted are novelty instruments, and were never used professionally for anything other than comedy musical acts. The Signal horn, discussed below, is rather common today, and is still manufactured in Germany.[1]

The Zobophone, sold by C. Bruno, is a relative of the kazoo, and was designed to look like a brass instrument. Often, Zobophones were made of either cardboard, or less commonly tin. Other such novelty instruments lurk on the periphery of musical instrument specialists, and rarely are collected, often due to their poor state of preservation. Included in this menagerie of kazoos is the Marxophone made by Marx (more known for making tin toys), and the Vocophone, which was sold by Lyon & Healy.

The signal horn, which is similar to a one-valve bugle, is given special attention here as experts are repeatedly asked about it, and very little information exists. The signal horn is a reed instrument related to the harmonica. It is usually stamped "Signal" on one of its bells, sometimes with other words in German, or even an arrow. No means of tuning the instrument exists, and on some examples an integral mouthpiece exists. The instrument has at least one valve that, at first, looks like a Périnet valve. The valve is directly attached to a bell, with many bells possible. By activating a valve, a metal reed is slid into place, and the wind passes through it to a bell. When depressing other valves only single pitches are produced. All this information is based upon examination of only a few working instruments. The tone is loud and raucous, and suitable for little other than the taxi part in George Gershwin's "An American in Paris." The instrument was even marketed as an automobile horn in some catalogs. The one-valve bugle can easily be distinguished from the signal horn, if only by the fact that the bugle has a detachable mouthpiece.

WHO MADE THE INSTRUMENT?

Examine the bell of the instrument. This is often where a name is stamped or engraved. If a name exists, it will either be of the maker, manufacturer, importer, general music retailer, trade name, or a previous owner. The maker/manufacturer's names, along with most of the important trade names are listed in *NLI*. The editors of *NLI*, according to Lloyd Farrar, chose not to actively pursue all the trade names and trademarks for the medium to lesser grade instruments. This is not to say that a name missing from *NLI* implies anything other than lack of information. Additionally, anyone can stamp a name on an instrument, even today. The more obscure the name, the more the instrument will invite investigation. If the name found on the bell is determined to be a general music dealer, the instrument will be of lesser importance. If the dealer was locally prominent, the instrument might increase in value in that area. If an instrument contains the name of a previous owner, and that owner was important (either regionally, or nationally) the instrument will have increased value. Determining this fact will require research, possibly using *NGDMM* or some other musical dictionary. The name on the mouthpiece usually does not correspond to the maker of the brass wind instrument.

WHAT IS THE SERIAL NUMBER ON THE INSTRUMENT?

The serial number, if one exists, might be stamped on the valve cluster, or possibly on the bell. Valves were often stamped with other numbers, such as 1, 2, and 3. Other times, valves were stamped with part numbers. The serial number is almost always stamped on one side of the second valve, above or below the valve numbers. Obviously instruments that were produced before the need for serial numbers will not have such. Additionally, serial numbers might help to date an instrument. Instruments without a serial number are quite difficult to date, unless some other information is available, such as a maker's mark, or an address. Researchers are actively reconstructing serial numbers lists, with approximate construction dates. However, the information found in *NLI* is quite incomplete, due to loss of most company data. Even so, most manufacturers seem to have used numbers consecutively. One fact that is commonly acknowledged is that C.G. Conn's instruments with numbers below 9,000 are especially interesting historically, though not necessarily commanding premium prices.

WHAT METAL IS USED TO CONSTRUCT THE INSTRUMENT?

The metal used to make an instrument is important. In the early 1800s, copper was a dominant metal used for making brass instruments. Copper gave way to brass rather quickly. Even so, some bugle-like instruments are still made in India, which are purely decorative. Most instruments made between about 1850 and 1920, consisted of varieties of brass, often overlaid with another metal, such a nickel silver, which is often called German silver. An easy way to determine the base metal is to examine the pipe into which the mouthpiece fits. Considerable wear will expose the base metal. Wear marks can also be found on prominent bends, and where the instrument is held during playing. Plated instruments were always considered more attractive, if only because the plating hid the joints where the sheets of metal were joined to form the body.

Many finer instruments were made of brass covered with silver. Some instruments were even made of solid silver or gold. Such instruments were often presentation instruments, with a date and other information engraved on the bell, along with elaborate engraving. These instruments are some of the most highly sought American brass instruments today, with most of them in museums. However, instruments could be engraved after they left the factory, and are probably nothing special in either construction or engraving. The quality of the engraving, and other ornaments will give a clue to the importance of the instrument.

German silver, as stated above, was used on brass instruments. In fact, it was probably the most common metal finish for the time. This metal has a dull silver color, but contains a large amount of nickel. An easy way to determine if the metal is German silver is to look for a green cast or substance that develops when an instrument made of German silver is left for a while. Often, a green pasty substance can be found in recesses, such as ornaments. German silver (Gs) over brass on instruments was considered to be just below silver in desirability.

Very few brass instruments were made of solid gold. In the U.S., E.G. Wright was known for making at least one cornet and a trumpet of gold. Gold was often applied to the bell in a thin wash, or to other ornamental points on instruments, particularly by C.G. Conn, and the H.N. White company. Instruments containing gold should be looked at by a specialist. Obviously, a poor-quality brass instrument would rarely have gold applied to it, unless done so after it left the factory. Any solid gold instruments should command prices well above the current market price for gold.

Aluminum was arguably more costly to smelt than gold during the 1800s. Aluminum surely began to be used in larger amounts with the increased availability of electricity. This metal has never fully gained acceptance among brass instrument makers, but staged some popularity when wars in the twentieth century dictated metal rationing. This is to say, that if an instrument was made using aluminum, either it was produced after circa 1930 or was a one-of-a-kind creation.

WHAT IS THE BODY DESIGN?

Of all brass instruments, cornets show possibly the widest (and most vexing) variety of body and valve designs. Two pitches of cornets were common, being E flat and B flat, with C cornets also in use but not generally considered a professional's instrument. Examine the tubing that runs from the mouthpiece to the valve cluster. On some instruments, the tubing might bend in a full arc, with a slight dip downward, as seen in many E flat cornets. Some specialists believe that the fewer the number of bends in the tubing, and the less acute the bends, the better the instrument will play. However, this opinion is subjective. A close examination of the various body designs found in this book can teach the reader what shapes existed.

Regarding design, consider the E flat cornets offered by Lyon & Healy found in this book. These instruments represent the classical design for such instruments. The tubing usually bends in a graceful arc. Also note that E flat cornets, like all E flat brass instruments, generally have less tubing than a close B flat relative. The tubing of B flat cornets generally begins to bend further back from the bell. Most B flat cornets often have 3 U-shaped bends between the mouthpiece and the valve cluster, while E flat cornets have just one U-shaped bend. Some of the European-style cornets have only a short tube between the mouthpiece and the valve cluster.

Identifying cornets is complicated by their body designs. Terms for some of the obscure designs were never standardized during the time. One can make a case for manufacturers and importers choosing different terms for exactly the same design, if only for commercial purposes. Such terms include orchestra, leader, band, short, long, and solo designs. In the Foote catalog, four other designs are shown, named for prominent cornet soloists. The difference between these types is so slight that only an expert would have the necessary ability to tell one from another. For the average person, the terms solo, leader, and orchestra tend to mean that the instrument was of superior construction.

Another difficulty exists in identifying small brass instruments. During the 19th century, the cornet was considered more desirable than the trumpet. During the early 20th century, however, the two instruments vied for popularity, with the trumpet emerging preeminent. During this transition (and possibly before that), cornets began to be made in trumpet shape, with only a slightly wider bore. Earlier, cornets were made with a rather wide look to them, if viewed from the side. Trumpets were made with less distance between the tubing. Put another way, trumpets generally are only as tall as their valves. Cornets rarely have valves extending below the tubing. Trumpets tend to be longer than cornets to account for a somewhat thinner look.

Another generality about brass instruments is of some value. Terms such as bugle and trumpet were used rather freely in trade catalogs to identify any valveless instrument. However, upon closer examination, bugles tend to flare out more after the last turn in the tubes, resulting in a fatter looking bell. Trumpets, on the other hand are supposed to be cylindrical and progressively larger throughout the entire length of the tube. Cornets are supposed to be conical throughout.

Though brass instruments also appear in pitches other than E flat and B flat, such examples tend to be uncommon. C Cornets, however, are quite common, and are rarely worth more than $150, unless some other feature is interesting, such as a rare maker. C and B flat Cornets look almost identical. Baines (p. 232-235) discusses the difference between the B flat and C Cornets. When in use, the C Cornet was designed for amateur use, often playing duets with a keyboard instrument.

Determining actual pitch presents a blizzard of possibilities. One could be examining a low pitch instrument; a high pitch instrument; an instrument with tubing that suggests a B flat cornet, but is in fact an E flat cornet; or an instrument that was pitched for local use. Experts can often determine actual pitch, often by using an electronic tuner.

Bell directions (BU, BF, OTS, or HD) is a clue to identifying the country where the instrument was made (Specialists tend to use the name of the city where the instrument was made and its local spelling, rather than the country, especially if made in eastern Europe).

Usually, German and Austrian instruments are often made with bells forward, or up. Instruments manufactured in France generally have bells forward. Instruments made in the U.S. can have any of the three mentioned. Generally, OTS instruments are unique to the U.S. and began to disappear after the Civil War, along with rotary valves on all but the French horn, and some bass trombones.

On a more specific level, virtually all OTS brass instruments have considerable value, with premium prices going to instruments in top condition. Many of these instruments currently sell for between $2,000 and $3,000. Even instruments in poor condition might sell for over $1,000. Obviously, instruments with the mark of important makers will sell for more than unsigned instruments. Instruments with forged makers' marks will sell for very little, often less than unsigned instruments.

After the Civil War ended, OTS instruments could not be sold easily, as tastes had changed. Thus, makers and manufacturers sold the instruments for substantially less than before the Civil War. This fact can be observed in the trade catalogs. Do not be confused by the prices found in the catalogs for OTS brass instruments. Collectors and Civil War enthusiasts avidly look for these instruments, regardless of when they were originally sold. Few types of antique brass instruments are as avidly sought as the OTS instruments.

Cornets and trumpets of student grade with bells forward and with no significant features (such as an extra valve, bell, history, etc.), but otherwise in playable condition might sell for about $100. Again, condition, history, mouthpiece, case, region of the country where it is being sold, etc. will affect the sale price. Differentiating student grade from professional grade instruments can be done by most competent brass players, or retail musical instrument shops with a patient staff. Also, an instrument that looks well made generally played well when new. Student-grade instruments rarely were engraved. Thus, engraved instruments sell for more than unengraved instruments.

Slide trombones with no special features rarely sell today for more than $200. Trombones with rotary valves will sell for more, but generally not much more. Trombones do not seem to command the attention of collectors that cornets, and even Saxhorn-style instruments command. If, however, the instrument is a historic sackbut and not a trombone, the instrument might command a very high price. The sackbut can be identified by having a relatively narrow bell, that flares out slowly. The sackbut was replaced by the trombone well before valves were invented. An actual historic sackbut is a museum piece. Reproduction sackbuts can be had today. See the glossary for more information about the sackbut.

Larger brasswind instruments, such as basses, and contra basses, despite selling for a considerable amount of money then and now, are difficult to sell today. This fact is partly due to the size of the instruments. One can store 20 cornets in the space that two basses might require. Another fact is that brass bands always needed more cornets than basses. Therefore, basses tend to be rarer and yet less interesting to many collectors, despite being as well made as cornets. Alto horns are totally ignored by most collectors.

WHAT TYPE AND NUMBER OF VALVES DOES THE INSTRUMENT HAVE?

Valves, as a concept, began in the early 1800s. Stoelzel is generally credited with inventing one of the earliest, practical valve systems. The Stoelzel valve has tubing coming from the bottom of the cylinder (see Baines, p. 185, example d, and p. 209). Cornopeans most often were made with Stoelzel valves, especially in France and England. The most common valve type is the Périnet valve (Baines, p. 185, example f) and is the dominant valve type found on instruments in this country. This thin, cylindrical valve has tubing entering and leaving from the sides of the cylinder.

Another common valve type is the rotary valve. Three types of rotary valve types have enjoyed some popularity. The first type is the Shaw valve, which is now quite rare, and which looks like an elegant rotary valve set on its side, activated by push rods (see Baines p. 213-214). The second rotary valve type has a string connecting the valve with a lever or touch key. A third type of rotary valve can be found on many German-made instruments. This valve is identified by having a touch key attached to an s-shaped piece of metal (instead of a string), which is then attached to the valve. Baines shows two instruments with this valve type on p. 238, one manufactured by Alexander, and the other by Moritz, both German.

Many less common valve types exist, including the Berliner pumpen (which looks like a very squat, fat Périnet valve), and the Vienna valve (see Baines p. 157, example 5, listed only as a Bass trumpet, and p. 209). The Vienna valve system is easy to identify, as it has double pistons, with tubes running out the bottom of the valve, and often a plate stabilizing the valve cluster.

Instruments made in Germany, Austria, and Bohemia will generally have any of the valve types mentioned. Instruments made in France will generally have Périnet-style valves, or less commonly rotary valves. Instruments made in England will often have Périnet-style valves. Early instruments might have Shaw valves, or even Vienna valves. Later instruments made in the U.S. will have either Périnet, or less commonly rotary (string) valves.

Périnet was a French instrument manufacturer, who in 1838 (according to *NLI* p. 299), created the prototype of a valve system. This system is pictured on pp.24-25 of this book, showing why this valve type is also called a piston valve. The initial design was as imperfect as almost every early valve system. Subsequently, an improved Périnet-style valve was perfected (possibly in France), and was described in countless catalogs as "light action French" valve system. Therefore, throughout this book the term "Périnet-style" refers to this second valve system. Existing instruments constructed using Périnet's early valve system are not at all common.

Many countries also had rare valve types (including square valves, hybrid valve systems, etc.) that were often unique to their own country. These valve types are quite rare, and tend to sell only at important auctions. Prices vary widely, based only partly on condition. Again, consult Baines for valve types. If an instrument has a valve type not pictured in this book, the instrument should be shown to an expert.

When examining a brass instrument, also examine the case, if it exists. Many American-made cases resemble small coffins. Very large brass instruments rarely came with cases that still survive. For smaller brass instruments, especially cornets and French horns, that generally date from before 1920, the case might include extra tubing. These tubes, called crooks (for bent tubes), and leader pipes or shanks (for straight tubes), allowed an instrument to change pitch, say from B flat to A. These tubes, unless badly damaged add to the overall value of the instrument.

In a few rare examples, cases even contained instruction books or other paperwork that might indicate the manufacturer, and date of construction. Some cases have been personalized with plaques or engravings that help to identify a previous owner. This is to say, the history of an instrument might increase the valve of the instrument. If the instrument had once been owned by John P. Sousa, the instrument would be more valuable than the same instrument owned by an unknown musician. In short, keep everything related to the instrument until an expert has a chance to examine it, even if damaged.

DOES THE INSTRUMENT HAVE ANY UNUSUAL FEATURES?

As stated elsewhere, manufacturers invented many features to entice people to buy their instruments, or to solve some other problem. For the most part, only those instruments that played well (i.e. were well made), and could fill an existing musical need (tenor, alto, etc.) had much success. Even so, some manufacturers persisted in creating novel instruments, some of which have value today to both collectors and performers. Double bell euphoniums are arguably the most common of these novel instruments. The instrument is easily identified by having two bells, and an additional valve to shift the wind from one bell to the other. For a short while in Europe, multiple-belled instruments enjoyed some popularity. These instruments are quite rare, and valuable.

Other novel inventions include echo attachments, or still earlier, valves attached to keyed bugles. Several echo attachments are documented in this book, other rarer novel contrivances are not documented here. If in doubt, take a photograph of the instrument, clearly showing the unusual feature, and show it to a qualified expert. Never ship an instrument without prior communication with the person to whom it will be sent.

Notes

[1.] Dr. Al Rice provided the following information about this curious instrument. "Max B. Martin of Markneukirchen took out three patents for three variations of "Signal Horns" on 16 August 1927 (#503951), 3 July 1928 (#540818); and 3 July 1928 (#543629). These are reproduced by Günther Dullat in *Blasinstrumente und Deutsche Patentschriften 1877-1970 Metallblasinstrument 1* (Nauheim: the Author, 1985), 103-4; 110-113. Apparently this firm manufactured a number of signal and multi-bell instruments starting in the late 1920's." Additionally, Lark in the Morning offered in its 1994 catalog (page 31) seven varieties of this instrument. In the catalog, these instruments are identified as being "Tyrolian many belled trumpets." The accompanying description states:

"These wonderful many belled horns are loud and raucous. they look like a trumpet with a bouquet of bells. Each bell has its own reed similar to an accordion reed. No embouchure required. A conversational piece at band rehearsal! ..."

3

Pricing Instruments

This chapter provides basic guidelines to determine if an instrument is a museum piece, extremely valuable, collectible, or common.[1] These terms, and variations thereof, are used without regard to actual values, simply because no consensus exists for pricing instruments, even among experts. Many dealers and collectors will have an opinion about prices that will often disagree with another expert. To arbitrarily apply prices given this quagmire of opinion invites problems. Therefore, this chapter gives basic information about unusual features, and quality makers and manufacturers with which the reader should be familiar.

If an instrument is described here as a museum piece, or highly collectible, the reader should consult an expert to find the current market value. Only an expert can give an adequate value for such instruments. The reader will also find Appendix C to be of value, being a list of current market values for instruments that were offered for sale by either dealers, or auction houses. The current market values for instruments illustrated in the trade catalogs used in this book were provided by a number of specialists, whose names can be found in the acknowledgment section of this book. These values have been incorporated into Appendix C.

Valuing brass instruments is more difficult than valuing other antiques. Most brass instruments do not appear in auction catalogs to any great extent, limiting the value of this resource. Further limiting the value of this resource, auction prices rarely equal prices offered by competent, long-time dealers of musical instruments. Even so, many of the most rare, museum-quality brass instruments rarely appear anywhere but in auction catalogs. Thus, prices from the Sotheby's catalogs dating from 1989 to the present have been included here. Inclusion of only Sotheby's prices is not meant to slight Christies, Phillips, Swann Galleries, or any of the many other reputable auction houses that offer instruments.

As a broad generality, brass instruments never sell for the prices of rare violins. Realistically, brass instruments have value for basically four reasons: they were made by an important maker or show some important development (such as

a rare valve action); they are beautiful either to play, or look at (or both); they have an important history, such as having been owned by an important person; or they are made of a valuable material, such as gold.

Condition of an instrument might greatly affect its value. If the valve cluster is damaged, it might be repairable. However, the repair cost might exceed the value of the instrument. In that case, the instrument could be sold "as is" for parts. If the instrument is determined by an expert to be rare, or otherwise unique, even in damaged condition, it might be highly collectible. If the instrument is dented, and the instrument is not historically significant, removing the dents is often acceptable. If the instrument was originally lacquered, never remove the lacquer. If the lacquer has already been removed, consult an expert about relacquering it. Relacquering instruments can severely damage the tone of instruments, even if done by an expert. Lacquering of brass instruments seems to have begun around 1920, and is therefore not discussed further in this book, as it is outside the time frame of this book.

Missing parts are always a concern. Missing bells and valve clusters detract substantially from the value of instruments, often by as much as 75 per cent. If the valve cluster is missing, the instrument might have value for parts only. Fabricating a new valve cluster rarely justifies the expensive. Missing mouthpieces do not alter the value of the instrument. However, some worthless instruments have been bought simply because they were offered with an interesting mouthpiece.

A very important point must be restated regarding all antique musical instruments. If the instrument might be valuable, do not restore it. Most museums and discriminating collectors will rarely pay much (if anything) for a restored instrument. If the restoration is questionable, the instrument could loose as much as half its value. If the instrument is repaired poorly, a second restoration would be needed to remove the mistakes. In such cases, the cost of restoration could not be recovered when the instrument is sold. The restored instrument might even sell for less than the unrestored instrument. By restoring a rare instrument, valuable information will probably be destroyed. Granted, an instrument with no special history could be restored which should increase the value of the instrument. Only a handful of qualified repairers of antique musical instruments exist, and can be found by contacting the libraries and museums listed in Appendix A of this book. These people regularly repair and restore instruments for major museums, and their work is generally considered above question. Do not take a rare instrument for repairs to just anyone! An apocryphal story describes how someone took a $100 violin, cut a hole in its back, and turned it into a $200 lamp. Delighted, he took a $2,000 violin, cut a hole in it and turned it into a $200 lamp.

Ornamentation can also influence an instrument's value. Instruments with heavy engravings will often increase the value of the instrument by $100. Finish also influences value. Gold wash, highly burnished, silver plate, and German silver are some of the more valuable finishes.

To begin identifying an instrument, first become familiar with the instrument in question simply by looking at. Notice the number of valves (if any), the way the bell points when being played (if possible), and the way the tubing bends. Then, with the instrument close at hand, begin thumbing through this book. If all else fails, find a trustworthy musician for assistance.

The number and type of valves on the instrument are important in valuing an instrument; yet less important in identifying the instrument. An instrument with no valves might be an inexpensive instrument or possibly a museum piece. Instruments with four valves, though uncommon, exist, and originally sold for more than a three valve version of the previous instruments. Instruments with more than four valves should be shown to an expert. For example, four-valved double-belled euphoniums currently sell for about $1,700.

Two common types of valves might be found. The first is the most common, and looks like a piston with tubing entering at the sides. This type, pictured on page 25 of this book, is called the Périnet-style valve, abbreviated here as PV. The second valve type is a rotary valve. This circular-shaped valve is commonly found on modern French horns, and involves half of the valve rotating while the other half remains stationary. Rotary valves might have a string as part of the valve action. Rotary valves can be either top action (TARV) or side action (SARV). Chapter 1 briefly discusses a larger number of valve types. A fuller discussion of valve types is left for Baines. The glossary of this book also provides more information. Illustrations of these and other valve types can be found elsewhere in this book.

Look at the way the tubing bends. E flat and B flat cornets, at first glance, look identical. B flat cornets, however, always have more tubing than E flat cornets. This is also true for the larger horns. Look at where the tubes bend. Does the instrument in question have the same bends in the tubes as found in this book? Learn how to read the "plumbing" of the instrument. This will take some time. Another common feature that will be of some general help is that B flat cornets generally have a "shepherd's crook" bend that appears below the mouthpiece in the tubing just before the valve cluster. Also, look at the two pages of this book that show some of the more common body designs for E flat and B flat cornets.

One might easily identify an instrument as a cornet, a valve trombone, or a bass instrument, but then decide that the instrument is pitched in the wrong key. This mistake might be more important to a musician than a collector. For example, an American-made E flat cornet, might be highly sought by one person, and totally ignored by another. By comparison, baritones, and basses from the same maker all sell for about the same price. One clear difference in prices between these instruments is when the instruments are heavily plated. Then the value of the metal would have to be factored into the instruments' CMV. Consider the following quote on the matter of preferred pitches, from The Boston Musical Instrument Manufactory *Illustrated Catalogue* of 1869 (p. 4).

"Of all instruments, the E flat Cornet is perhaps the most difficult to bring under control; it requires great strength of lip and strength of lungs together with many years of practice to make a good E flat Cornet player. In Europe this instrument is treated by writers as a Chorus Instrument, while here, all the grand arias of the great Prima Donnas are adapted to it. There is no instrument in the selection of which a performer should use greater caution than in the purchase of an E flat Cornet. They are about as numerous as Violins and in almost as great a variety, good ones being exceedingly rare."

Valuing an instrument often begins by determining who made it. In this book, a maker is identified as any person who personally constructed instruments, and might have also employed people in his shop. A manufacturer is any person who employed others to make the instruments, while he ran the company. No women musical instrument manufacturers have yet been identified. The difference here is that instruments that were manufactured will often exist in larger numbers than instruments that were made by hand. Also, manufactured instruments will tend to be more uniform than hand-made instruments. Unsigned instruments tend to sell for the least amount to collectors, unless the instrument is clearly old. Very old instruments (pre-1700) were often unsigned, or signed with an ornamental mark, and should be assumed to be of museum quality until examined by an expert.

Makers and manufacturers of woodwind instruments regularly sold their unsigned rejected instruments. These inferior instruments could then be stamped with someone else's name, such as an importer or a retail store. This situation is more a concern for woodwind instruments. For brass makers and manufacturers, inexpensive lines of instruments were regularly offered for sale to others who could put their name on these cheap instruments. As such, verifying that a name on an instrument is the actual maker or manufacturer will help considerably in determining a value. These instruments were often derided as being "stencil instruments" and have value mainly to musicians, if the instrument plays well. By now, it should be obvious that advertisement information prior to about 1920 was little scrutinized for accuracy. Names of importers, etc. are not to be confused with brand names that began to appear around 1880. Fortunately, *NLI* helps sort out this complex problem.[2]

Lyon & Healy is one company that deserves special attention regarding names found on instruments. Current thinking is that the company obtained parts from various sources, and might have assembled, or more likely simply prepared instruments for sale. *NLI* (p. 245) states that the company only manufactured instruments between 1923-1930. However, that book also points out that all the company's records were destroyed in fires. Also, considering the somewhat obscure comments in other catalogs, Lyon & Healy could have assembled instruments as early as 1896. Many instruments bearing the Lyon & Healy name exist. If one were to find evidence to the contrary, the value of Lyon & Healy instruments might increase. The information would even have value to collectors and researchers.

When valuing an instrument, its history can be extremely important. For example, if an unvalved instrument can be shown to have been in a family for over 200 years (i.e. made before the development of valve systems), the instrument should be shown to an expert. If the instrument can be proven to have been made before 1700, the instrument might be extremely valuable. As ever, the more valuable an instrument, the more likely that it might have been forged or somehow altered, thereby driving down the price.

Almost any instrument brought back from World War I or II, especially if found around southern Germany should be examined by an expert. Makers from this area were famous for centuries for their workmanship, and are still not fully documented. Some of these instruments are very old and have been passed over as forgeries, owing to their poor condition.

For that matter, the older any quality musical instrument is, the more likely that it is valuable, even if hopelessly damaged. Such instruments tend to be museum specimens of potentially great value. Instruments that were cheap when made, no matter how old will still be cheap today. Here again, even museum-quality brass instruments rarely command the prices of rare violins.

Fragments of ancient instruments (such as from ancient Rome or Egypt) are unique museum specimens, and have no value as a useable musical instrument. One might find such instruments in an archaeological dig, or in an old collection. As early as the 1600's, nobility and other wealthy people discovered the social status associated with collecting antiquities. This practice came to the U.S. around the end of the nineteenth century. Within a number of these collections, truly rare specimens have been discovered. However, probably all such known musical instrument collections have been examined for such items. Some collectors even commissioned reproductions of antiquities or were duped by forgers.

Any accompanying documentation related specifically to the instrument in question should improve the value of the instrument. Any associated paperwork documenting the instrument's history can increase the value by possibly as much as 25 per cent, or more, depending upon the significance of the instrument. For example, an instrument that can be proven to have been used in a significant event such as the funeral ceremonies of President Lincoln will command a higher price than the same instrument without a pedigree. Yet, that instrument with a forged history, will sell for less than it might without the forgery.

Regarding forgeries, collectors always face this potential problem. Beginning sometime during the end of the nineteenth century, Americans began collecting artwork, often as a status symbol. This interest eventually encompassed musical instruments. Some of the prominent collections of today began this way. Most of these collections were limited to keyboard instruments and members of the violin family. Some collectors were very poorly educated as to what to buy, and bought very unwisely, resulting in a market for forged instruments. Today, only the name Franciolini is known.

Collectors have often been duped into buying forged items. For musical instruments, Mr. Franciolini is the most famous forger. Though he actually sold genuine antique musical instruments, he regularly fabricated instruments often from miscellaneous parts and sold the composites as genuine. As a result of his highly illegal antics, any instrument with a Franciolini pedigree must be viewed with considerable suspicion until authenticated by at least one highly-qualified expert. Mr. Ripin has republished Franciolini's catalogs (see the bibliography). From this resource, one can see that Franciolini rarely dealt in brass instruments.

Forging an item can often be expensive. Forging less valuable items is rarely financially worth the effort. Even so, the collector must exercise caution when buying an instrument. Fortunately for brass instruments, forged instruments are rarely found. As recent U.S. makers and manufacturers produced so many instruments, and so many of them survived, no market exists for forged brass instruments. The same is not true for violins, keyboard instruments, and possibly brass instruments made before the Renaissance, because they can sell for many thousands of dollars. Additionally, few people are either qualified, or interested in reproducing antique brass instruments. In short, if the instrument is well made, and in good condition, it is probably authentic, and worth something, either to a performer or a collector, or both.

Valuing antique brass instruments is like shooting at a moving target in the dark. Put another way, give an instrument to three experts, and you might get four different prices, as one expert might be unsure of something. When more credible research has been done in identifying rare model numbers, creating a pricing guide similar to most collectibles should be possible. A final note, the Internet is currently a popular source of information about rare model numbers, etc. However, great care is cautioned in the quality of this information. Hopefully, these comments, along with Appendix C, should help to value most antique brass instruments found in the United States.

Notes

[1] See also chapter 1, which touches on many of the points made in this chapter, though from a different perspective. "Extremely valuable" throughout this book is synonymous with "museum specimen." Such instruments must be examined by experts not just to verify information, and to value the instrument, but also to suggest an appropriate means of selling the instrument, if that is desired.

[2] The Martin Brothers' *Band Instruments and Celebrated Guitars* catalog found in this book includes on page 18 an interesting paragraph. "In offering this line of improved piston light valve instruments, we beg to consider that we do not import same in parts and have them soldered together here as in other shops, (like others finish similar instruments), so as to leave only the little trouble to stamp them, and after this sell them for American Make Instruments, as ours are original with us, and made entirely under our own supervision, in our own factory."

Examples of Rare and Unusual Instruments and Related Illustrations

This section of the book contains artwork showing a number of unrelated features. The section is provided here to help the reader understand what to look for in a brass instrument. To this end, one page shows a cornet with names of its various parts. These parts also apply to virtually every brass instrument. Following that page are three pages showing valve designs. Next are pages showing various body designs for cornets. The reader is strongly advised to become familiar with these pages. Following these pages are illustrations of rare brass instruments that do not appear in the catalogs found in this book. Any instrument found in this section should be considered to be rare, and quite probably a museum piece. Values of these instruments are quite beyond the scope of this book.. This section ends with a page showing instruments that might at first be thought to be brass instruments. In fact, the instruments on the top of the page are Signal horns, and are discussed in the glossary of this book. The remaining instruments on this page are toys, and are called Zobophones.

They are related to the kazoo, and are also discussed in the glossary of this book. None of these instruments are discussed in *NGDMM*, or any other scholarly work to the utter annoyance of musical instrument curators, who regularly receive questions about these instruments. No CMVs could be located for any of these inexpensive instruments.

The purpose of pages 28 and 29 is to show some body designs for the E flat and B flat cornets, as cornets show the most variations in their body designs of all the brass musical instruments. Not all the types of cornets found in this book are shown on these pages. The accompanying list provides basic information about most of these designs. Abbreviations found here are defined in the glossary of this book and below.

Once one understands the various features of cornets, one should then be able to examine the catalogs excerpted in this book to locate an instrument, if it exists in this book.

Abbreviations Found Throughout This Book

BF:	bell forward body design
BPV:	Berliner pumpen valves
BMIM:	The Boston Musical Instrument Manufactory
BU:	Bell up body design
Br:	Brass
CMV:	Current market value
Go:	Gold
GS:	German silver
HD:	Helicon body design
Ni:	Nickel
OTS:	Over-the-shoulder body design
RV:	an unidentfied type of rotary valve, most likely either SARV or TARV
SARV:	Side action rotary valve
TARV:	Top action rotary valve

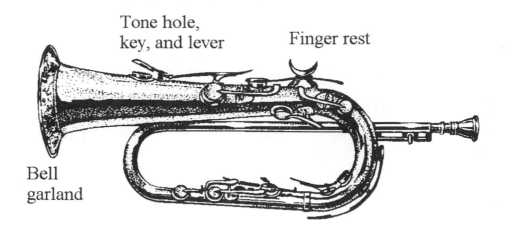

Tone hole, key, and lever

Finger rest

Bell garland

Keyed bugle from: Musical Instruments of the World, p. 73.

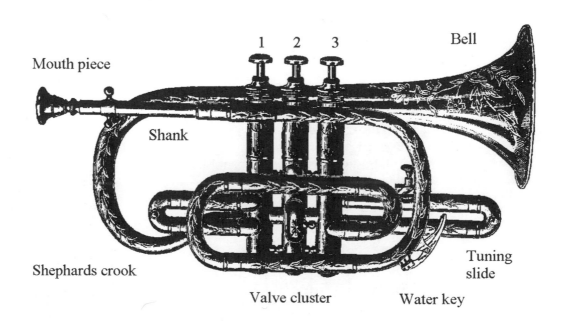

Mouth piece

1   2   3

Bell

Shank

Shephards crook

Tuning slide

Valve cluster

Water key

Cornet from Lyon & Healy's Campaign catalog of 1896, p. 39

LESS COMMON VALVE TYPES

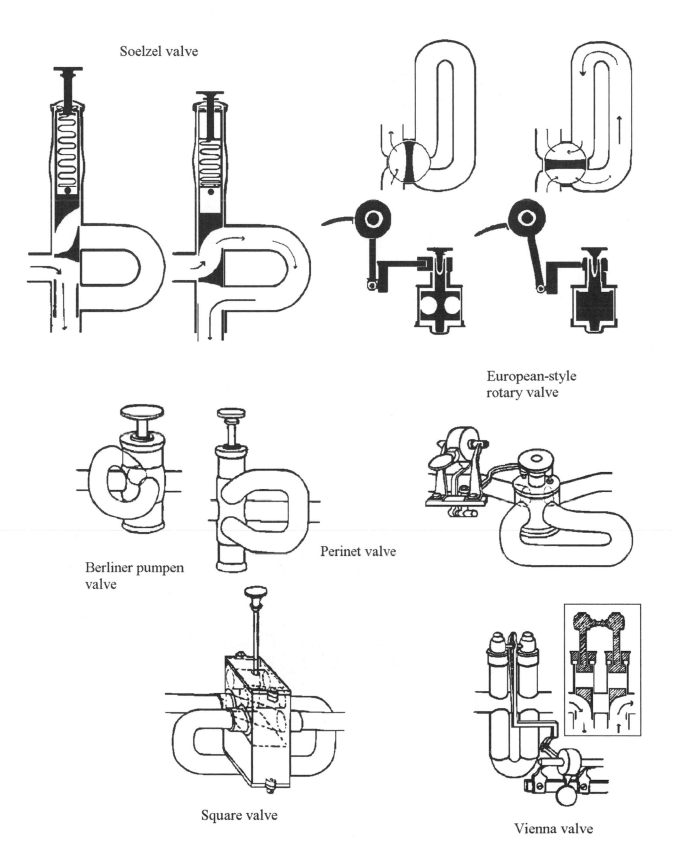

Soelzel valve

European-style
rotary valve

Berliner pumpen
valve

Perinet valve

Square valve

Vienna valve

Artwork adapted from Curt Sachs' "Sammlung alter Musikinstrumente" p. 207

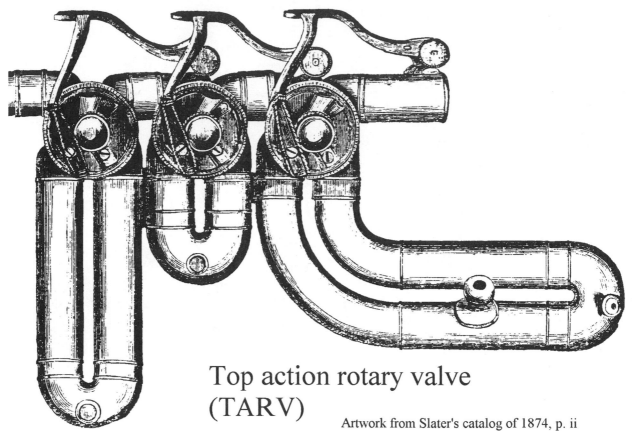

Top action rotary valve (TARV)

Artwork from Slater's catalog of 1874, p. ii

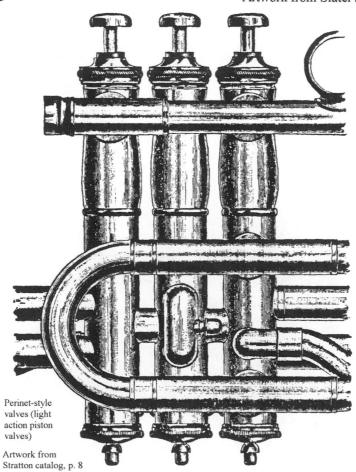

Perinet-style valves (light action piston valves)

Artwork from Stratton catalog, p. 8

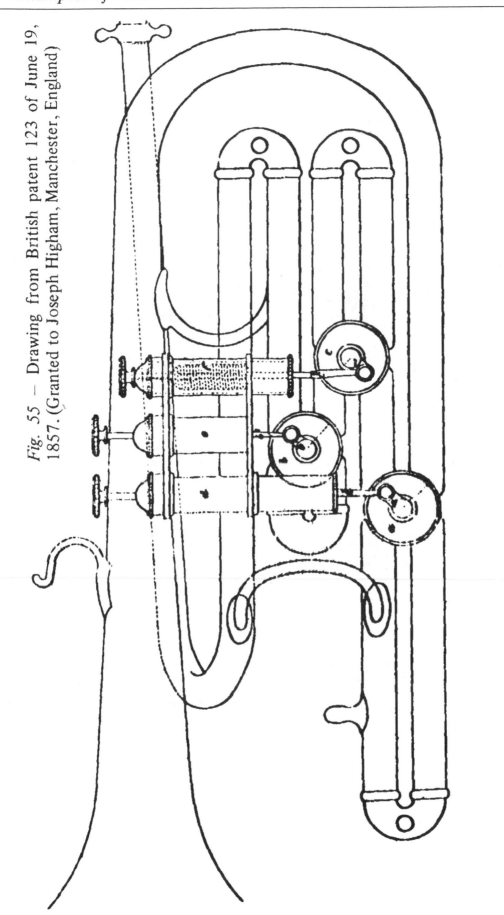

Fig. 55 – Drawing from British patent 123 of June 19, 1857. (Granted to Joseph Higham, Manchester, England)

Artwork from: Robert E. Eliason's Early American Brass Makers, p. 45

Examples of 19th century
E FLAT CORNETS

1. HD, TARV.
2. BF, SARV. B
3. BF, PV. Shepherd's crook below mouthpiece.
4. OTS, TARV.
5. HD, SARV.
6. BF, PV. Shepherd's crook below mouthpiece. Often described as "Distin" model distinguished by the bent tube near the bell.
7. BF, SARV. Often identified as an orchestral or solo design. Not a common body design.
8. BF, SARV. Often identified as a "long" pattern.
9. BU, TARV. Though E flat cornets were rarely made in this design, the design was common for larger brasses. The design is often called the "Saxhorn."
10. BF, TARV. Solo model. Unusual extra loop of tubing below bell.
11. BF, BPV.
12. BF, TARV.
13. BF, TARV. Pocket model.
14. BF, SARV. Pocket model.
15. BF, PV.

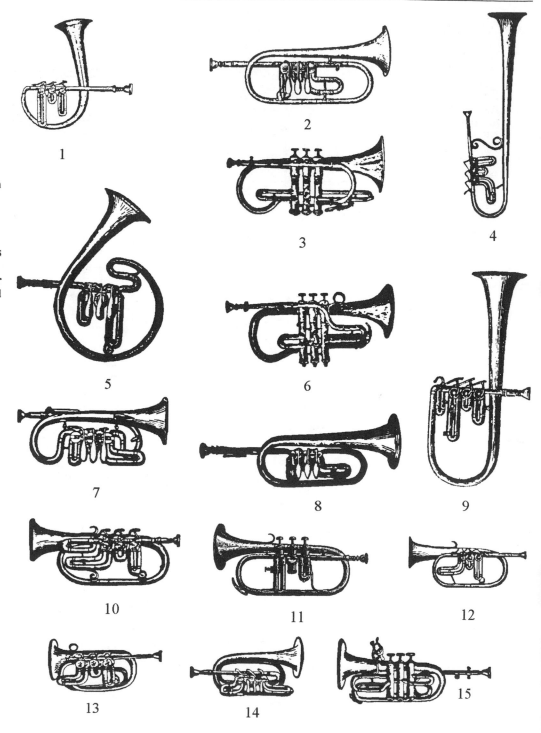

Examples of 19th century
E FLAT CORNETS

1. HD, TARV.
2. BF, PV. Shepherd's crook below mouthpiece.
3. OTS, TARV.
4. BF, TARV. Shepherd's crook below mouthpiece.
5. BF, SARV.
6. BF, TARV.
7. BF, BPV.
8. BF, SARV.
9. BU, TARV. Saxhorn design.
10. BF, SARV. Rare body design.
11. BF, TARV. Short model; note the extra loop in the lowest tube.

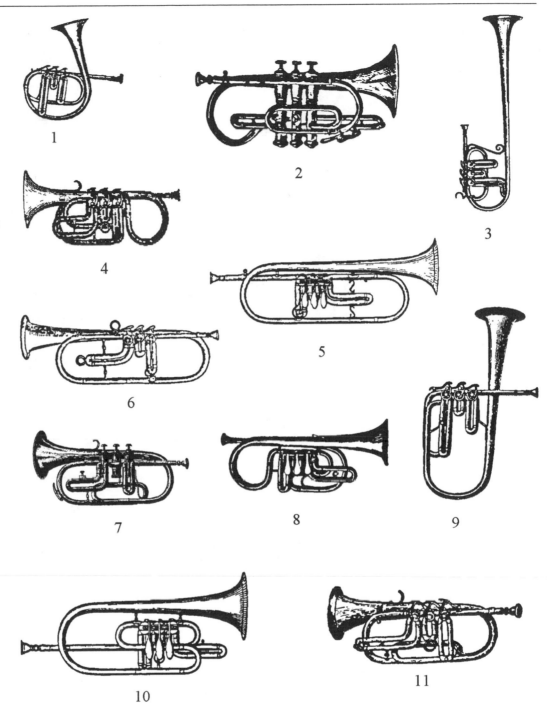

Examples of early brass instruments.

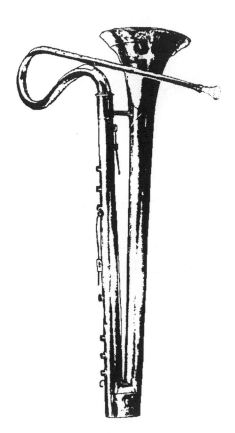

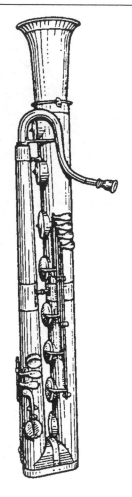

Bass horn, 6 finger
holes, 2 keys,
original artwork

Russian bassoon,
from Bahnert, p. 29

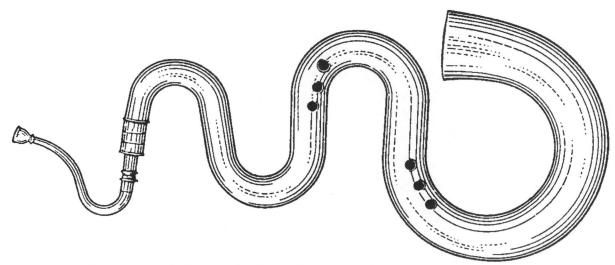

Serpent, 6 finger holes, from Bahnert, p. 27

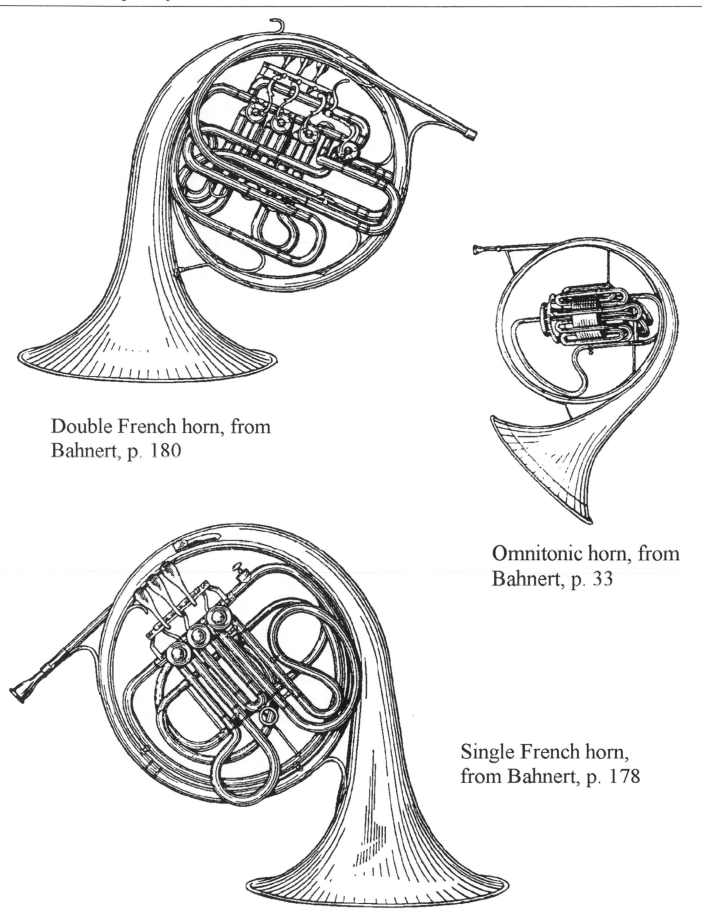

Double French horn, from
Bahnert, p. 180

Omnitonic horn, from
Bahnert, p. 33

Single French horn,
from Bahnert, p. 178

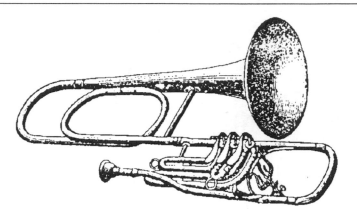

Tenor trombone in B flat, BF, SARV, Centennial model

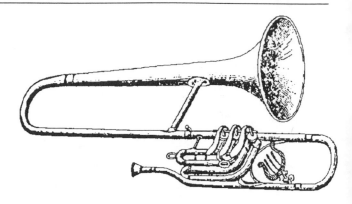

Alto trombone in E flat, BF, PV, Centennial model

Tenor or Baritone horn in B flat, BF, SARV, Centennial model

Bass horn in [B flat], BF, SARV, Centennial model

From an undated fragment, Henry G. Lehnert's patented "Centennial" models are shown. The top two instruments are trombones, while the bottom two instruments are horns. Centennial model instruments are extremely rare, and sell for the same prices as OTS instruments.

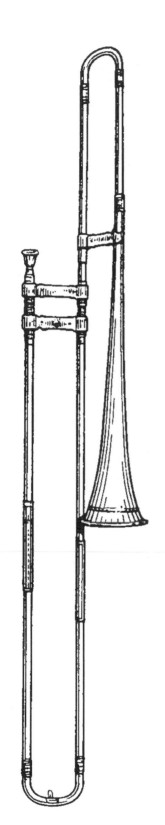

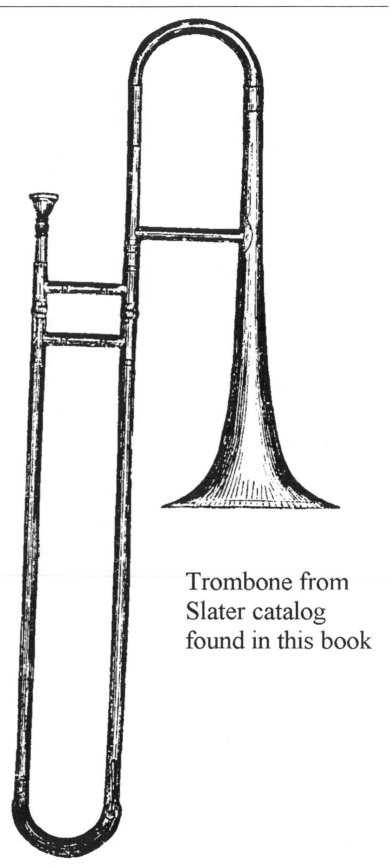

Trombone from
Slater catalog
found in this book

Sackbut, from
Bahnert, p. 29

Patent Lever Trombone, and Patent Lever Cornopean made by Köhler of London. Illustrations taken from Baines page 214.

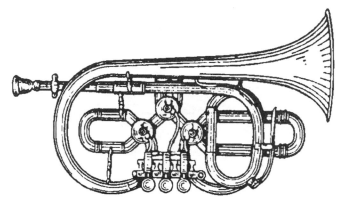

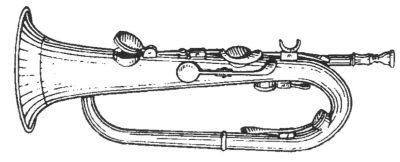

Keyed bugle in [B flat?], 4 keys,
from Bahnert, p. 33

Cornet in ?, BF, SARV,
siggestive of Shaw valves,
water key, from Bahnert, p. 49

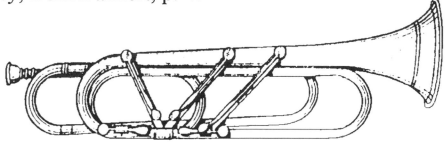

Keyed trumpet in ?, BF, from Bahnert, p. 33

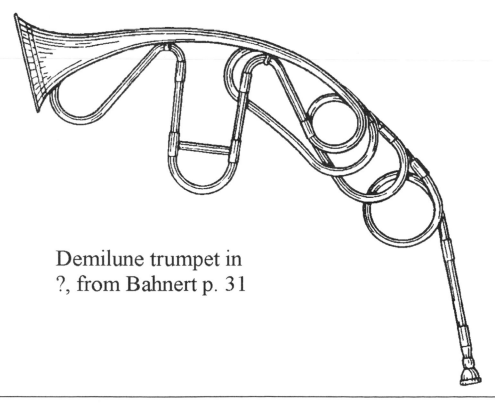

Demilune trumpet in
?, from Bahnert p. 31

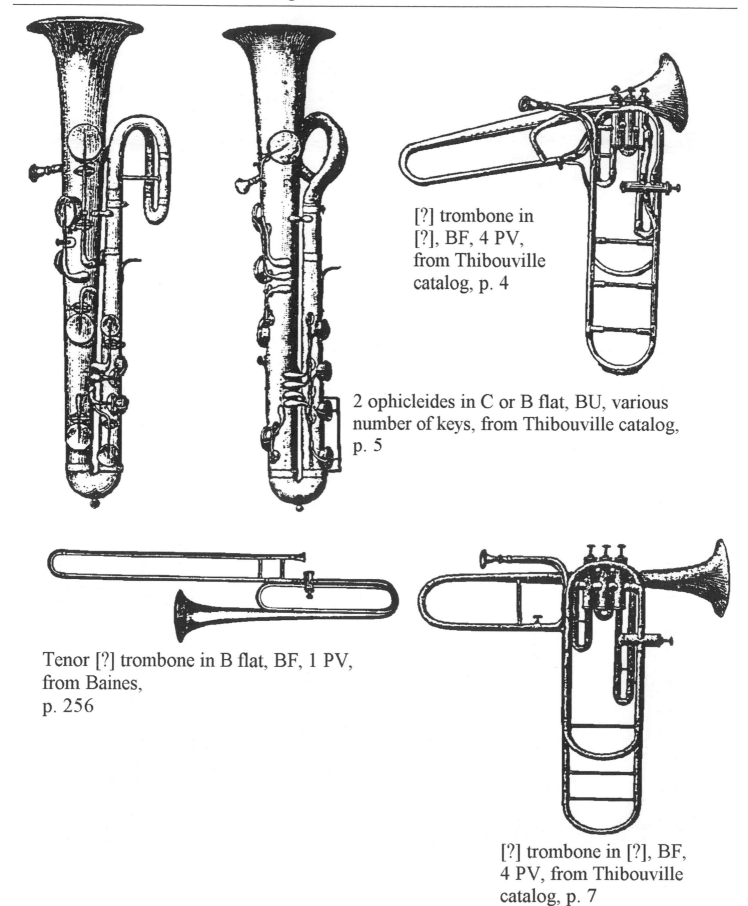

[?] trombone in
[?], BF, 4 PV,
from Thibouville
catalog, p. 4

2 ophicleides in C or B flat, BU, various
number of keys, from Thibouville catalog,
p. 5

Tenor [?] trombone in B flat, BF, 1 PV,
from Baines,
p. 256

[?] trombone in [?], BF,
4 PV, from Thibouville
catalog, p. 7

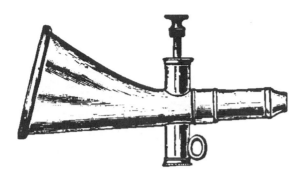

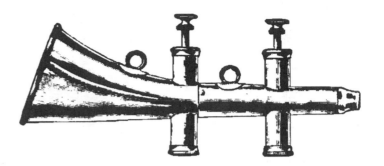

Signal horn, BF, 1 psudo-Perinet style valve

Signal horn, BF, 2 psudo-Perinet style valves

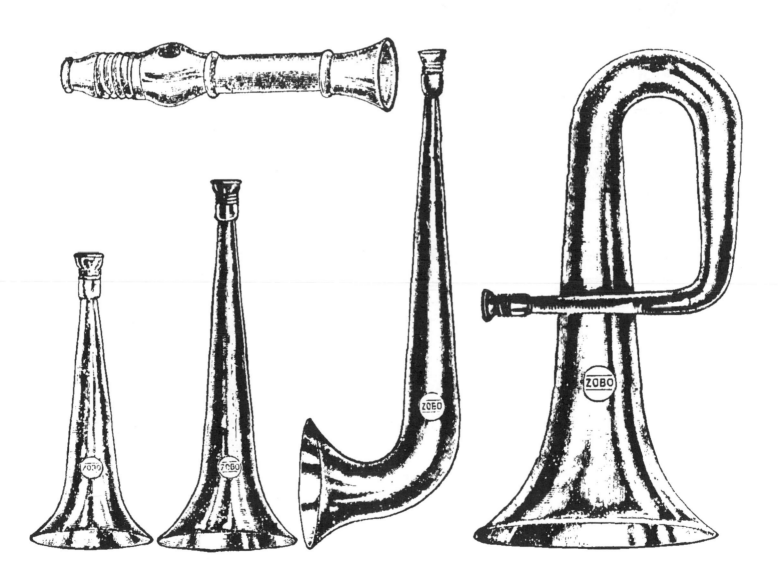

Family of Zobophones

Boston Musical Instrument Manufactory Catalogs of 1869, 1874, &1887?

The Boston Musical Instrument Manufactory is arguably one of the most important United States brass instrument manufacturers of the mid to late 19th century. *NLI* (p. 42) states that this company began in 1869, "by the amalgamation of the partners and workers of Graves & Co. and E.G. Wright & Co." Succeeding these two very important U.S. brass instrument manufacturers, the Boston Musical Instrument Manufactory Company (consisting of Henry Esbach, L.F. Hartman, and W.G. Reed) continued to manufacture instruments using the older patterns, and tools. As stated in the preface to the 1874 catalog, the company received first medals at the following exhibitions: the Massachusetts Charitable Mechanics' Association, 1865; the Middlesex Mechanics' Association, 1867; the Massachusetts Charitable Mechanics' Association, 1869; and the St. Louis Agricultural and Mechanics' Association, 1871. The catalog evidently exaggerated by stating it had been variously named: Wright, Esbach & Hartman; E.G. Wright & Co.; Wright, Gilmore & Co.; and the Boston Musical Instrument Manufactory. These statements, if true, give an earlier date than found in *NLI*, and includes the association of Wright, Gilmore & Co., which is also not listed in *NLI*. By implication, authentic instruments stamped with "Wright, Gilmore & Co.," are probably quite rare.

Characteristics of this company's instruments include rotary valves with either top or side actions, high-quality workmanship, and a cornet design where the tube from the mouthpiece passes directly into the valve cluster. This design is more characteristic of Germanic instruments. These instruments do not have the characteristic "shepherd's crook" found on many U.S.-made instruments. The company did also manufacture cornets with the shepherd's crook design, being the more common design. For their side action instruments, the touch keys can be very long tear-drop shapes. Instruments made in Germany and Austria still have all these features, and are not to be confused with this company's instruments. The top action instruments (always shown from the side in their catalogs) have touch keys that look more like the trigger of a gun. In fact, these keys are very similar to the side action keys. Though top action valves are especially associated with this company, in the 1869 catalog (p. 6), the following statement appears: "French and English cornet players still adhere to the old fashioned piston valve, while in Germany and America the rotary valve is much more in use. Recently, however, many of the most distinguished American cornet players are returning to the piston valves, and as our illustrations will show, we are prepared to apply either action agreeable to the wish and taste of the purchaser. ..."

The company's 1874 catalog (p.4) includes an interesting statement. "We have long endeavored to reduce the size of the E flat cornet, from the old-fashioned model to something smaller, giving a more brilliant quality of tone; and have already, in the "Medium," "Second Size," and "Leaders" E flat cornets, done as much as it would seem possible to do; ... This little cornet is 9 3/4 inches in length, about 4 inches in width, ..." All this implies that the company's catalog was not totally precise in what it offered, and probably repeated information from earlier catalogs. These facts are surely indicative of a company that was primarily a manufacturer, not a company that relied on subcontractors.

The company's catalogs present some problems. As stated in the preface, the 1869 catalog includes no prices. Due to the curious nature of the 1874 catalog, information has been restructured here. The numbers found here are editorial.

Special attention should to be given to the placement of SARV touch keys for this company. Most companies only offered instruments with the keys pointing in one direction throughout their catalog. This company offers either left-handed or right-handed instruments for some of its instruments. The rarity of these variations is currently uncertain.

The 1874 catalog includes an interesting statement on page 3:

"Infantry bugles, cavalry trumpets, and every description of Br, Copper and Gs Instruments made to order. Also, Snare and Bass drums, Fifes, Clarionets, Cymbals, and all the requirements of a Military Band, furnished at the shortest notice. ... We would state to our customers, that we pay particular attention to special instructions in the manufacturer of instruments, by their orders. Copper Instruments, with Gs trimmings, same price as all Gs. Instruments with Br bells, same price as all Gs. Instruments of Br, with Gs trimmings, one-half the difference in price of Br and Gs, in addition to the price of Br."

Though it is quite unlikely that this company manufactured woodwind instruments and drums, any custom-made brass wind instrument that can be documented as having been made by this company will greatly interest collectors.

The Boston Musical Instrument Manufactory catalog of 1869 included neither prices nor catalog numbers. The 1874 catalog does include prices on pages 2 and 3. The 1869 catalog is missing pages 2 and 3, which surely included a price list. Thus, the artwork from this catalog has been rearranged here, and the format used for this catalog is not followed elsewhere in this book. Instead, information taken from the catalogs has been excerpted.

Additionally, a fragment of an 1897 (?) catalog has been included. As the 1869 and 1874 catalogs include some of the same instruments, the second appearance of the instrument will not be included.

For the collector, the company's Boston Three Star trumpets are sought. These instruments are distinguished by having three stars stamped into the instrument near the company's name. Even so, considering the quality of workmanship from this company, all BMIM produced instruments will command attention by collectors, especially the company's earlier instruments. Some performers of period music even use this company's instruments today.

According to Rubb Stewart, the firm began stamping serial numbers in 1880. Instruments without serial numbers are rarer and more valuable to collectors than numbered instruments.

Boston Musical Instrument Manufactory catalog 1869. Instruments produced by the Boston Musical Instrument Manufactory. All instruments have three valves unless otherwise indicated. The original sales prices for these instrument were not available. Any original sales prices listed here were obtained from the 1874 catalog.

Cornet in E flat, BF, SARV
CMV $1200.00

Cornet in E flat, BF, 4 TARV
CMV $2000.00+

Corno (rare cornet variant) in B flat, BF, TARV
CMV $2000.00 - $3500.00

Cornet in B flat, BF, 3+1 SARV, orchestra type
Br $55.00
Gs $65.00
CMV $1200.00 - $1800.00

Cornet in B flat, BF, PV
Br $55.00
Gs $65.00
CMV $600.00 - $1000.00

Alto horn in E flat, BF, SARV
CMV $600.00 - $900.00

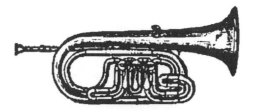

Alto in E flat, BF, SARV

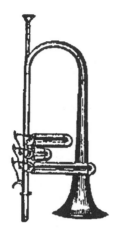

Corno [cornet variant] in B flat, BF, TARV

Cornet in B flat, BF, 4 SARV, Orchestra type

Cornet in B flat, BF, SARV

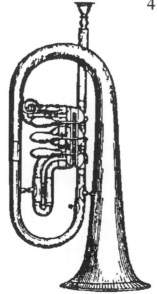

Cornet in E flat, BF, SARV

Cornet in E flat, BF, 4 SARV

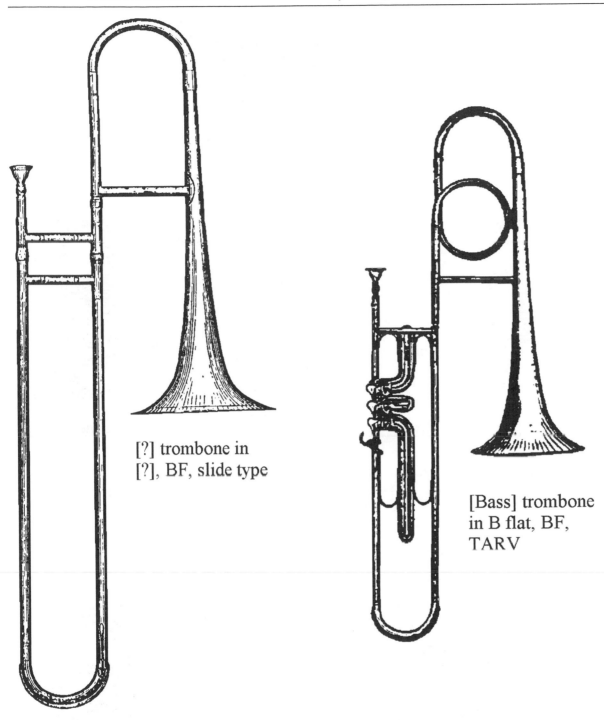

[?] trombone in
[?], BF, slide type

[Bass] trombone
in B flat, BF,
TARV

Tenor Trombone in B flat,
BF. slide type,
CMV $200-400

Tenor Trombone in B flat,
BF, RV,
CMV $600-$900
(SARVs sell for less than TARVs)

Boston Musical Instrument Manufactory catalog 1869. Instruments produced by the Boston Musical Instrument Manufactory. Instruments found on this page were constructed using a design identified in the catalog as being a "newly improved pattern," and having been introduced in 1869. Mouthpieces are pictured to the right of the instruments.

Alto horn in E flat, BU, SARV
Br $53.00
Gs $67.00
CMV $800.00 - $1100.00

Tenor horn in B flat, BU, SARV
Br $65.00
Gs $78.00
CMV $800.00 - $1100.00

Baritone horn in B flat, BU, SARV
Br $72.00
Gs $85.00
CMV $800.00 - $1100.00

Bass horn in B flat, BU, SARV
Br $75.00
Gs $98.00
CMV $800.00 - $1100.00

Bass horn in E flat, BU, SARV (shown with four valves)
Br $100.00
Gs $130.00
CMV $1200.00 - $1700.00

Alto in E flat, BU, SARV

Tenor in B flat, BU, SARV

Baritone in B flat, BU, SARV

Bass in B flat, BU, SARV

Bass in E flat, BU, 4 SARV

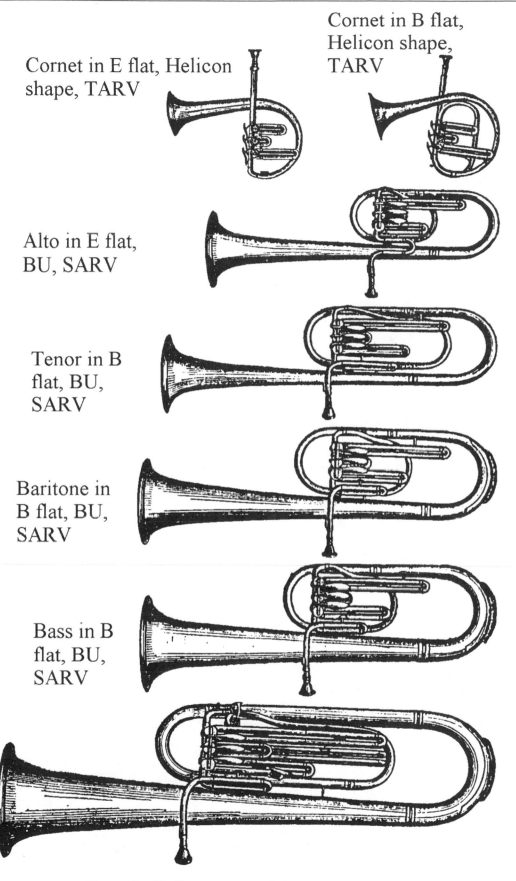

Cornet in E flat, Helicon shape, TARV

Cornet in B flat, Helicon shape, TARV

Alto in E flat, BU, SARV

Tenor in B flat, BU, SARV

Baritone in B flat, BU, SARV

Bass in B flat, BU, SARV

Bass in E flat, BU, 4 SARV

Cornet in E flat, HD, TARV
Br $45.00
Gs $55.00
CMV $2500.00 - $3500.00

Cornet in B flat, HD, TARV
Br $45.00
Gs $55.00
CMV $2500.00 - $3500.00

Alto horn in E flat, BU, SARV
Br $53.00
Gs $67.00
CMV $800.00 - $1100.00

Tenor horn in B flat, BU, SARV
Br $65.00
Gs $78.00
CMV $800.00 - $1100.00

Baritone horn in B flat, BU, SARV
Br $72.00
Gs $85.00
CMV $800.00 - $1100.00

Bass horn in B flat, BU, SARV
Br $75.00
Gs $98.00
CMV $800.00 - $1100.00

Bass horn in E flat, BU, 3+1 SARV
Br $100.00
Gs $130.00
Three valve CMV $600.00 - $1000.00
Four valve CMV $1000.00 - $1600.00

Cornet in E flat, OTS, TARV
Br $45.00
Gs $55.00
CMV $2500.00 - $3000.00

Cornet in B flat, OTS, TARV
Br $45.00
Gs $55.00
CMV $2500.00 - $3000.00

Alto horn in E flat, OTS, TARV
Br $53.00
Gs $67.00
CMV $2500.00

Tenor horn in B flat, OTS, TARV
Br $65.00
Gs $78.00
CMV $2500.00

Baritone horn in B flat, OTS, TARV
Br $72.00
Gs $85.00
CMV $2500.00

Bass horn in B flat, OTS, TARV
Br $75.00
Gs $98.00
CMV $2500.00

Bass horn in E flat, OTS, 1 SARV, 3 TARV
Br $100.00
Gs $130.00
CMV $2500.00 +

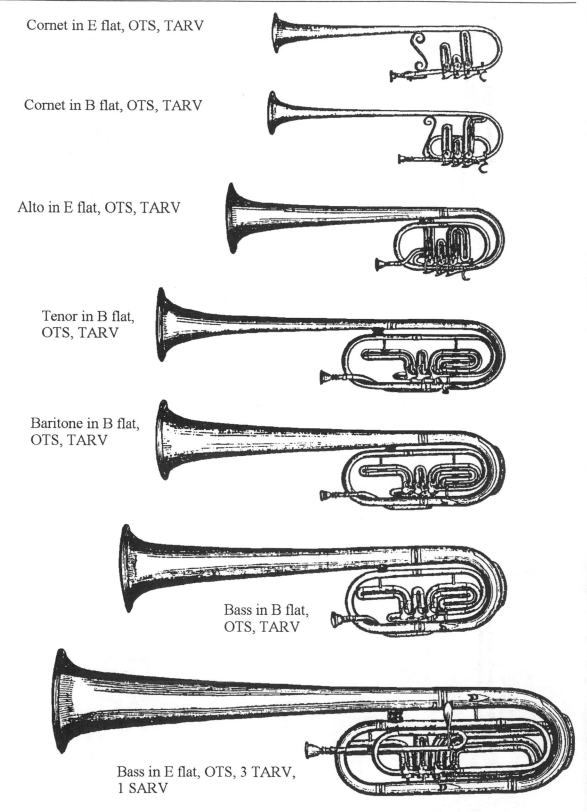

Cornet in E flat, OTS, TARV

Cornet in B flat, OTS, TARV

Alto in E flat, OTS, TARV

Tenor in B flat, OTS, TARV

Baritone in B flat, OTS, TARV

Bass in B flat, OTS, TARV

Bass in E flat, OTS, 3 TARV, 1 SARV

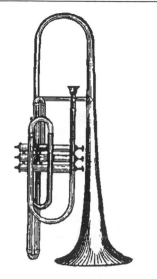

Alto in E flat,
BF, PV

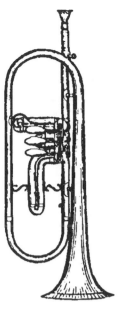

Alto horn in E flat, BF, PV
CMV $400.00 - $600.00

Cornet [Trumpet] in B flat,
BF, SARV (unusual design)
CMV $2000.00 - $3500.00

Cornet in B flat, BF, SARV
CMV $1000.00 - $1500.00

French horn [in F?], SARV
CMV $200.00 - $400.00

Cornet in E flat.
BF, SARV, leader model
CMV $1200

Cornet in B flat, BF,
SARV

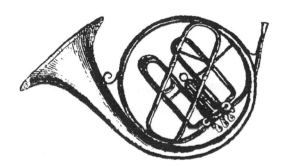

French horn, SARV

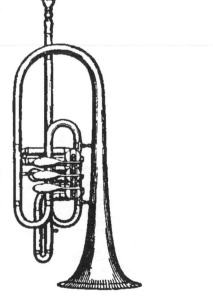

Cornet in B flat, BF,
SARV

Cornet in E flat,
BF, SARV

Boston Musical Instrument Manufactory catalog 1874. Instruments produced by the Boston Musical Instrument Manufactory. All instruments have three valves unless otherwise indicated. The catalog indicates that all prices for instruments on this page apply to OTS and BF designs, and SARV or TARV systems. All instruments listed in this catalog, except the pocket cornet, the C cornet, all trombones, and the French horn, are offered with a fourth valve for an additional $10.00. The CMV (current market value) for an item follows all other prices for that item, when the CMV could be determined. Instruments with the fourth valve sell for above the given CMV. Though the catalog offered OTS, SARV, and TARV instruments for the same price, their CMV's are considerably different. The structure of this catalog has presented some problems which might not have been fully ameliorated here.

Cornet in E flat, BF or OTS, SARV or TARV
Br $45.00
Gs $55.00
Si plated $70.00
Pure Si $160.00
CMV OTS $2500-$3000
CMV BF, SARV $1200
CMV BF, SARV $1200-$1400

Cornet in E flat, BF, RV, Leader model, Br $45, GS $55
CMV $1200

Cornet in E flat, BF, RV, Pocket shape, CMV $1500-$2000

Gold plated Cornets sell for above the given CMVs.

Cornet in E flat, BF, SARV

Cornet in E flat, BF, SARV

Cornet in E flat, BF, TARV

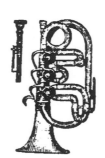

Cornet in E flat, BF, TARV, Pocket shape

Cornet in E flat, BF, SARV, Pocket shape

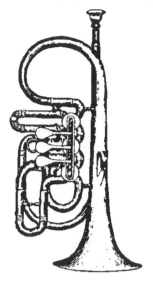

Cornet in B flat,
BF, TARV

Cornet in B flat,
BF, SARV

Boston Musical Instrument Manufactory catalog 1874.
Instruments produced by the Boston Musical Instrument Manufactory. The following instruments are identified as being orchestra instruments.

Cornet in B flat, BF, RV or PV
Br $55.00
Gs $65.00
CMV RV $1200.00 - $1400.00
CMV PV $600.00 - $1000.00

Cornet in B flat, BF, 3 PV and 1 SARV, and echo attachment (not shown)
Br $85.00
Gs $95.00
CMV $1200.00 - $1400.00

Solo alto in E flat, BF, RV,
CMV $600-$900

Tenor trombone in B flat, BF, RV
CMV $600-$900

Cornet in B flat,
BF, PV

Solo alto in E flat,
BF, SARV

[?] Trombone in B flat, BF, SARV

Boston Musical Instrument Manufactory catalog 1869. Instruments produced by the Boston Musical Instrument Manufactory.

Cornet in E flat, HD, TARV (not shown)
Br $45.00
Gs $55.00
CMV $2500-$3500

Cornet in B flat, HD, TARV (not shown)
Bf $45.00
Gs $55.00
CMV $2500-$3500

Alto horn in E flat, BU, SARV
Br $53.00
Gs $67.00
CMV $800.00-$1100.00

Tenor horn in B flat, BU, SARV
Br $72.00
Gs $85.00
CMV $800.00-1100.00

Baritone horn in B flat, BU, SARV
Br $72.00
Gs $85.00
CMV $800.00-$1100.00

Bass horn in B flat, BU, SARV
Br $75.00
Gs $98.00
CMV $800.00-$1100.00

Bass horn in EE flat, HD, 3 SARV
Br $120.00
Gs $150.00
CMV $800.00

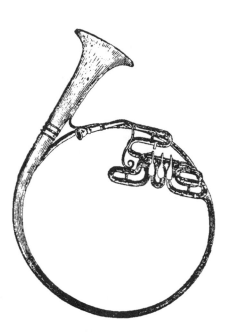

Alto in E flat, Helicon style, SARV

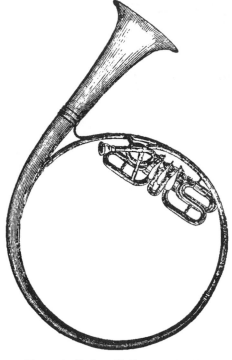

Tenor in B flat, Helicon style, SARV

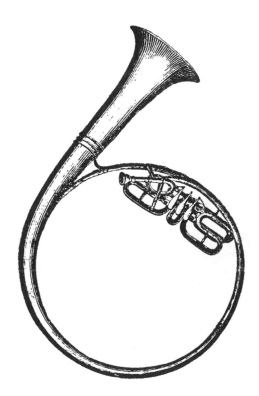

Baritone in B flat, Helicon style, SARV

Bass in B flat, Helicon style, SARV

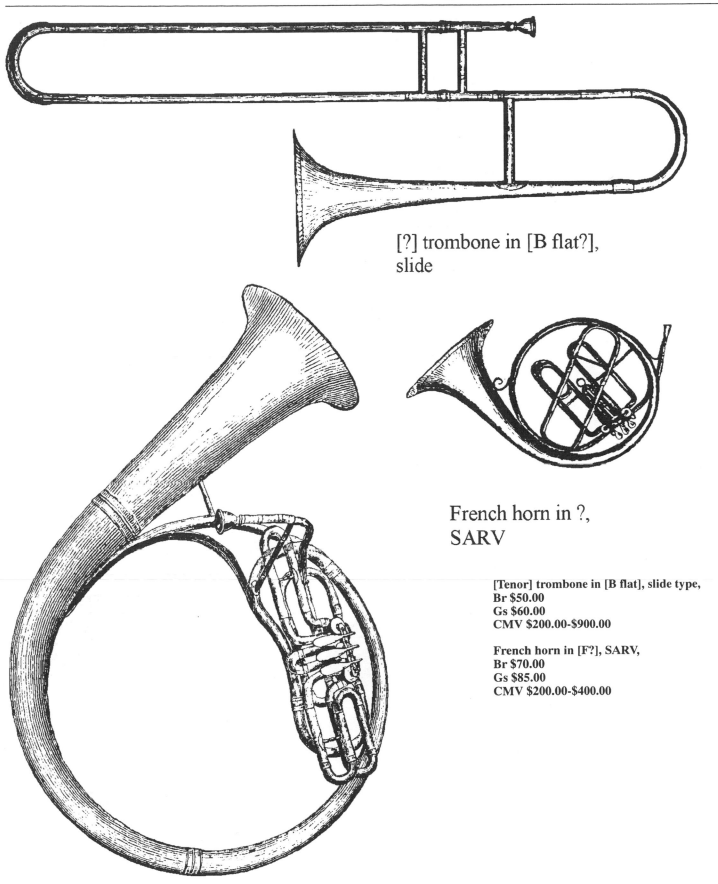

[?] trombone in [B flat?], slide

French horn in ?, SARV

Contrabass in [E flat], Helicon shape, SARV

[Tenor] trombone in [B flat], slide type,
Br $50.00
Gs $60.00
CMV $200.00-$900.00

French horn in [F?], SARV,
Br $70.00
Gs $85.00
CMV $200.00-$400.00

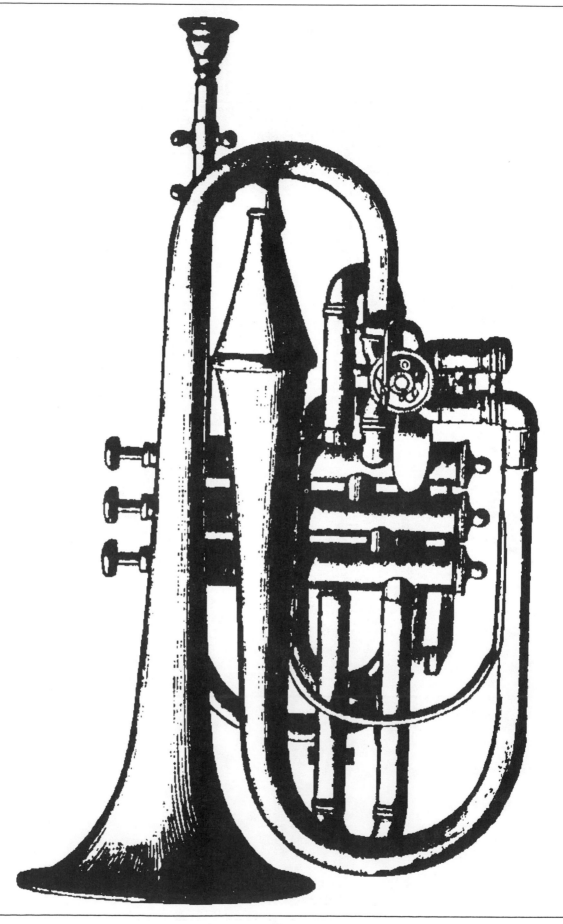

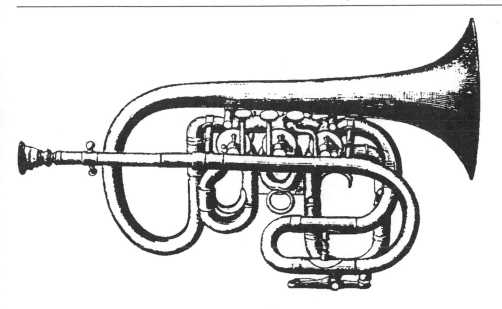

Cornet in B flat and A, BF, PV, water key

Boston Musical Instrument Manufactory catalog fragment of 1887? Instruments produced by the Boston Musical Instrument Manufactory. The patent cornet incorporates a valve system patented April 22, 1879, and, from the artwork, appears to be an improved SARV system. The body design is also uncommon. The echo cornet has a SARV valve which activates the echo attachment. Current market values for these instruments are not possible due to their rarity. Speculatively, the cornet with the echo attachment should sell for at least $1200.00, depending upon condition. This assumption is based upon the CMV for a similar, though not as ornate cornet offered in the 1874 catalog.

Cornet in B flat and A, C and B flat, BF, SARV, patent model, water key
Br $55.00
Gs $65.00
Si plate $65.00

Cornet in B flat, BF, 3 PV and 1 SARV, echo model
Br $85.00
Gs $95.00
Si plate $95.00

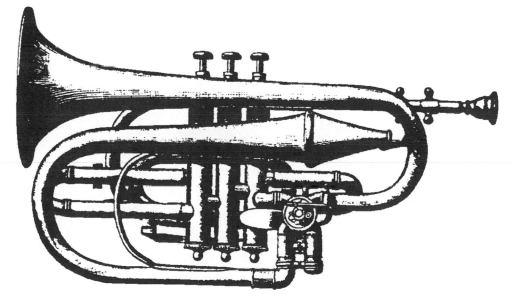

Cornet in B flat, BF, 3 PV and 1 SARV, echo attachment

Fragments of Undated Distin-related Catalogs

The Distin family was quite prolific as instrument makers, and performers, beginning in London. With Henry John Distin, the family came to the U.S. Henry Distin worked in London from 1850-1868. In the U.S., he worked in New York from 1877-1882. Next, he worked in Philadelphia from 1882-1890. Finally, he worked in Williamsport, PA from 1886-1909, opening his factory there. Until the Williamsport factory opened, Distin designed instruments, but had others actually manufacture them for him. During his life, he associated himself with M. Slater, F.W. Busch, and later J.W. Pepper, all of whom most certainly manufactured instruments for Distin. Distin retired and sold out to Keefer. A more complete biography of Distin is found in *NLI*, page 90.

After Distin ended his business relationship with M. Slater, Slater continued to sell Distin model instruments. He stated in a circa 1881 catalog the following:

"The bells [of the Distin model instruments] are all of large dimensions, therefore producing a very powerful tone, combined with a harmonious and very pleasing effect, the valve notes being equal to the open notes. ... I beg to call attention to my Solo Bb cornet No. 2, patent light piston valve, Distin model, made by the same workmen that made the Distin Cornets for me when I was connected with Mr. Distin. These instruments are made of the same material and have the same bell and valves as the genuine Henry Distin Bb cornets, and I will guarantee them to be equal to the genuine Henry Distin in every respect. Yet I offer them at a great deal less money."

Henry Distin invented at least one instrument, and made improvements to others. Distin invented the melody horn, evidently also called the altophone, sometime after 1860. He, M. Slater (after the two ended their business relationship), and Keefer all produced this now rare instrument. Originally, the instrument was produced in either F or E flat. A later fragment of a catalog stated that instruments made in F came with an E flat slide. An early M. Slater catalog (circa 1880) showed three models of melody horns. The first was a circular design with the bell pointing up. The second design was a circular design with the bell pointing down. The third design was a saxhorn design, with the bell pointing up. All instruments were offered with PV. Sadly, the artwork in the catalog was not usable for this book.

Distin's history is quite complicated. This is to say that an instrument with the Distin name on it might sell for as little as $25 or as much as $2,500. Great care must be taken in determining what instrument is in hand, and where, and when it was made. For the collector, Distin's instruments made in London are of two totally different classes. The first class, instruments bearing Distin's name and London, are collectible, bringing $500 for cornets. Instruments, however, with the Distin name, London, and the Boosey name are worth very little. These instruments should have a logo of a trumpet with a Distin banner. Distin instruments made in New York or Philadelphia command high prices for the collector, but not necessarily for the performer. Instruments from Williamsport, PA are not as interesting to the collectors, yet are quite valuable to today's performer looking for a period cornet. Condition here is very important. Farrar states that prior to World War I, Keefer, who bought out Distin in 1909, produced some of the highest-grade band instruments in the U.S. After that time, the quality of the instruments deteriorated. Below is a chart that should help in identifying Distin instruments. Valuing Distin instruments might still require an expert. Most of the information from this chart was provided by Farrar.

Distin's instruments almost always have logos (or trade marks) and trade names stamped on them. The logo (and absence of a logo) can help to identify the quality of the instrument, and more. A description of the logo is followed here by a discussion of collectiblity.

1. Henry Distin Band Instrument Company and London: instruments made by Distin, and are very collectible instruments. Cornets tend to sell for upwards of $500 today.

2. Distin banner with a trumpet, and London: instruments made by Boosey, and are worth very little.

3. Eagle with trumpet: instruments made by or for Distin in the U.S. Here, the city stamped on the instrument determines who might be interested in collecting the instrument. Do not confuse model type, such as London, Berlin, etc. for where the instrument was made.

   A. New York: Instruments are collectible. Yet, musicians often find them not playable.

   B. Philadelphia: Same as New York.

C. Williamsport, PA. Collectors are less interested in these instruments. Yet, performers will pay as much as $2,000 for a cornet in excellent condition (i.e. all the set pieces, and case) and requiring no repairs.

4. Eagle with the U.S. Capital dome: very rare transitional logo. Exceptionally few of these instruments survive. Instruments with this logo must be appraised by an expert.

5. No logo: two classes of instruments. Either the instrument is very early and valuable, or a cheap European import. Here is one of the few times in this book where no directions can be given, except to consult an expert. Condition and quality of workmanship might lead one to conclude that the instrument is a cheap instrument, when in fact the instrument might or might not actually be a very old instrument in poor condition. Also, Paris model instruments evidently never had a logo, being rather cheap instruments. Even so, these instruments are collectible.

6. Keefer trade mark on Distin instruments, made before WW I are in demand by performers. See also 3C above.

7. As a final point, instruments with serial numbers of 10,000 and lower are worth more to performers than those with higher numbers. All these instruments should have the Keefer trade mark on them.

As can be seen, providing current market values for Distin instruments is quite involved. By comparing the above information with the instrument, one should be able to determine if the instrument is a student or professional instrument. Only two Distin instruments were found in dealers' lists, and have been included in Appendix C. However, no information was included about where they were made, or even their model names. By inference from their prices, one might assume that these were student-grade instruments or better-grade instruments in poor condition.

Distin (and Keefer) instrument models generally had names. These names help to identify the quality of the instrument. Highest grade is the professional model, and is found throughout the entire line of brass instruments, i.e. cornet through basses. The Oxford model is based upon the Highest grade model. The most noticeable difference is that the Oxford model does not have as much engraving as the Highest grade. The Oxford model sold for almost as much as the Highest grade. The American model is a moderately priced instrument, designed for a student. The Orchestral model "is practically our Oxford Model Cornet with minor modifications." However, the fragment does not indicate what those modifications were. The only visible difference from the fragment is the orchestral model has a quick-change slide to allow the musician to quickly change key from B flat to A. The musician can also change tuning slides for low or high pitch. The Vienna model sold for a modest price, and was possibly a student instrument. The Paris model was imported from Paris, and is not considered to be his best model. The Berlin model sold for the least of all his identified models, and was probably an amateur instrument.

Distin, like most makers also produced larger instruments. As stated throughout this book, larger instruments originally sold for more than smaller instruments. Yet, today, the larger instruments rarely sell as well as the smaller instruments. Since only fragments of Distin catalogs could be found, a complete line of Distin's instruments is not documented here, especially his larger instruments.

No complete trade catalog has been identified from the Distin company. Only fragments are currently known, which are also collected. Thus, if one complete catalog were to come to light, it too would command an interesting price, possibly at least $100, depending upon contents, condition, and page count.

A welcome feature of some fragments is the inclusion of dimensions for instruments. Though these dimensions are not uniformly given in the fragments, all such information is gladly added to this book.

Retail prices and detailed descriptions could not be obtained for most of the instruments found in the fragments used for this book. Furthermore, the artwork in a Slater catalog of circa 1880 was too faded to be useable here. The scant information from this catalog, however, is provided here to give some insight into the variety of instruments offered by Slater, based upon his association with Distin. In a circa 1895 Slater fragment, the melody horn was not offered. Instruments in this fragment were offered with either brass, triple plated Si, or triple plated Si with Go lined bell, mounts, and points. An illustration of an altophone (a probable trade name invented by Keefer for the melody horn) appears in this book. See the Glossary of this book for a discussion of the terms ballad horn, mellophone, altophone, and melody horn.

Though Henry Distin is a very important maker, information about him obtained for this book does not give a clear picture of him, his output, or the current market values for his instruments. This section is therefore offered with great care and hope that no errors exist, but with no guarantees. Frankly, Distin is the most vexing of all makers documented in this book. No CMVs were found for most of Distin's instruments.

Fragment of a probable Keefer catalog of circa 1910? Instruments produced by the Keefer Mfg. Co., Williamsport, PA and are heavily, and completely engraved.

Alto horn in E flat, BF, PV, Highest grade
Length 19 inches, width 7 1/4 inches, bell diameter 7 inches
Br $37.50
Si plate, with burnished points and bell $47.50
Low-pitch slide $5.00 extra

Altophone in F or E flat, Bell down, PV, Highest grade model, water key
Brass $60.00
Si plated, satin finish, Go mounted $75.00

Low pitch slide $5.00

Extra slides for string orchestra
E natural slide $4.00
D natural slide $3.50
C slide $4.50

Fragment of a probable Keefer catalog of circa 1910? Instruments produced by the Keefer Mfg. Co., Williamsport, PA.

Alto horn in E flat, BU, PV, Highest grade, water key, heavily engraved
Length 20 1/2 inches, width 8 inches, bell diameter 8 inches
Br $37.50
Si plate, with burnished points and bell $47.50
Full burnishing $5.00 extra
Low-pitch slide $5.00 extra

Fragment of a Keefer catalog of circa 1920? Instrument produced by the Keefer Mfg. Co., Williamsport, PA

Altophone in E flat, BU, PV, water key, engraving on bell
Br $70.00
Quadruple Si plate, satin finish, Go mounted $80.00
Full burnishing $5.00 extra
Also offered in F with E flat slide for the same price

Illustrations of four Distin trade marks.

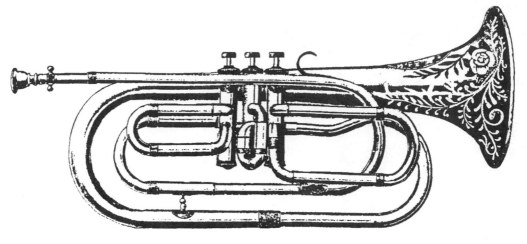

Alto in E flat, BF, PV, Highest grade model

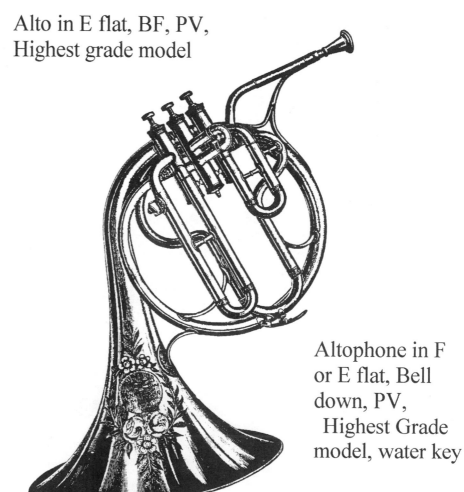

Altophone in F or E flat, Bell down, PV, Highest Grade model, water key

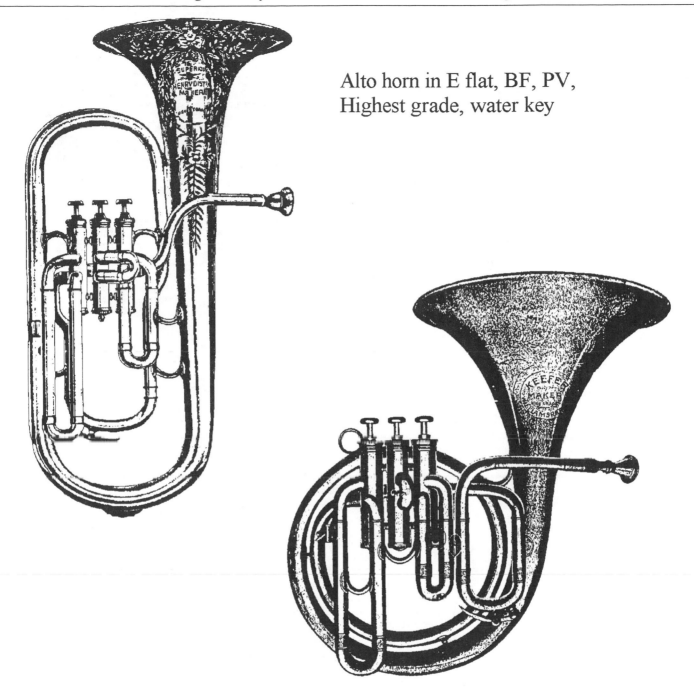

Alto horn in E flat, BF, PV,
Highest grade, water key

Altophone in E flat, BU, PV, water key

Four of Distin's trade marks

Fragment of a probable Keefer catalog of circa 1910? Instruments produced by the Keefer Mfg. Co., Williamsport, PA and are heavily, and completely engraved.

Cornet in E flat, BF, PV, American model, water key [Br or Si plate no price found.]

Cornet in B flat, BF, PV, American model, A and B shank, and water key Length 13 1/2 inches, width 6 1/2 inches, bell diameter 5 inches Br $22.50 Si plate, sating finish $30.00 Low-pitch slide $2.50 extra CMV $100

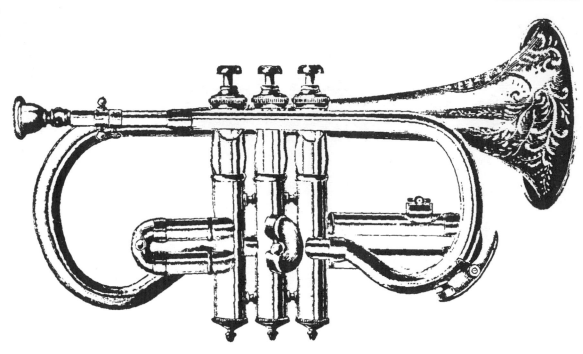

Cornet in E flat, BF, PV, American model, water key

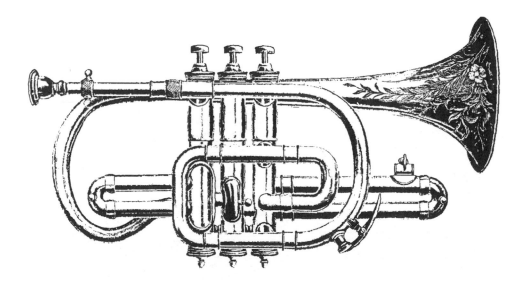

Cornet in B flat, BF, PV, American model, water key

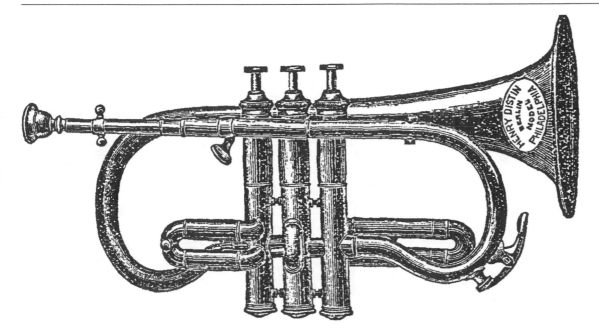

Fragment of a Henry Distin catalog of circa 1878. Instruments produced by unidentified manufacturer for Distin.

Cornet in E flat, BF, PV, Berlin model, water key
Br $12.00
Ni plate $15.00
Si plate, satin finish $17.00
Si plate, burnished, and Go plate $19.00

Cornet in B flat, BF, PV, Berlin model, water key
Br 12.00
Ni plate $15.00
Si plate, satin finish $18.00
Si plate, burnished, and Go plate $20.00

Cornet in E flat, BF, PV, Berlin model, water key

Cornet in B flat, BF, PV, Berlin model, water key

Fragment of a probable Keefer catalog of circa 1910?. Instruments produced by the Keefer Mfg. Co., Williamsport, PA.

Cornet in B flat, BF, PV, Highest grade model, heavily engraved throughout, pearl button tops, A and B shanks, tuning bit, low-pitch slide, and double water key
Length 12 1/2 inches, width 6 1/2 inches, bell diameter 5 inches
Br $45.00
Triple Si plate, full burnished, Go mounted $60.00
Go plate, full burnished $85.00

Cornet in B flat, BF, 3+1 PV, Solo model, echo attachment, water key
[Br version probably produced]
Si plate $27.00
CMV $900.00 - $2500.00 (Price based upon condition.)

Cornet in B flat, BF, PV, Orchestral model, water key. Offered in B flat, low-pitch, with extension slides and gage (seen at the bottom of the instrument) for quick change to either A high-pitch or A low-pitch,
Br $60.00
Triple Si plate, Go mounted $70.00
"The orchestral model is practically our Oxford model cornet with minor modifications."

Fragment of a Distin catalog of circa 1882.
Instrument produced by unidentified manufacturer while Distin was in Philadelphia, using a model designed in 1882.

Cornet in B flat, BF, PV, water key
Br $75.00
Triple Si plate, engraved and burnished $90.00
Triple Si plate, Go inside and all points $125.00

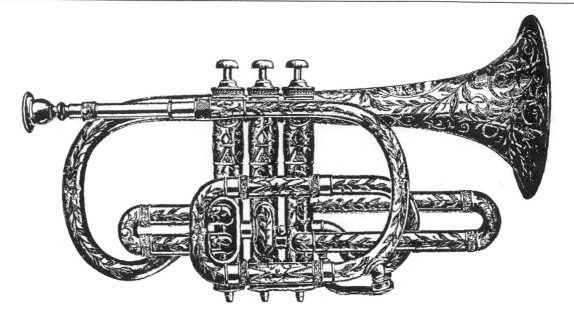

Cornet in B flat, BF, PV, Highest grade model, double water key

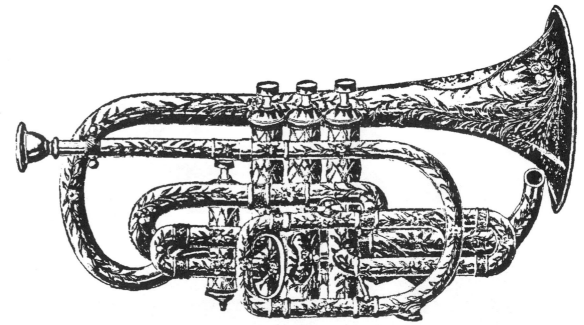

Cornet in B flat, BF, 3 + 1 PV, echo attachment, water key

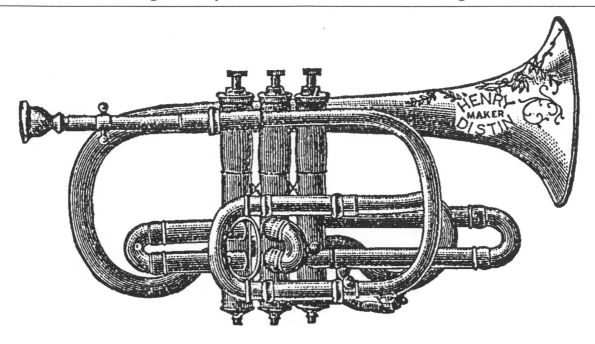

Cornet in B flat, BF, PV, water key

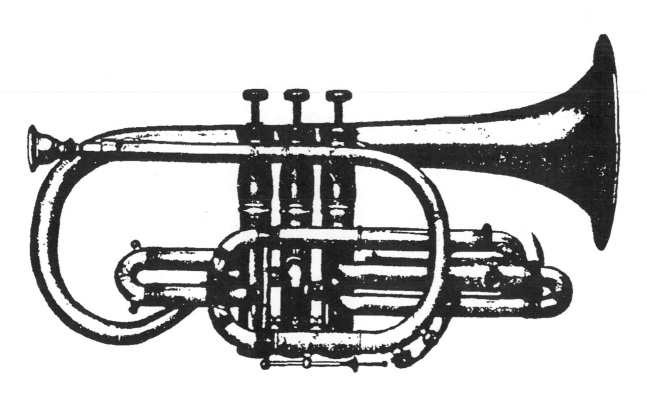

Cornet in B flat, BF, PV, Orchestral model, water key

Fragment of a probable Keefer catalog of circa 1910? Instruments produced by the Keefer Mfg. Co., Williamsport, PA and are heavily, and completely engraved.

Double bell euphonium, BU, 3 and 2 PV, engraved mounts and main bell, Highest grade
Br $100.00
Si plate $125.00
Low-pitch slide $5.00 extra

Fragment of a probable Keefer catalog of circa 1920? Instruments produced by the Keefer Mfg. Co., Williamsport, PA and are heavily, and completely engraved.

Double bell euphonium, BU, 3 and 2 PV, engraved mounts and main bell. Length 25 inches, diameter of baritone bell 11 1/2 inches, diameter of tenor bell 7 inches. Marked "Keefer maker Highest grade Williamsport, PA." Despite subtle differences between the two shown instruments, the above measurements might apply to the Distin instrument.
[Not shown here. No prices given in the fragment.]

Double bell Euphonium, BU and bell forward, 3 + 2 PV

Bass horn
[in E flat],
HD, PV

Fragment of a probable
Keefer catalog of circa 1910
[?]. Instrument produced by
the Keefer Mfg. Co.,
Williamsport, PA.

Bass horn in E flat, HD,
PV, highest grade, water key.
Br $100.00
Gs $135.00
Full burnished, extra $12.00
Low pitch slide, extra $5.00

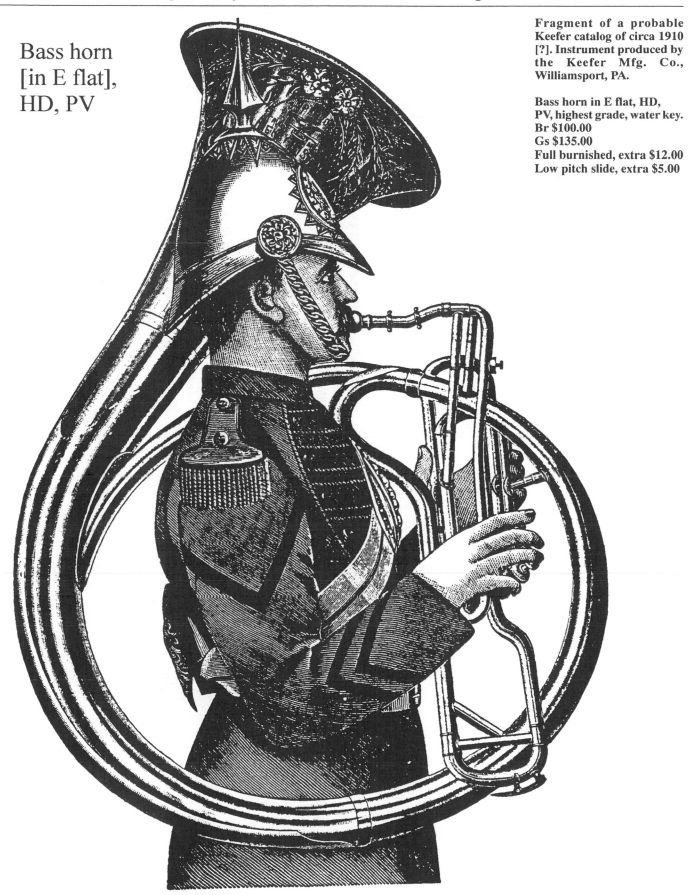

Fragment of a probable Keefer catalog of circa 1920? Instruments produced by the Keefer Mfg. Co., Williamsport, PA and are heavily, and completely engraved.

Cornet in B flat, BF, PV, London model, water key, engraved. Length 12 1/2 inches, width 6 1/2 inches, bell diameter 4 1/2 inches.
Br $40.00
Quadruple Si plate, satin finish, Go mounted $50.00
Low pitch slide $2.50
CMV $500 - $600
Same as above without engraving CMV $200

Fragment of a probable Keefer catalog of circa 1910? Instruments produced by the Keefer Mfg. Co., Williamsport, PA and are heavily, and completely engraved.

Cornet in B flat, BF, PV, Oxford model, water key.
Br $45.00
Triple Si plate, satin finish, engraved $55.00
Go plated $85.00
Full burnished, Go mounted $5.00 extra

Fragment of a Keefer catalog of circa 1920?
Instruments produced by the Keefer Mfg. Co., Williamsport, PA and are heavily, and completely engraved.

Cornet in B flat, BF, PV, Oxford model, water key.
This instrument has no lap joint below the third finger button, unlike the one pictured in this book. The engraving on the tubing over the tuning slide suggests an X, instead of a floral pattern found on the circa 1910 version. Length 12 1/2 inches, width 6 1/2 inches, bell diameter 4 1/2 inches.
Br engraved, enamel inlay finger buttons $55.00
Quadruple Si plate, full burnished or satin finish, Go mounted $70.00
Quadruple Go plate $90.00

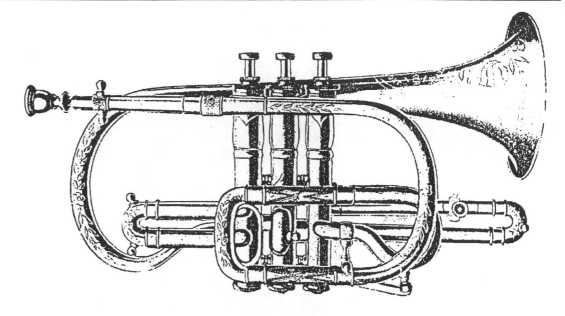

Cornet in B flat, BF, PV, London model, water key

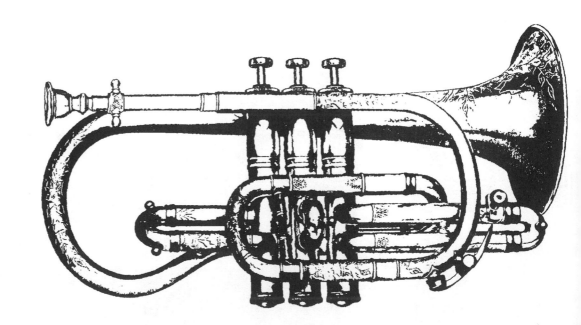

Cornet in B flat, BF, PV, Oxford model, water key

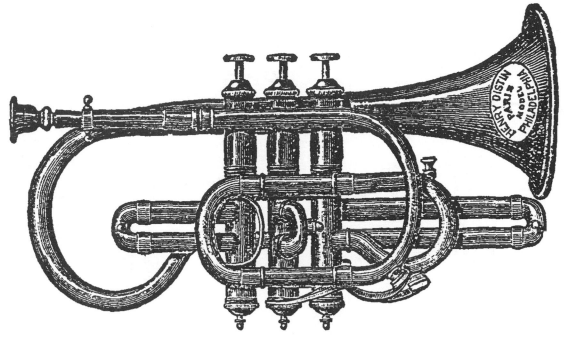

Cornet in B flat, BF, PV, Paris model, double water key

Trumpet in E flat, BF, PV, Cabaret Caliber. Length 23 inches, width 6 1/2 inches, bell diameter 4 1/2 inches. [No prices given, and the original artwork is not useable here.]

Fragment of a Henry Distin catalog of circa 1878. Instrument produced by unidentified manufacturer.

Cornet in B flat, BF, PV, Paris model, double water key, with A shank
Br $18.00
Ni plate $21.00
Si plate, satin finish $22.00
Si plate, burnished, Go plated bell $25.00

Cornet in B flat, BF, PV, Vienna model, water key, with A shank
Br $12.00
Ni plate $15.00
Si plate, satin finish $18.00
Si plate, burnished, Go plate $20.00

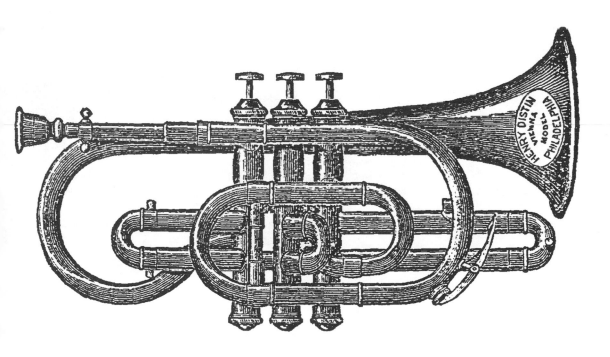

Cornet in B flat, BF, PV, Vienna model, water key

Tenor trombone in B flat, BF, PV, Highest grade model, Government model, water key.
Br $50.00
Si plate, Go in bell and points $65.00
"Tuning slide can be pulled to low pitch."
CMV not available.

Tenor trombone in B flat, BF, PV.
Highest grade model, water key.
Length 32 inches, bell diameter 7 inches.
Br $40.00
Si plate, Go in bell $52.00
Full burnished, extra $5.00
Low pitch slide $5.00

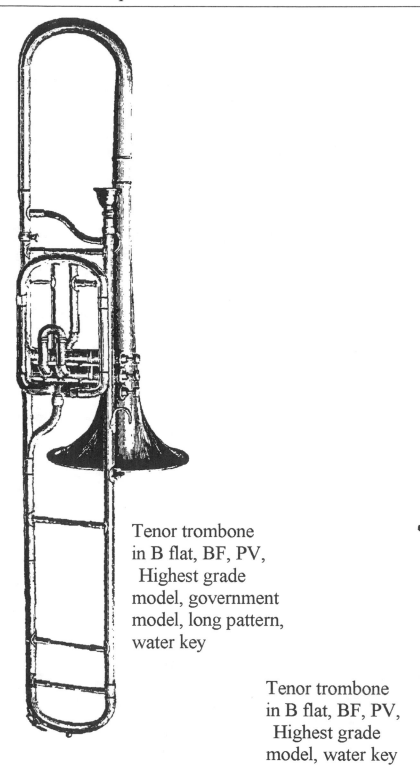

Tenor trombone
in B flat, BF, PV,
 Highest grade
model, government
model, long pattern,
water key

Tenor trombone
in B flat, BF, PV,
 Highest grade
model, water key

Fiske Catalog of 1868 & 1881

Issac Fiske was an important manufacturer of quality brass instruments used during the U.S. Civil War. His instruments are highly collected. He also experimented in various types of valves, some of which are depicted in the small catalogs reproduced in their entirety here. Some of his former employees formed their own companies, copying traits from Fiske, which no doubt caused some legal difficulties. One such company was McFadden & Beaumont. As stated throughout this book, any instrument made with a typical valve systems are highly sought by collectors, more than performers. Fiske is known to have used various early types of rotary valves, piston valves, and Vienna valves. He also patented a valve arrangement where the valves are activated by what at first appears to be a Périnet-style valve, with a push rod running out the bottom of the piston (variant 1). A variant of this has the rod coming out the top (variant 2). [Fiske did not make these distinctions in his catalog; they have been provided by this editor.] His patent is very much like the Higham patent found on page 25 of this book. Fiske advertised this valve type as a "rotary valve, piston action." On some of Fiske's instruments, the rotary valves are arranged in a straight line. On other examples, the valves are arranged in a triangular formation, which produces a very decorative and more desirable instrument.

All instruments in these two catalogs were produced by this company. In the 1881 catalog, the instruments were offered with black walnut cases for an extra $10.00.

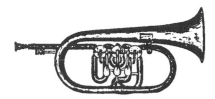

Cornet in E flat, BF, SARV, Number 1

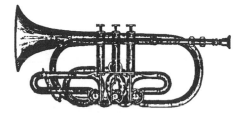

Cornet in B flat, BF, Push rod rotary valve, Number 4

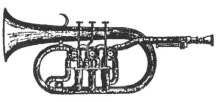

Cornet in E flat, BF, Push rod rotary valve, Number 2

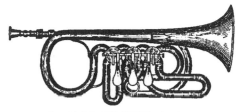

Cornet in B flat, BF, SARV, Number 5

Cornet in E flat, OTS, SARV, Number 3

Cornet in B flat, OTS, SARV, Number 6

Fiske, Isaac. Illustrated catalogue of musical instruments. Worcester, MA: Edward R. Fiske & Son, 1868. Instruments produced by Fiske & Son.

Cornet in E flat, BF, SARV
Number 1 Br $55.00
Number 1 Gs $65.00
CMV $1400.00 - $1700.00

Cornet in E flat, BF, Push rod rotary valve (variant 1)
Number 2 Br $60.00
Number 2 Gs $70.00
CMV $1800.00 - $2400.00

Cornet in E flat, OTS, TARV
Number 3 Br $55.00
Number 3 Gs $65.00
CMV $2500.00 - $3500.00

Cornet in B flat, BF, Push rod rotary valves (variant 2)
Number 4 Br $60.00
Number 4 Gs $70.00
CMV $1600.00 - $2200.00

Cornet in B flat, BF, SARV (offered in two sizes of calibers, both for the same price)
Number 5 Br $55.00
Number 5 Gs $65.00
CMV $1400.00 - $1800.00

Cornet in B flat, OTS, SARV
Number 6 Br $55.00
Number 6 Gs $65.00
CMV $3500.00 +

Alto horn in E flat, BU, SARV (offered in two sizes of calibers, both for the same price)
Number 7 Br $70.00
Number 7 Gs $85.00
CMV $1200.00 - $1700.00

Alto horn in E flat, OTS, SARV (offered in two sizes of calibers, both for the same price)
Number 8 Br $70.00
Number 8 Gs $85.00
"I make two sizes of calibre, both same price."
CMV $2200.00 - $2700.00

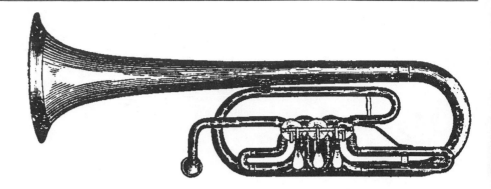

Alto in E flat, BU, SARV, Number 7

Alto in E flat, OTS, SARV, Number 8

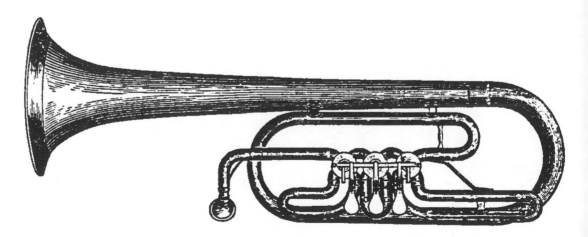

Tenor in B flat, BU, SARV, Number 9

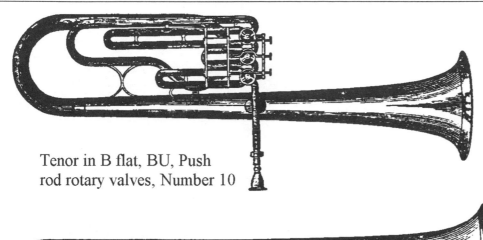

Tenor in B flat, BU, Push
rod rotary valves, Number 10

Tenor in B flat, OTS,
SARV, Number 11

Bass in E flat, BU, SARV, Number 12

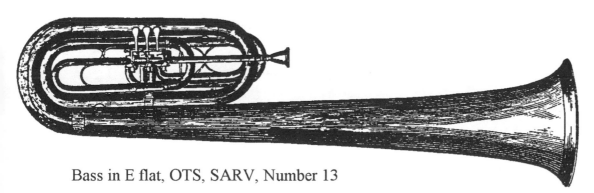

Bass in E flat, OTS, SARV, Number 13

**Tenor horn in B flat, BU,
SARV**
Number 9 Br $80.00
Number 9 Gs $95.00
CMV $1400.00 - $1800.00

**Baritone horn in B flat, BU,
SARV**
Number 9 Br $85.00
Number 9 Gs $100.00
(Same style as the tenor number 9 above, therefore not shown here.)
CMV $1400.00 - $1800.00

The following six instruments share the same catalog number, as they share the same basic body design, resulting in only one illustration.
Page ?. Instruments produced by Fiske & Son.

**Alto horn in E flat, BU, Push
rod rotary valves (variant 1)**
Number 10 Br $70.00
Number 10 Gs $85.00
CMV $2200.00 - $2800.00

**Tenor horn in B flat, BU,
Push rod rotary valves (variant 1)**
Number 10 Br $80.00
Number 10 Gs $95.00
CMV $2200.00 - $2800.00

**Baritone horn in B flat, BU,
Push rod rotary valves (variant 1)**
Number 10 Br $85.00
Number 10 Gs $100.00
CMV $2200.00 - $2800.00

**Bass horn in B flat, BU, Push
rod rotary valves (variant 1)**
Number 10 Br $100.00
Number 10 Gs $125.00
CMV $2200.00 - $2800.00

**Bass horn in E flat, BU, Push
rod rotary valves (variant 1)**
Number 10 Br $130.00
Number 10 Gs $150.00
CMV $2200.00 - $2800.00

**Bass horn in E flat, extra
large calibre, BU, Push rod
rotary valves (variant 1)**
Number 10 Br $155.00
Number 10 Gs $175.00

Fiske, Isaac. Illustrated catalogue of musical instruments. Worcester, MA: Edward R. Fiske & Son, 1868. Instruments produced by Fiske & Son.

Tenor horn in B flat, OTS, SARV
Number 11 Br $80.00
Number 11 Gs $95.00
CMV $2200.00 - $2400.00

Baritone horn in B flat, OTS, SARV
Number 11 Br $85.00
Number 11 Gs $100.00
CMV $2200.00 - $2400.00

Bass horn in E flat, BU, SARV
Number 12 Br $130.00
Number 12 Gs $150.00
CMV $1500.00 - $2000.00

Bass horn in B flat, BU, SARV
Number 12 Br $100.00
Number 12 Gs $125.00
CMV $1700.00 - $2400.00

Bass horn in E flat, OTS, SARV
Number 13 Br $130.00
Number 13 Gs $150.00
CMV $1600.00 - $2200.00

Bass horn in E flat, large calibre, OTS, SARV
Number 13 Br $155.00
Number 13 Gs $175.00
CMV $1600.00 - $2200.00

Bass horn in B flat, OTS, SARV
Number 13 Br $100.00
Number 13 Gs $125.00
CMV $1400.00 - $2400.00

Cornet in E flat, BF, PV
Number 1 Br $45.00
Number 1 Br, Si plated $57.00
Go inside of bell, extra $5.00
CMV $1400.00-$1700.00

Cornet in E flat, BF, PV
Number 2 Br $45.00
Number 2 Br, Si plated $57.00
Go inside of bell, extra $5.00
CMV not available.

Cornet in E flat, BF, SARV, Number 1

Cornet in E flat, BF, PV, Number 2

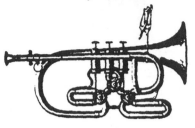

Cornet in E flat, BF, Push rod rotary valves, Number 3

Cornet in E flat, BF, Push rod rotary valves, Number 4

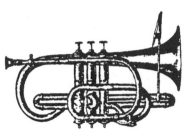

Cornet in B flat, BF, PV, Number 5

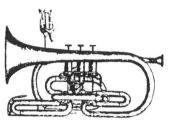

Cornet in B flat, BF, Push rod rotary valves, Number 6

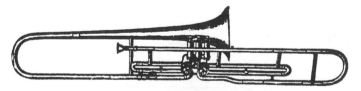

Cornet in B flat, BF, Push rod rotary valves, Number 7

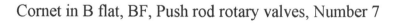

Tenor trombone in B flat, BF, Push rod rotary valves, Number 8

Cornet in E flat, BF, Push rod rotary valves (variant 1), with water key
Number 3 Br $45.00
Number 3 Br, Si plated $57.00
Go inside of bell, extra $20.00
CMV $1300.00-$2400.00

Cornet in E flat, BF, Push rod rotary valves, improved model
Number 4 [No prices given. Possibly same price as above.]
CMV not available.

Cornet in B flat, BF, PV, double water key
Number 5 Br $55.00
Number 5 Br, Si plated $67.00
Number 5 Br, Si plated, and gilded $75.00
CMV not available.

Bass in E flat, BU, Push rod rotary valves, Number 9

Cornet in B flat, BF, Push rod rotary valves
Number 6 Br $55.00
Number 6 Br, Si plated $67.00
Number 6 inside of bell and points gilded $75.00
CMV $1600.00-$2200.00

Cornet in B flat, BF, Push rod rotary valves, double water key, set piece for A
Number 7 same price as Number 6

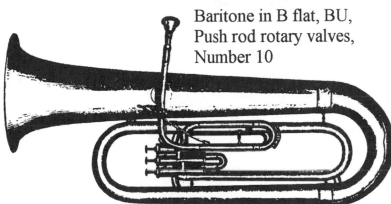

Baritone in B flat, BU, Push rod rotary valves, Number 10

Tenor trombone in B flat, BF, Push rod rotary valves
Number 8 Br $65.00
Number 8 Br, Si plated $85.00
Number 8 piston valves $65.00
Number 8 Br, piston valves $85.00
CMV not available.

Bass horn in E flat, BU, Push rod rotary valves [not shown to scale]
Number 9 Br $110.00
Number 9 Br, Si plated $145.00
CMV $2200.00-$2800.00

Baritone horn in B flat, BU, Push rod rotary valves
Number 10 Br $75.00
Number 10 Br, Si plated $100.00
CMV $2200.00-$2800.00

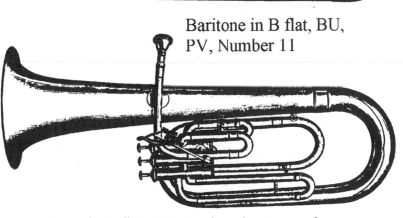

Baritone in B flat, BU, PV, Number 11

Tenor in B flat, BU, Push rod rotary valves
Number 10 Br $70.00
Number 10 Br, Si plated $90.00
CMV $2200.00-$2800.00

Baritone horn in B flat, BU, Push rod rotary valve
Number 11 Br $75.00
Number 11 Br, Si plated $100.00
"Length of instrument 29 inches; weight 5 1/2 pounds."
CMV $2200.00-$2800.00

Tenor horn in B flat, BU, Push rod rotary valves
Number 11 Br $70.00
Number 11 Br, Si plated $90.00
CMV $2200.00-$2800.00

Bass horn in E flat, BU, Push rod rotary valves
Number 12 Br $110.00
Number 12 Br, Si plated $145.00
CMV $2200.00-$2800.00

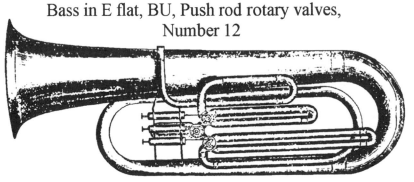

Bass in E flat, BU, Push rod rotary valves, Number 12

J. Howard Foote Catalog of 1893

According to *NLI* (p. 120), J. Howard Foote was a dealer and importer of musical instruments, not a manufacturer. He was located in New York City between 1863-1896. So, instruments stamped with the name of Foote were manufactured for, but not by Foote. Who actually manufactured all these instruments is conjectural. However, all the brass instruments for which a manufacturer is identified in this catalog were produced by Antonie Courtois of Paris, one of the finest French manufacturers of the time, and highly collected today.

This catalog also includes a very rare and valuable Brass wind instrument family invented by Mr. Courtois. This novel instrument family is so rare that it does not appear in Baines' book, and many other similar works. The family's name is Antoniophone. Mr. Foote even registered the trade-mark of Antoniophone, receiving No. 13,696. Sadly, the catalog includes artwork of this type of instrument that is too blurred to be reproduced here. Fortunately, a Thibouville-Lamy catalog includes an illustration of the instrument, which is there identified as a "Parlor horn." That illustration is used here. The family is uniformly identified by having a bell that sweeps down and then back up, in an "S" shape. Thus, the bell is below the valve cluster, and points slightly upward. Being so novel, Antoniophones sold very poorly, and are now quite valuable.

This catalog includes descriptions of bore sizes for some cornets, a feature rarely found in catalogs of the time. Four bore sizes are included but no dimensions are given. The four sizes are named for prominent cornet players of the time, being Arban (also known as Reynold's model, medium bore), Emerson (big bore), Arbuckle (also medium bore), and Levy (small bore). The only visible difference found in the catalog between Arban and Emerson is that the forward bend, just before the tube enters the valve cluster, bends up slightly on the Arban model. The catalog implies that these bores were available on instruments Numbers 12-21. The prices for these instruments are as they appear, and are quite exceptional for their time. Few manufacturers or makers commanded such prices for their instruments.

No CMVs were found for Courtois' instruments, but are surely quite high. Also, most instruments listed here are not shown.

J. Howard Foote. Catalogue of Musical Instruments, Strings, etc. 1893. Instruments produced by Courtois.

Cornet in B flat, BF, PV, double water key
Number 12 Br $143.50
Number 13 Elegantly Si plated and burnished $166.00
Number 14 Elegantly Si plated and burnished, Go plated bell $174.00
Number 15 Elegantly Si plated and burnished, Go engraving on bell $190.00
Number 16 Elegantly Si plated and burnished, Go engraving on bell $200.00 (not further identified)
Number 18 Elegantly Si plated and burnished, Go plated ferrules, pillars, braces, water key, valve caps, piston rods, finger buttons, and mouthpiece. $185.00
Number 19 Same as Number 18, inside of bell Go plated and burnished $193.00
Number 20 Same as Number 18, with beautiful Go engraving on bell, pearl and Go finger buttons $240.00

Number 21 Same as Number 20, different case $260.00
Number 24 Elegantly Si plated and burnished, inside of bell Go plated and burnished, beautiful Go engraving on bell and slides, richly embossed or engraved Go plated ferrules, Go plated pillars, braces, water key, valve caps, piston rods, and mouthpiece, pearl and Go finger buttons $295.00
Number 25 Same as Number 24 in different case $315.00

Cornet in B flat, BF, PV, tourist model [other manufacturers called this a pocket model]
Number 30 Br $143.00
Number 31 Elegantly Si plated and burnished $166.00
Number 32 Same as Number 31, with beautiful Go engraving on bell $190.00
Number 33 Elegantly Si plated and burnished, Go engraving on bell, pearl and Go finger buttons $185.00
Number 34 Same as Number 33, inside of bell Go plated and burnished, beautiful Go engraving on bell, pearl and Go finger buttons $240.00

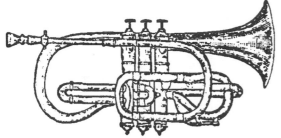

Cornet in B flat, BF, PV,
Arban model, Number 12

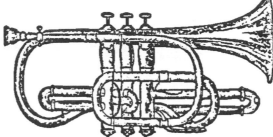

Cornet in B flat, BF, PV,
Emerson model, Number 12

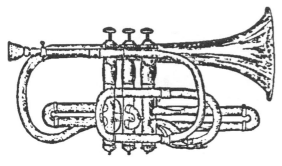

Cornet in B flat, BF, PV,
Arbuckle model, Number 12

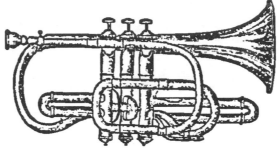

Cornet in B flat, BF, PV,
Levy model, Number 12

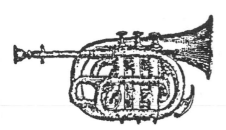

Cornet in B flat, BF, PV,
tourist's model, Number 30

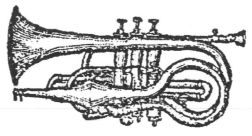

Cornet in B flat, BF, PV, solo
model, with echo attachment,
Number 36

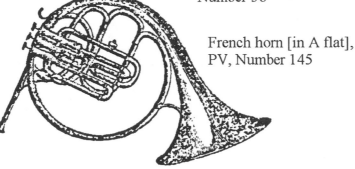

French horn [in A flat],
PV, Number 145

Number 35 Same as Number 33, very beautiful Go engraving on bell and slides, richly embossed or engraved Go plated ferrules, $290.00

Cornet in B flat, BF, PV, with echo or mute attachment
Number 36 Br $200.00
Number 37 Same as Number 36, elegantly Si plated and burnished $226.00
Number 38 Same as Number 37, with beautiful Go engraving on bell $260.00
Number 39 Same as Number 37, with Go plated ferrules, pillars, braces, water key, valve caps, piston rods, finger buttons, and mouthpiece $255.00
Number 40 Same as Number 39, inside of bell Go plated and burnished, beautiful Go engraving on bell, pearl and Go finger buttons $315.00
Number 41 Same as Number 39 very beautiful Go engraving on bell and slides, richly embossed or engraved Go plated ferrules $375.00

French horn in A flat, PV
Number 145 Br 4 crooks in A, G, F, and E $180.00
Number 146 Br, Si plated, satin finished, 4 crooks in A, G, F, and e $220.00
Number 147 Same as Number 146, gild engraving on bell $320.00

French horn in B flat, PV
Number 148 Br, chromatic, with 10 crooks $210.00
Number 149 Br, with 10 crooks, Si plated, satin finish $270.00
Number 150 Same as Number 149, Go engraving on bell $380.00

**Trumpet in D, PV, water key
D flat crook**
Number 130 Br $120.00
**Number 131 Br, Si plated
and burnished $140.00**
**Number 132 Br, Si plated, Go
engraving on bell $175.00**

**Trumpet in G, PV, water key
crooks in F, E, E flat, D flat,
and C**
Number 133 Br $128.00
**Number 134 Br, Si plated
and burnished $150.00**
**Number 135 Br, Si plated, Go
engraving on bell $190.00**

**Trumpet in F, PV, water key
crooks in E, E flat, D flat, and
C**
Number 136 Br $125.00
**Number 137 Br, Si plated
and burnished $147.00**
**Number 138 Br, Si plated, Go
engraving on bell $187.00**

**Melody horn in C, PV, water
key crooks in B flat**
Number 140 Br $170.00
**Number 141 Br, Si plated
and burnished $210.00**
**Number 142 Br, Si plated, Go
engraving on bell $300.00**

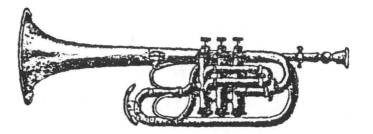

Trumpet in D, BF, PV, with D flat crook, Number 130

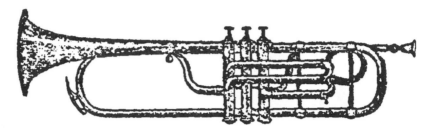

Trumpet in G, BF, PV, with F, E, E flat,
D, D flat, and C crooks, Number 133

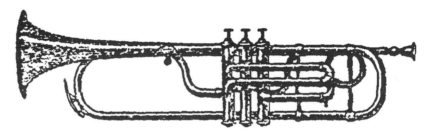

Trumpet in F, BF, PV, with E, E flat, D,
D flat, and C crooks, Number 136

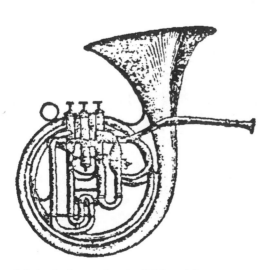

Melody horn in C, PV, with
B flat crook, Number 140

Antoniophone [in various
keys], Number 380

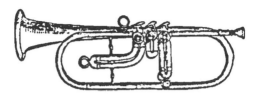

Cornet in E flat, OTS, TARV, Number 507

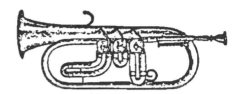

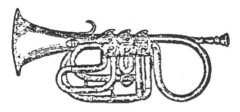

Cornet in B flat, BF, TARV, Number 544

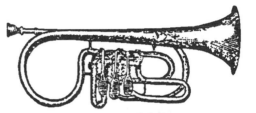

Cornet in E flat, BF, TARV, Number 528

Cornet in B flat, BF, TARV, Number 547

Cornet in B flat, BF, SARV, Number 548

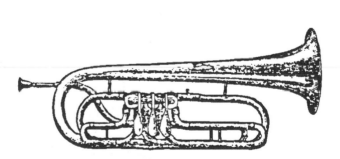

Alto in E flat, BF, SARV, solo model, Number 549

Alto in E flat, BU, TARV, Number 550

Cornet-Antoniophone in B flat, PV
Number 380 Br $142.00
Number 382 Br, elegantly Si plated, satin finish $165.00
Number 382 Br, elegantly Si plated and Go mounted $195.00

Contra-alto-Antoniophone in B flat, PV
Number 383 Br $170.00
Number 384 Br, elegantly Si plated, satin finish $146.00
Number 385 Br, elegantly Si plated and Go mounted $200.00

Alto-Antoniophone in F and E, PV
Number 386 Br $165.00
Number 387 Br, elegantly Si plated, satin finish $200.00
Number 388 Br, elegantly Si plated and Go mounted $250.00

Tenor-Antoniophone in C and B flat, 4 PV
Number 389 Br $220.00
Number 390 Br, elegantly Si plated, satin finish $257.00
Number 391 Br, elegantly Si plated and Go mounted $310.00

Baritone-Antoniophone in C and B flat, 5 PV
Number 392 Br $235.00
Number 393 Br, elegantly Si plated, satin finish $275.00
Number 394 Br, elegantly Si plated and Go mounted $325.00

Bass-Antoniophone in B flat, 4 PV
Number 395 Br $240.00
Number 396 Br, elegantly Si plated, satin finish $300.00
Number 397 Br, elegantly Si plated and Go mounted $360.00

J. Howard Foote. Catalogue of Musical Instruments, Strings, etc. 1893. Instruments produced by unidentified manufacturer.

Cornet in E flat, OTS, TARV Number 507 Br $16.00

Cornet in B flat, OTS, TARV Number 508 Br $16.00

Alto horn in E flat, OTS, TARV Number 509 Br $20.00

Tenor horn in B flat, OTS, TARV Number 510 Br $24.00

Baritone horn in B flat, OTS, TARV Number 511 Br $26.00

Bass horn in B flat, OTS, TARV Number 512 Br $30.00

Bass horn in EE flat, OTS, TARV Number 513 Br $36.00

Bass horn in EE flat, OTS, TARV, large bell Number 514 Br $38.00

Cornet in E flat, OTS, TARV Number 517 Gs $22.00

Cornet in B flat, OTS, TARV Number 518 Gs $24.00

Alto horn in E flat, OTS, TARV Number 519 Gs $28.00

Tenor horn in B flat, OTS, TARV Number 520 Gs $32.00

Baritone horn in B flat, OTS, TARV Number 521 Gs $34.00

Bass horn in B flat, OTS, TARV Number 522 Gs $40.00

Bass horn in EE flat, OTS, TARV Number 523 Gs $54.00

Bass horn in EE flat, OTS, TARV, large bell Number 524 Gs $60.00

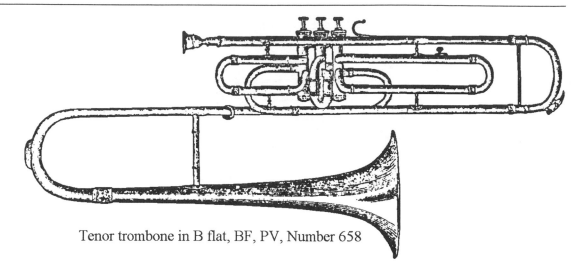

Tenor trombone in B flat, BF, PV, Number 658

Tenor trombone in B flat, BF, slide model, Number 667

French horn in B flat, PV, with crooks to E flat, Number 5156

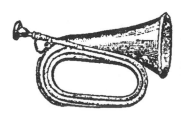

Bicycle buglet [in ?], BF, Number 709

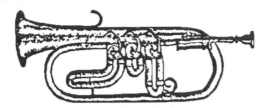

Cornet in E flat, BF, TARV,
pocket model, Number 5015

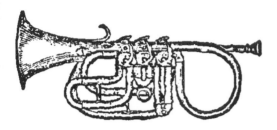

Cornet in B flat, BF,
TARV, Number 5020

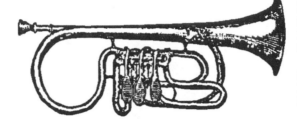

Cornet in B flat, BF,
SARV, Number 5022

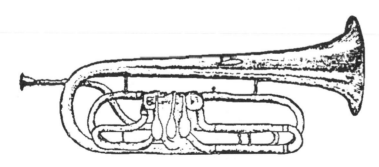

Alto in E flat, BF, SARV, Number 5023

Solo cornet in B flat, BF, TARV, with G crook
Number 544 Gs $25.00

Leader's cornet in E flat, BF, 3 RV
Number 528 Gs, long pattern, top action $24.00
Number 529 Gs, long pattern, side action $25.00

Cornet in B flat, HD, TARV, Dodworth Model.
Number 540 Gs $25.00
[not shown]

Cornet in B flat, BF, RV, short pattern
Number 547 Gs, top action $25.00
Number 548 Gs, side action $27.00

Solo alto in E flat, BF, SARV
Number 549 Gs, with water key $30.00

Alto horn in E flat, BU, TARV, improved model
Number 550 Gs $30.00

Tenor horn in B flat, BU, TARV, improved model
Number 551 Gs $34.00

Baritone horn in B flat, BU, TARV, improved model
Number 552 Gs $36.00

Bass horn in EE flat, BU, TARV, improved model
Number 553 Gs $55.00

Bass horn in EE flat, BU, TARV, large bell, improved model
Number 554 Gs $62.00

Cornet in E flat, OTS, 3 Sax pistons, best quality. American military band style
Number 578 Gs $14.00

Cornet in B flat, 3 Sax pistons, best quality. American military band style
Number 579 Gs $16.00

Alto horn in E flat, OTS, 3 Sax pistons, best quality. American military band style
Number 580 Gs $19.00

Tenor horn in B flat, OTS, 3 Sax pistons, best quality. American military band style
Number 581 Gs $23.00

Baritone horn in B flat, OTS, 3 Sax pistons, best quality. American military band style
Number 582 Gs $26.00

Bass horn in EE flat, OTS, 3 Sax pistons, best quality. American military band style
Number 583 Gs $28.00

Bass horn in EE flat, OTS, large bell, 3 Sax pistons, best quality. American military band style
Number 584 Gs $30.00

J. Howard Foote. Catalogue of Musical Instruments, Strings, etc. 1893. Instrument "Challenge superior" trade mark produced by unidentified manufacturer. [This trade mark is not listed in *NLI*.]

Tenor trombone in B flat, BF, PV, trumpet model
Number 658 Br $48.00
Number 659 Si plated $78.00

Baritone trombone in B flat, BF, PV, trumpet model
Number 661 Br $53.00
Number 662 Si plated $87.00
[Not shown]

Bass trombone in G, BF, PV, trumpet model
Number 664 Br $66.00
Number 665 Si plated $96.00
[Not shown]

Tenor trombone in B flat, slide model
Number 667 Br $38.00
Number 668 Si plated $55.00

Bass trombone in G, slide model
Number 670 Br $49.00
Number 671 Si plated $68.00

The catalog also states "The silver plated slide trombones can be burnished finish, if desired, at same prices, when plated to order."

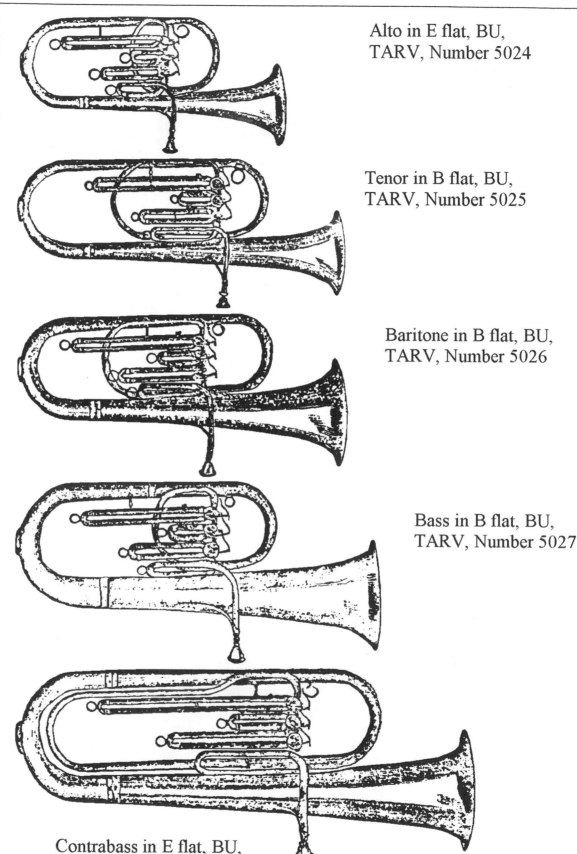

Alto in E flat, BU, TARV, Number 5024

Tenor in B flat, BU, TARV, Number 5025

Baritone in B flat, BU, TARV, Number 5026

Bass in B flat, BU, TARV, Number 5027

Contrabass in E flat, BU, TARV, Number 5028

Alto in E flat, BU,
PV, Number 5135

Tenor in B flat, BU, PV,
Number 5137

Baritone in B flat, BU, PV,
Number
5139

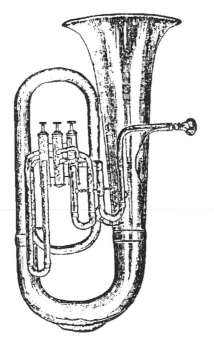

Bass in B flat, BU,
PV, Number 5141

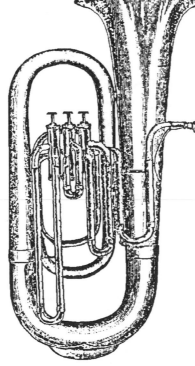

Contrabass in E flat,
BU, PV, Number 5143

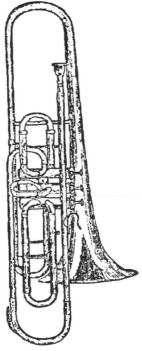

Tenor trombone in B flat,
BF, PV, Number 5149

French or concert horn in B flat, PV, with crooks to E flat. French model
Number 5156 Br $90.00

Bicycle buglets
Number 708 Br, genuine English, oval bell, 3 turns $7.50
Number 709 Br, genuine English, oval bell, 3 turns, with chain, the best made, Gs mountings $15.00
Number 714 The same as 708, Si plated $13.00
Number 715 The same as 709, Si plated $23.00
Number 716 The same as 709, Si plated, and Go mountings $28.50

Coaching horns
Number 728 Co, 40 inches long, genuine English "Tally ho," Gs mountings $9.20
Number 729 Co, 40 inches long, genuine English "Tally ho," Gs mountings, in basket $15.00
Number 732 The same as Number 728, Si plated $17.00
Number 734 The same as Number 729, Si plated, and Go mountings $28.50

J. Howard Foote. Catalogue of Musical Instruments, Strings, etc. 1893.
Instruments produced by unidentified manufacturer.

Pocket cornet in E flat, BF, TARV
Number 5015 Br $20.00

Leader's cornet in E flat, BF, 3 RV
Number 5016 Br, top action $20.00
Number 5017 Br, side action $21.00

Cornet in B flat, BF, 3 RV
Number 5020 Br, top action $22.00
Number 5022 Br, side action $23.00

Alto horn in E flat, BF, SARV

Number 5023 Br $28.00

Alto horn in E flat, BU, TARV, improved model Number 5024 Br $28.00

Tenor horn in B flat, BU, TARV, improved model Number 5025 Br $30.00

Baritone horn in B flat, BU, TARV, improved model Number 5026 Br $33.00

Bass horn in B flat, BU, TARV, improved model Number 5027 Br $36.00

Bass horn in EE flat, BU, SARV, improved model Number 5028 Br $50.00

Bass horn in EE flat, BU, large bell, TARV, improved model Number 5029 Br $55.00

Army or infantry bugles in C, BF. [not shown in catalog] Number 5162 Br, Officer's Pattern, best quality, "Challenge" $4.00 Number 5163 Si plated, Officer's Pattern, best quality, "Challenge" $12.50

Infantry, cavalry or artillery trumpets. Number 5166 F trumpet, Br, U.S. regulation, best quality [$10.00?] Number 5166 1/2 F trumpet, Br, U.S. regulation, best quality, with C crook [$10.00?] Number 5168 G trumpet, Br, U.S. regulation, best quality, with F slide, "Challenge" $10.00

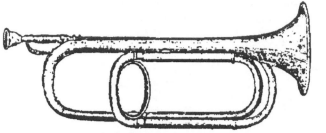

Trumpet in F, BF, Number 5168

Officer's bugle, BF, Number 5162

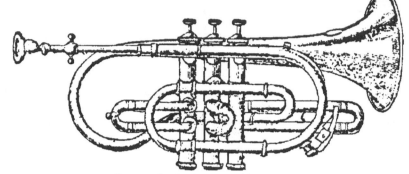

Cornet in B flat, BF, PV, Number 5067

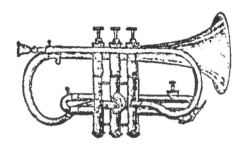

Cornet in E flat, BF, PV, Number 5124

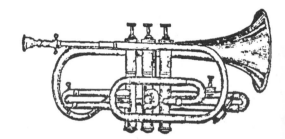

Cornet in B flat, BF, PV, Number 5127

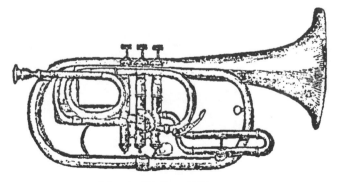

Alto in E flat, BF, PV, Number 5133

Number 5168c The same as Number 5168, with C crook $12.60
"Number 5168 The "Challenge" U.S. Regulation trumpet, can be played in unison with Number 5166 by drawing the F slide; and by adding the C crook can ben used with the C bugles Number 5162-5163. It is the most serviceable trumpet made, for all arms." [*NLI* states that a clarinet marked "Challenge, Paris" was reported.]

Cornet in B flat, BF, PV, "Amateur" model, water key
Number 5067 Br $21.00
Number 5068 Br, Ni plated $23.50
Number 5069 Br, finely Si plated $37.50

All instruments on the rest of this page carry Foote's "Eureka" trademark. Foote describes this grade of instruments as "Prices not higher than the cheapest quality in the market, considering superiority of the Eurekas." "Eureka" instruments were made with light action PV. Foote also stated that, if desired, his name would also be stamped on the instrument. The Eureka trademark is not listed in *NLI*.

Cornet in E flat, BF, PV, with water key
Number 5124 Br $19.00
Number 5125 Br, Ni plated $22.00

Cornet in B flat, BF, PV, with water key
Number 5127 Br, with B flat and A set pieces $20.00
Number 5128 Br, Ni plated $22.50

Cornet in C, BF, PV, water key and, C and B flat set pieces
Number 5131 Br $20.00
Number 5132 Br, Ni plated $22.50
Alto horn in E flat, BF, PV, with water key
Number 5133 Br $25.50
Number 5134 Br, Ni plated $30.50

Alto horn in E flat, BU, PV, water key
Number 5135 $25.50
Number 5136 Br, Ni plated $30.50

Tenor horn in B flat, BU, PV, water key
Number 5137 Br $30.50
Number 5138 Br, Ni plated $36.00

Baritone horn in B flat, BU, PV, water key
Number 5139 Br $33.75
Number 5140 Br, Ni plated $40.00

Bass horn in B flat, BU, PV, water key
Number 5141 1/2 Br $36.00
Number 5142 Br, Ni plated $43.00

Bass horn in EE flat, BU, PV, water key
Number 5143 Br $53.25
Number 5144 Br, Ni plated $63.00
Number 5145 Br, large calibre $64.00
Number 5146 Br, Ni plated, large calibre $74.00

Alto trombone in E flat, BF, PV, trumpet model, water key
Number 5149 Br $25.50
Number 5150 Br, Ni plated $30.00

Tenor trombone in B flat, BF, PV, trumpet model, water key
Number 5151 Br $30.50
Number 5152 Br, Ni plated $36.00

D. C. Hall Catalog
Circa 1879

More research is clearly needed regarding this interesting brass instrument manufacturer. *NLI* provides a brief account of this company's complex history. Persons associated with D.C. Hall at various times include the Quinby brothers, and E.G. Wright. The catalog used here was originally undated. However, comparing the company's name and address with the *NLI* citation, the catalog was not printed before 1879. The following year, the company was in a different location. Even so, this catalog is dated here as circa 1879. The catalog used here is either not complete, or not all instruments described here were pictured in this catalog.

The company both manufactured, and imported instruments. This fact partly explains the existence of a cornopean in this catalog. See the Glossary for more information about this instrument. In general, cornopeans attract interest, but do not always sell well, as many of these instruments were poorly made by modern standards.

One feature that has been corrected throughout this catalog is the use of the word tenor. In this catalog, "tenor" was applied to tenor horns (pitched in B flat) and also alto horns (pitched in E flat), a feature common during the time. Thus, when a tenor pitched in E flat was found in this catalog, the name of the instrument has been changed here to reflect current usage.

Yet another problem with this catalog is that descriptions of instruments do not match depicted instruments, and some information appears to be missing. Correcting these problems will require more research by others.

The name Quinby is often found in current retail catalogs, and some reference books but with an alternate spelling of Quimby. Farrar believes that this is nothing more than a spelling error that has been repeatedly copied. This catalog only uses the spelling Quinby.

This catalog does not offer Quinby Brothers instruments equipped with the rare Allen valve type. Allen valves are easily identified by their very flat, long appearance, which requires triangular pieces of tubing between the round pipes and the flatter valves. Instruments from Quinby Bros. with Allen valves should sell for between twenty five to fifty per cent above the prices for other valve types.

| Cornopean in B flat, BF, 3 Stoelzel valves, Number 450 | Cornet in B flat, BF, PV, Number 460 | Cornet in B flat, BF, PV, Number 492 | Cornet in E flat, BF, PV, Number 502 |

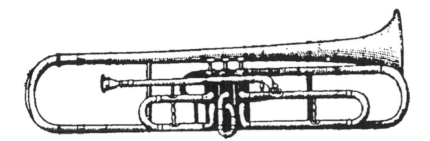

[Tenor ?] trombone in B flat and C, BF, PV, Number 579

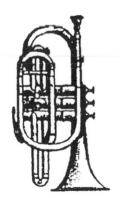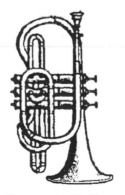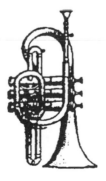

| Cornet in B flat, BF, PV, Number 533 | Cornet in B flat, BF, PV, Number 534 | Cornet in B flat, BF, PV, Number 539 |

Hall, D.C. Musical instruments. [1879].
Instruments produced by A. Lecomte & Co., Paris. Unless otherwise indicated, the catalog did not include the metal used to make these instruments.

Cornopean in B flat [listed as a cornet], BF, 3 Stölzel valves
Number 450 $10.32
CMV $400.00 - $800.00

Cornet in B flat, BF, 2 PV, and 1 large bore valve
Number 460 $15.40
CMV $200.00 - $400.00

Cornet in B flat, BF, 3 large PV
Number 492 $18.12
CMV $200.00 - $400.00

Cornet in E flat, BF, PV
Number 502 best make $32.00
CMV $300.00 - $600.00

Cornet in [B flat], BF, PV
Number 533 Model P.O., oval bore $32.00
CMV $200.00 - $400.00

Cornet in [B flat], BF, PV
Number 534 Courtois shape, Arban & Levy's latest pattern $32.00
CMV $200.00 - $400.00

Cornet in E flat, BF, PV
Number 539 Champion, best make $32.00
CMV $250.00 - $450.00

Tenor trombone in B flat and C, BF, PV
Number 579 $26.00
Number 580 $30.00
Number 587 Champion, $42.00
CMV $400.00

Hall, D.C. Musical instruments. [1879].
Instruments produced by A. Lecomte & Co., Paris. All instruments came with a large bore. The metal is also not given.

Bass horn in BB flat, Champion best make
Number 100 $130.00
CMV $100.00 - $300.00

Bass horn in E flat, Champion best make
Number 103 $65.00
CMV $100.00 - $300.00

Bass horn in B flat, 3+1 PV, Champion best make
Number 104 $60.00
CMV $250.00 - $500.00

Bass horn in B flat, Champion best make [Not shown]
Number 105 $48.00
CMV $50.00 - $150.00

Tenor horn in B flat, Champion best make
Number 106 $42.00
CMV $150.00 - $300.00

Alto horn in E flat, Champion best make
Number 107 $35.00
CMV $50.00 - $150.00

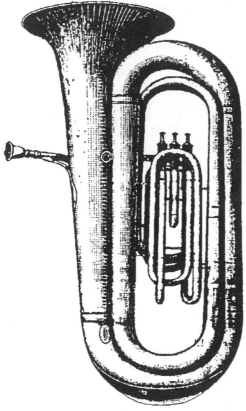

Contrabass in B flat, BU, PV, Number 100

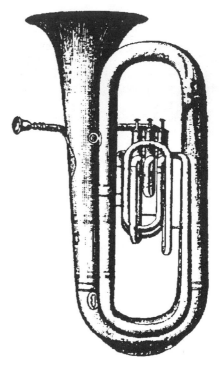

Bass in E flat, BU, PV, Number 103

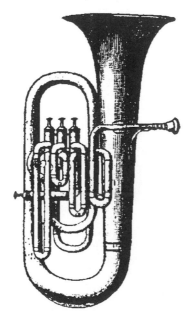

Bass in B flat, BU, 4 PV, Number 104

Tenor in B flat, BU, PV, Number 106

Alto in E flat, BU, PV, Number 107

Bass in B flat, BU, SARV, Number 26

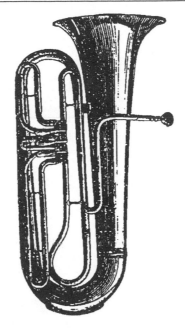

Bass in E flat, BU, SARV, Number 27

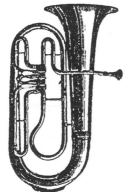

Baritone in B flat, BU, SARV, Number 25

Tenor in B flat, BU, SARV, Number 24

Alto in E flat, BU, SARV, Number 23

Cornet in B flat, BF, TARV, Number 47

Cornet in C and B flat, BF, SARV, Orchestra shape, Number 19

Cornet in E flat, BF, SARV, Number 20

Cornet in E flat, BF, SARV, Pocket shape, Number 45

Cornet in B flat, BF, TARV, Orchestra shape, Number 46

Hall, D.C. Musical instruments. [1879]. Instruments produced by Quinby Bros.

Cornet in C and B flat, BF, SARV, orchestra shape
Number 19 Br $45.00
Number 19 Gs $55.00
CMV $1400.00 - $1800.00

Cornet in E flat, BF, SARV, long pattern
Number 20 Br $45.00
Number 20 Gs $55.00
CMV $1400.00 - $1800.00

Alto horn in E flat, BU, SARV
Number 23 Br $53.00
Number 23 Gs $67.00
CMV $1200.00 - $1500.00

Tenor horn in B flat, BU, SARV
Number 24 Br $65.00
Number 24 Gs $78.00
CMV $1200.00 - $1500.00

Baritone horn in B flat, BU, SARV
Number 25 Br $72.00
Number 25 Gs $78.00
CMV $1200.00 - $1500.00

Bass horn in B flat, BU, SARV
Number 26 Br $75.00
Number 26 Gs $96.00
CMV $1200.00 - $1600.00

Bass horn in E flat, BU, SARV
Number 27 Br $100
Number 27 Gs $180.00
CMV $1200.00 - $1600.00

Cornet in E flat, BF, SARV, pocket model
Number 45 Br $45.00
Number 45 Gs $55.00
CMV $1500.00 - $2200.00

Cornet in B flat, BF, TARV, orchestra model
Number 46 Br $45.00
Number 46 Gs $55.00
CMV $1500.00 - $2200.00

Cornet in B flat, BF, SARV, orchestra model
Number 47 Br $45.00
Number 47 Gs $55.00
CMV $1500.00 - $2000.00 +

Tenor trombone in B flat, TARV
Number 16 Br $65.00
Number 16 Gs $78.00
CMV $400.00 - $600.00

Bass trombone in B flat, TARV [same number as above]
Number 16 Br $72.00
Number 16 Gs $85.00

Alto horn in E flat, BF, PV
Number 22 Br $53.00
Number 22 Gs $67.00
CMV $125.00 - $250.00

Tenor trombone in B flat, slide model
Number 34 Br $45.00
Number 34 Gs $55.00
CMV $150.00 - $400.00

Bass trombone in B flat, slide model [same number as above]
Number 34 Br $50.00
Number 34 Gs $60.00
CMV not available

French horn in F and C, with crooks, SARV
Number 35 Br $60.00
Number 35 Gs $75.00
CMV $300.00 - $700.00

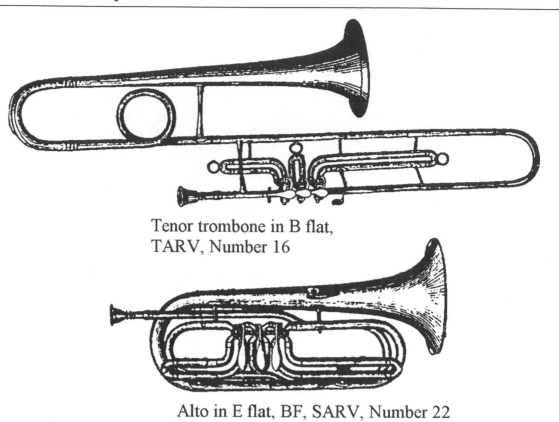

Tenor trombone in B flat,
TARV, Number 16

Alto in E flat, BF, SARV, Number 22

Bass trombone in B flat, BF, Slide, Number 34

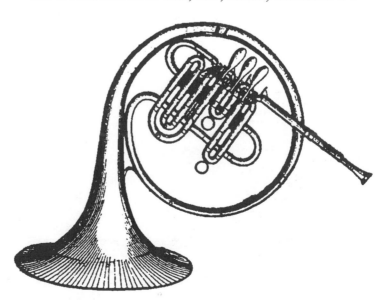

French horn in [F], SARV, Number 35

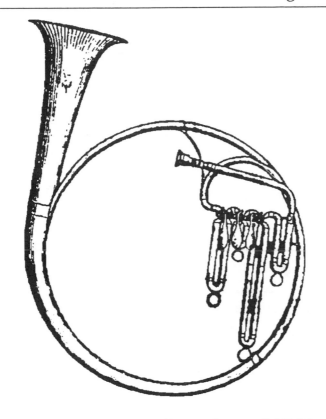

Alto in E flat, Helicon shape, SARV,
Number 39

Alto horn in E flat, HD, SARV
Number 39 Br $60.00
Number 39 Gs $75.00
CMV $800.00 - $1400.00

Tenor horn in B flat, HD, SARV
Number 40 Br $70.00
Number 40 Gs $85.00
CMV $900.00-$1500.00

Baritone horn in B flat, HD, SARV
Number 41 Br $80.00
Number 41 Gs $95.00
CMV not available.

Bass horn in E flat, HD, SARV
Number 42 Br $90.00
Number 42 Gs $100.00
CMV $700.00-$1000.00

Bass horn in B flat, HD, SARV
Number 43 Br $120.00
Number 43 Gs $150.00
CMV $700.00 - $1000.00

Bass horn in B flat, HD, SARV
Number 44 Br $200.00
Number 44 Gs $240.00
CMV $1000.00 - $1500.00

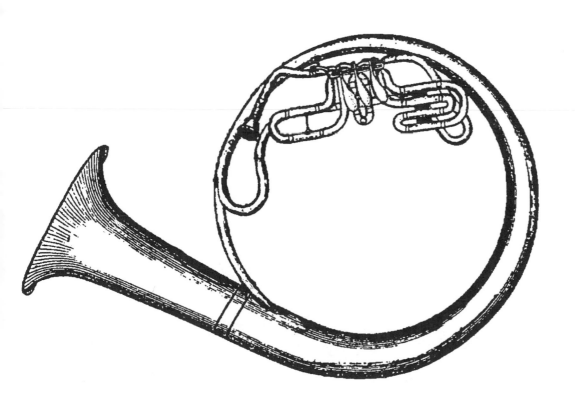

Bass in B flat, Helicon shape, SARV, Number 42

Contrabass in E flat, Helicon shape, SARV, Number 43

Bass in BB flat, Helicon shape, SARV, Number 4 4

Lyon & Healy
Campaign Catalog of 1896

Lyon and Healy began in the music business possibly around 1874, according to the company's 1895 catalog. The company produced some of the largest and finest musical instrument trade catalogs. The 1895 catalog (page 1) states that the company is "the largest band supply house in the world, ..." It goes on to claim that the company has been selling musical instruments for thirty-one years. A picture of its sizable factory is shown, located at the corner of Ogden and Randolph. The company had a retail store at the corner of Wabash and Adams St. *NLI* (p. 245) states that the company manufactured wind instruments between 1923-1930. However, due to the loss of the company's records in fires, the company possibly manufactured before that date.

The catalogs of 1895 and 1896 provide some interesting clues to this company's activities. On the cover of these catalogs appears "100,000 musical instruments [were] produced annually at our factory." The company listed various instruments on the last page of both catalogs that they manufactured. Included in this list are plucked stringed instruments, under the Washburn name. These plucked stringed instruments include banjos, banjores, guitars, mandolins, zithers, dulcimers, etc. Even to this date, this company is rightly famous for its professional concert harps. The company also claimed to have manufactured tambourines, drum sticks, drums, presentation instruments (unidentified type), keyboard instruments, band uniforms, etc. The catalog further states that the company manufactured the Nightingale Flageolet, a folk wind instrument. In short, the company manufactured a wide variety of stringed instruments, without manufacturing bowed stringed instruments, preferring to import them from Europe.

Regarding brass instruments, the company is known to have used subcontractors to manufacture instruments and parts of instruments. The subcontractors who actually made instruments sold by Lyon & Healy can not always be determined. The same is true for the instruments that Lyon & Healy imported from European manufacturers. The instruments and parts were then either assembled by Lyon & Healy's workers, or were plated in their factory. On page 130 of the 1896 catalog, the company claims "We are Gold, Silver, Copper, Bronze and Nickel platers." This catalog also offers (front cover) Lyon & Healy's Si Piston instruments, and Beau Ideal instruments. One might suppose that the company manufactured these instruments, and might well be wrong. Clearly, more research is needed here.

On page 113 of the 1896 catalog, the company offers to either repair instruments, plate them, or replace old valve clusters with new French ones. Yet, the catalog never specifically states that it manufactures brass instruments. One can understand why *NLI* is so careful about describing the company as a manufacturer of wind instruments. Lyon & Healy is especially important to the U.S. as a great many instruments are still in circulation that came from this company.

Current market values found in Appendix C have been added to this section. These CMV's are indicated with a *. Thus, the prices should not be taken as gospel, merely the best information currently available.

All Lyon & Healy catalogs seem to use a unique system of catalof numbers. As these numbers recur, these numbers are not changed here. Also, not all instruments listed are shown.

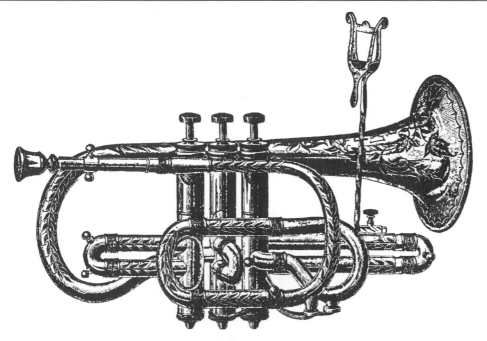

Cornet in B flat, BF, PV, Number 903

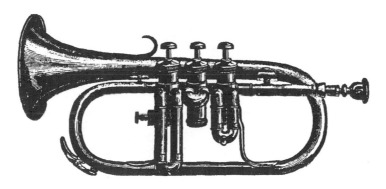

Cornet in E flat, BF, BPV, Number 50

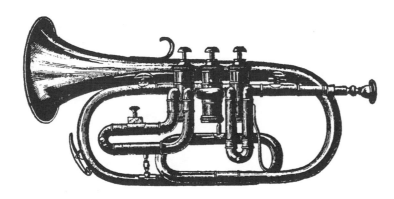

Cornet in B flat, BF, BPV, Number 51

Lyon & Healy Campaign edition. 1896.
Instruments produced by unidentified manufacturer, with "genuine heavy triple Silver plate," and elaborate engravings.

Cornet in B flat, BF, PV, double water keys, solo model
No. 903 Br, Si plated, satin finish $42.95
No. 904 Br, Si plated, satin finish, Go trimmed $52.00
No. 906 Br, Si plated, elegantly burnished, with Go bell and tips $58.55
CMV $450.00 - $550.00

Cornet in E flat, BF, BPV, water key
No. 50 Br $7.40
No. 050 Br, Ni plated $9.65
CMV $450.00 - $750.00

Lyon & Healy Campaign edition. 1896.
Instruments produced by unidentified manufacturer. Improved short pattern instruments.

Cornet in B flat, BF, BPV, water key
No. 51 Br $7.40
No. 051 Br, Ni plated $9.65
CMV $450.00 - $750.00

Tenor in B
flat, BU,
BPV, Number
53

Alto in E flat, BU,
BPV, Number 52

Alto trombone in E flat, BF, BPV, water key
No. 68 Br $10.00
No. 69 Br, Ni plated $14.65
CMV $250.00 - $400.00

Trombone in B flat, BF, BPV, water key
No. 65 Br $13.00
No. 66 Br, Ni plated $17.35
CMV $200.00 - $400.00

Alto horn in E flat, BU, BPV, water key
No. 52 Br $10.00
No. 052 Br, Ni plated $14.65
CMV $100.00 - $175.00

Tenor horn in B flat, BU, BPV, water key
No. 53 Br $13.00
No. 053 Br, Ni plated $17.35
CMV $125.00 - $175.00

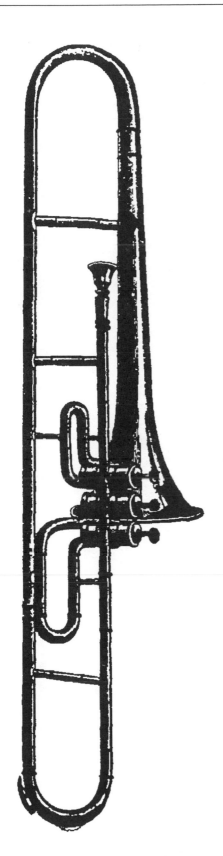

**Alto trombone in E flat, BF, PV,
Number 68**

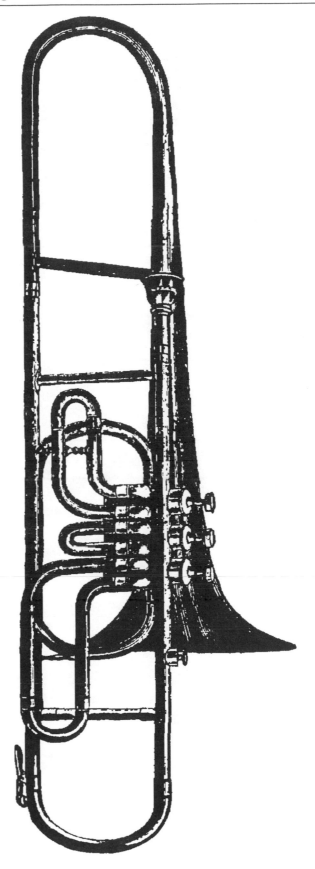

**Trombone in B flat, BF, PV,
Number 65**

Baritone in B flat,
BU, BPV,
Number 54

Baritone horn in B flat, BU, BPV
No. 54 Br $15.35
No. 054 Br, Ni plated $20.00
CMV $175.00 - $250.00

Bass horn in B flat, BU, BPV
No. 55 Br $17.00
No. 055 Br, Ni plated $21.35
CMV $175.00 - $250.00

Bass horn in E flat, BU, BPV
No. 56 Br $23.10
No. 056 Br, Ni plated $31.75
CMV $175.00 - $250.00

Bass horn in EE flat, BU, BPV (not shown)
No. 57 Br $26.65
No. 057 Br, Ni plated $33.35
CMV $175.00 - $250.00

Bass in E flat, BU,
BPV, Number 56

Bass in B flat, BU,
BPV, Number 55

Lyon & Healy Campaign edition. 1896.
Page 35 Lyon & Healy light action Si piston valves. Instruments produced by unidentified manufacturer. All light action instruments equipped with Gs PVs, and water keys.

Cornet in B flat, BF, PV, London model, furnished with B flat and A set pieces (crooks)
No. 440 Br $13.35
No. 441 Br, Ni plated $16.35
No. 440 1/2 Br, Si plated, satin finish $21.00
No. 441 1/2 Br, Si plated, finely burnished $23.00
No. 442 Br, Si plated, burnished, with Go plated bell and tips $28.00
CMV $95.00 - $300.00

Cornet in B flat, BF, PV, Artists' model, furnished with B flat and A set pieces (crooks)
No. 460 Br $14.80
No. 461 Br, Ni plated $17.80
No. 462 Br, Si plated, satin finish, with Go plated bell $23.00
No. 463 Br, Si plated, finely burnished $25.00
No. 464 Br, Si plated, burnished, with Go plated bell and tip $30.00
CMV $95.00 - $300.00

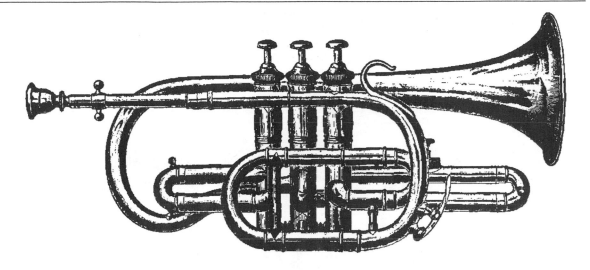

Cornet in B flat, BF, PV, Number 440

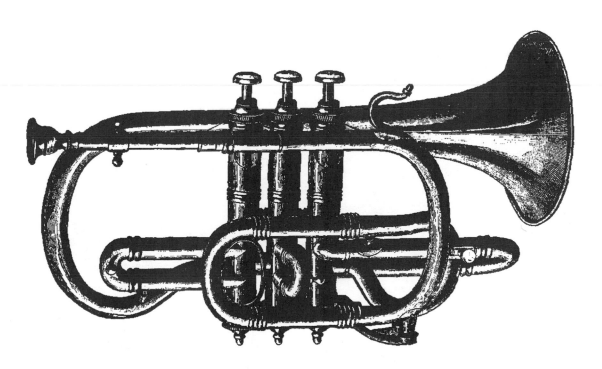

Cornet in B flat, BF, PV, Number 460

Alto in E flat, BU, PV, Number 404

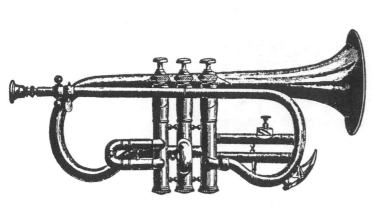

Cornet in E flat, BF, PV, Number 400

Cornet in E flat, BF, PV,
Artist model, Number 445

Tenor in B flat, BF, PV,
Number
406

Alto in E flat, BF, PV,
Solo type, Number 424

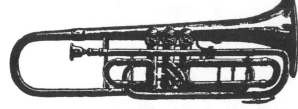

Alto trombone in E flat, BF, PV, Number 422

Lyon & Healy Campaign edition. 1896.
Page 36 Lyon & Healy light action Si piston valves. Instruments produced by unidentified manufacturer.

Cornet in E flat, BF, PV, water key
No. 400 Br $8.75
No. 401 Br, Ni plated $11.25
No. 400 1/2 Si plated, satin finish $18.00
No. 401 1/2 Si plated, finely burnished $20.00
CMV $150.00 - $450.00

Alto horn in E flat, BU, PV, water key
No. 404 Br $14.30
No. 405 Br, Ni plated $20.40
No. 404 1/2 Si plated, satin finish $29.00
No. 405 1/2 Si plated, finely burnished $36.45
CMV $75.00 - $150.00

Tenor horn in B flat, BU, PV, water key
No. 406 Br $17.00
No. 407 Br, Ni plated $23.30
No. 406 1/2 Si plated, satin finish $30.00
No. 407 1/2 Si plated, finely furnished $40.00
CMV $125.00 - $175.00

Alto horn in E flat, BF, PV, solo model, water key
No. 424 Br $14.30
No. 424 1/2 Si plated, satin finish $29.00
No. 425 Br, Ni plated $20.40
No. 425 1/2 Si plated, finely burnished $36.45
CMV $75.00 - $250.00

Alto trombone in E flat, BF, PV, water key
No. 422 Br $14.30
No. 423 Br, Ni plated $20.40
No. 422 1/2 Si plated, satin finish $20.00
No. 423 1/2 Si plated, finely burnished $36.45
CMV $250.00 - $400.00

Cornet in E flat, BF, PV, artist model, water key
No. 445 Br $13.35
No. 446 Br, Ni plated $16.30
No. 447 Si plated, satin finish $22.00
No. 449 Si plated, burnished Go bell and tips $29.55
CMV $150.00 - $500.00

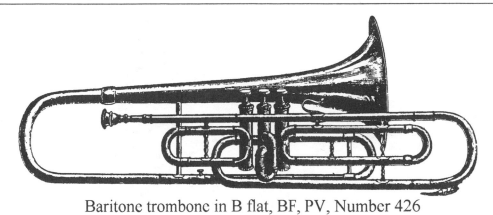

Baritone trombone in B flat, BF, PV, Number 426

Bass in B flat, BU,
PV, Number 410

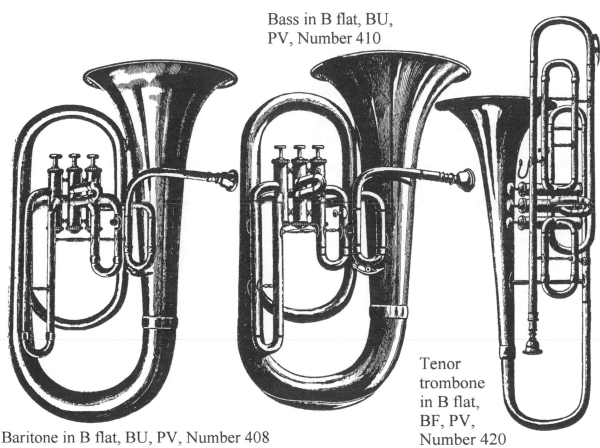

Baritone in B flat, BU, PV, Number 408

Tenor
trombone
in B flat,
BF, PV,
Number 420

Lyon & Healy Campaign edition. 1896.
Lyon & Healy light action Si piston valves. Instruments produced by unidentified manufacturer.

Baritone trombone in B flat, BF, PV, water key
No. 426 Br $20.00
No. 427 Br, Ni plated $26.00
No. 426 1/2 Br, Si plated, satin finish $42.00
No. 427 1/2 Br, Si plated, finely burnished $50.00
CMV $150.00 - $300.00

Baritone horn in B flat, BU, PV, water key
No. 408 Br $20.00
No. 409 Br, Ni plated $26.00
No. 408 1/2 Si plated, satin finish $42.00
No. 409 Si plated, finely burnished $50.00
CMV $125.00 - $275.00

Bass horn in B flat, BU, PV, water key
No. 410 Br $22.50
No. 411 Br, Ni plated $29.05
No. 410 1/2 Si plated, satin finish $48.00
No. 411 1/2 Si plated, finely burnished $53.70
CMV $125.00 - $275.00

Tenor trombone in B flat, BF, PV, water key
No. 420 Br $17.00
No. 421 Br $23.30
No. 420 1/2 Si plated, satin finish $26.00
No. 421 1/2 Si plated, finely burnished $40.00
CMV $150.00 - $300.00

Bass horn in E flat, BU, PV, water key
No. 412 Br $32.00
No. 413 Br, Ni plated $40.00
No. 412 1/2 Br, Si plated, satin finish $60.00
No. 413 1/2 Br, Si plated, finely burnished $70.00
CMV $125.00 - $300.00

Bass horn in EE flat, BU, PV, (water key, not pictured)
No. 414 Br $37.25
No. 415 Br, Ni plated $42.20
No. 414 1/2 Br, Si plated, satin finish $67.90
No. 415 1/2 Br, Si plated, finely burnished $78.50
CMV $125.00 - $300.00

Bass horn in E flat, HD, PV, water key
No. 416 Br $50.00
No. 417 Br, Ni plated, satin finish $59.60
No. 416 1/2 Br, Si plated, satin finish $91.65
No. 417 1/2 Br, Si plated, finely burnished $105.00
CMV $275.00 - $500.00

Bass in E flat, Helicon shape, PV, Number 416

Bass in E flat, BU, PV, Number 412

Lyon & Healy Campaign edition. 1896.
Champion (trade name used by Lyon & Healy). Instruments produced by unidentified manufacturer, with Gs PVs.

Cornet in B flat, BF, PV, water key, B flat and A set pieces
No. 375 Br $12.00
No. 376 Br, Ni plated $14.75
No. 377 Br, Si plated, satin finish, with Go plated bell $19.70
No. 378 Br, Si plated, finely burnished $21.00
No. 379 Br, Si plated, burnished, with Go plated bell $24.00
CMV $150.00 - $350.00

Cornet in B flat, BF, PV, Artists' model, double water key, B flat and A set pieces
No. 475 Br $17.00
No. 476 Br, Ni plated $20.00
No. 477 Br, Si plated, satin finish, with Go plated bell $24.00
No. 478 Br, Si plated, finely burnished $25.25
No. 479 Br, Si plated, finely burnished, with Go plated bell $28.50
CMV $150.00 - $350.00

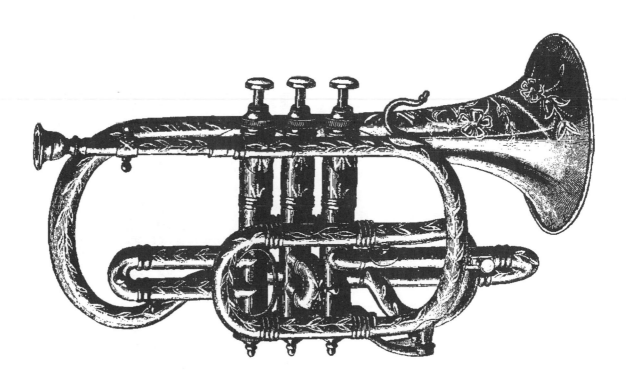

Cornet in B flat, BF, PV, Number 475

Lyon & Healy Campaign edition. 1896.
Page 41. Instruments produced by F. Jaubert & Co., Paris. All instruments on this page are made with French piston valves. None are shown.

Cornet in B flat, BF, PV, artist model, double water keys
No. 1260 Br $19.25
No. 1261 Br, Ni plated $22.25
No. 1262 Br, Si plated, satin finish $29.05
No. 1263 Br, Si plated, finely burnished $31.05
CMV $50.00 - $250.00

Cornet in B flat, BF, PV, artist model, double water keys, elegantly engraved
No. 1275 Br $26.65
No. 1276 Br, Ni plated $29.25
No. 1277 Br, Si plated, satin finish $36.00
No. 1278 Br, Si plated, finely burnished $39.00
No. 1279 Br, Si plated, finely burnished and Go tipped $44.00
CMV $150.00 - $400.00

Cornet in B flat, BF, PV, artist model, double water keys, C attachment
No. 1296 Br $22.00
No. 1297 Br, Ni plated $25.00
No. 1296 1/2 Br, Si plated, satin finish $31.65
No. 1297 1/2 Br, Si plated, finely burnished $33.65
No. 1298 Br, Si plated, finely burnished and Go tipped $38.00
CMV $75.00 - $350.00

Cornet in B flat, BF, PV, water key, C attachment
No. 1290 Br $19.25
No. 1291 Br, Ni plated $22.25
No. 1290 1/2 Br, Si plated, satin finish $26.25
No. 1291 1/2 Br, Si plated finely burnished $28.25
CMV $75.00 - $350.00

Cornet in E flat, BF, PV, water key
No. 1200 Br $13.95
No. 1201 Br, Ni plate $16.95
No. 1200 1/2 Si plated, satin finish $21.50
No. 1201 1/2 Si plated, finely burnished $23.25
CMV $125.00 - $400.00

Cornet in B flat, BF, PV, water key
No. 1202 Br $14.85
No. 1203 Br, Ni pate $17.80
No. 1202 1/2 Si plated, satin finish $22.50
No. 1203 1/2 Si plated, finely burnished $25.50
CMV $75.00 - $350.00

Alto horn in E flat, BF, PV, solo model, water key
No. 1224 Br $22.75
No. 1225 Br, Ni plate $27.75
No. 1224 1/2 Si plated, satin finish $36.00
No. 1225 1/2 Si plated, finely burnished $40.00
CMV $50.00 - $250.00

Alto trombone in E flat, BF, PV, water key
No. 1222 Br $22.75
No. 1223 Br, Ni plate $27.75
No. 1222 1/2 Si plated, satin finish $36.00
No. 1223 1/2 Si plated, finely burnished $40.00
CMV $200.00 - $300.00

Alto horn in E flat, BU, PV, water key
No. 1204 Br $22.75
No. 1205 Br, Ni plated $27.75
No. 1204 1/2 Si plated, satin finish $36.00
No. 1205 1/2 Si plated, finely burnished $40.00
CMV $50.00 - $150.00

Tenor horn in B flat, BU, PV, water key
No. 1206 Br $24.30
No. 1207 Br, Ni plated $29.30
No. 1206 1/2 Si plated, satin finish $42.00
No. 1207 1/2 Si plated, finely burnished $48.00
CMV $125.00 - $200.00

Tenor trombone in B flat, BF, PV, water key
No. 1220 Br $24.30
No. 1221 Br, Ni plated $29.30
No. 1220 1/2 Br, Si plated, satin finish $42.00
No. 1221 1/2 Br, Si plated, finely burnished $48.00
CMV $150.00 - $250.00

Baritone trombone in B flat, BF, PV, water key
No. 1226 Br $26.00
No. 1227 Br, Ni plated $33.00
No. 1226 1/2 Br, Si plated, satin finish $50.00
No. 1227 1/2 Br, Si plated, finely burnished $56.00
CMV $150.00 - $250.00

Baritone horn in B flat, BU, PV, water key
No. 1208 Br $26.60
No. 1209 Br, Ni plated $33.00
No. 1208 1/2 Si plated, satin finish $50.00
No. 1209 1/2 Si plated, finely burnished $56.00
CMV $125.00 - $200.00

Bass horn in B flat, BU, PV, water key
No. 1210 Br $32.10
No. 1211 Br, Ni plated $40.00
No. 1210 1/2 Si plated, satin finish $56.00
No. 1211 1/2 Si plated, finely burnished $63.00
CMV $125.00 - $200.00

Bass horn in EE flat, BU, PV, water key
No. 1214 Br $44.32
No. 1214 1/2 Br, Si plated, satin finish $73.65
No. 1215 Br Ni plated $54.32
No. 1215 1/2 Br, Si plated, finely burnished $86.00
CMV $125.00 - $300.00

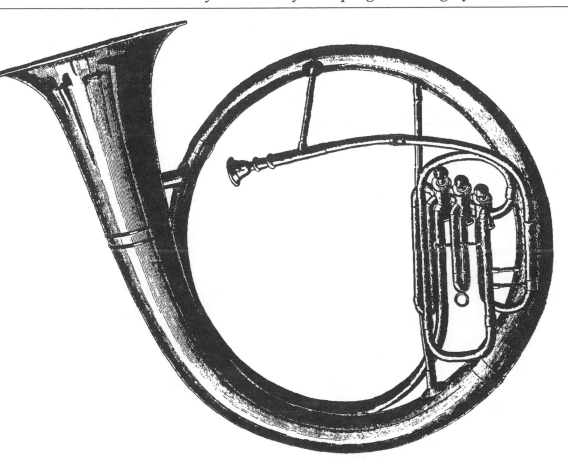

Bass horn in E flat, BU, PV, water key
No. 1212 Br $40.80
No. 1213 Br, Ni plated $47.55
No. 1212 1/2 Br, Si plated, satin finish $68.00
No. 1213 1/2 Br, Si plated, finely burnished $78.00
CMV $125.00 - $300.00

Bass horn in EE flat, HD, PV
No. 1216 Br $53.00
No. 1217 Br, Ni plated $60.00
No. 1216 1/2 Si plated, satin finish $94.00
No. 1217 1/2 Si plated, finely burnished $106.00
CMV $200.00 - $500.00

Contrabass in E flat, Helicon style, PV, Number 1216

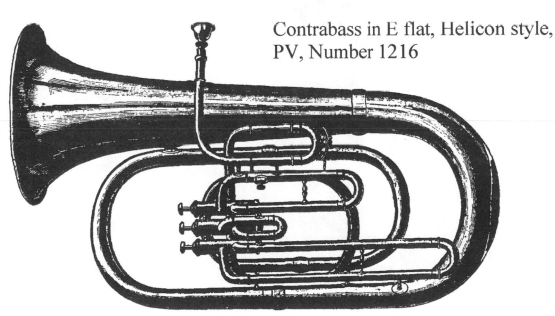

Bass in E flat, BU, PV, Number 1212

Bass horn in BB flat, BU, PV, water key, diameter of bell 13 inches (not shown)
No. 1218 Br $66.00
No. 1219 Br, Ni plated $78.25
No. 1218 1/2 Br, Si plated, satin finish $120.00
No. 1219 1/2 Br, Si plated, finely burnished $135.00
CMV $150.00-$500.00

Bass horn in BB flat, BU, PV, monster pattern, diameter of bell 16 1/2 inches
No. 1228 Br $92.00
No. 1229 Br, Ni plated $107.00
No. 1228 1/2 Br, Si plated, satin finish $140.00
No. 1229 1/2 bras, Si plated, finely burnished $160.00
CMV $150.00-$500.00

Cornet in B flat, BF, PV, pocket model (length 8 1/2 inches, height 5 inches, diameter of bell 3 inches), water key (not shown)
No. 1232 Br $21.00
No. 1233 Br, Ni plated $23.75
No. 1232 1/2 Br, Si plated, satin finish $30.00
No. 1233 1/2 Br, Si plated, finely burnished $31.55
No. 1234 Br, Si plated, Go bell and tips $36.00
CMV $500.00 - $800.00

Alto horn in E flat, PV, Concert French horn model, French horn mouthpiece, water key (not shown)
No. 1236 Br $37.65
No. 1237 Br, Ni plated $42.00
No. 1236 1/2 Br, Si plated, satin finish $52.00
No. 1237 1/2 Br, Si plated, finely burnished $60.00
CMV $125.00 - $200.00

Double bell euphonium [in B flat], BF and BU, 4 PV, water key (not shown)
No. 1240 Br $63.00
No. 1241 Br, Ni plated $72.00
No. 1240 1/2 Br, Si plated, satin finish $86.00
No. 1241 1/2 Br, Si plated, finely burnished $98.00
CMV $500.00 - $1200.00

Double bass in B flat, BU, PV,
Number 1228

Lyon & Healy Campaign edition. 1896.
"Beau Ideal" (trade name used by Lyon & Healy), also stamped "Chicago," light action valves, improved short model, Gs pistons and mouthpiece, richly engraved on mounts, and bells, produced by unidentified French manufacturer. All Beau Ideal instruments are heavily engraved on the bell and mounts. "The larger instruments are ordinarily kept only in Br and are plated to order, which requires a few days' time after order is received."

Cornet in E flat, BF, PV, water key
No. 1400 Br $26.75
No. 1401 Br, Ni plated $29.40
No. 1400 1/2 Br, Si plated, satin finish $34.75
No. 1401 1/2 Br, Si plated, burnished $36.00
No. 1401 3/4 Br, Si plated, burnished, Go plated bell and mountings, very rich $47.75
CMV $150-400

Cornet in B flat, BF, PV, double water key
No. 1460 Br $27.75
No. 1461 Br, Ni plated $29.40
No. 1460 1/2 Br, Si plated, satin finish $34.75
No. 1461 1/2 Br, Si plated, burnished $36.00
No. 1461 3/4 Br, Si plated, burnished, Go plated bell and mountings, very rich $47.75
CMV $125.00 - $400.00

Alto horn in E flat, BU, PV, water key
No. 1404 Br $32.00
No. 1405 Br, Ni plated $37.30
No. 1404 1/2 Br, Si plated, satin finish $46.00
No. 1405 1/2 Br, Si plated, burnished $50.00
No. 1405 3/4 Br, Si plated, burnished, Go plated bell and mountings, very rich $64.00
CMV $50.00 - $150.00

Tenor horn in B flat, BU, PV, water key
No. 1406 Br $36.25
No. 1407 Br, Ni plated $42.90
No. 1406 1/2 Br, Si plated, satin finish $54.00
No. 1407 1/2 Br, Si plated, burnished $57.75
No. 1407 3/4 Br, Si plated, burnished, Go plated bell and mountings, very rich $72.00
CMV $125.00 - $200.00

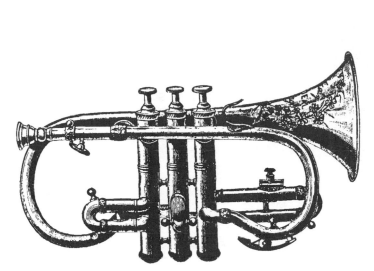

Cornet in E flat, BU, PV, Number 1400

Alto in E flat, BU, PV, Number 1404

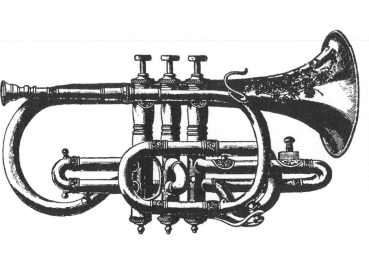

Cornet in B flat, BF, PV, Number 1460

Tenor in B flat, BU, PV, Number 1406

Lyon & Healy Campaign edition. 1896.
"Beau ideal" (trade name used by Lyon & Healy), also stamped "Chicago" light action valves, improved short model, produced by unidentified French manufacturer, etc. Instruments on this page are not shown.

Alto horn in E flat, BF, PV, solo model, water key
No. 1424 Br $32.00
No. 1425 Br, Ni plated $37.30
No. 1424 1/2 Br, Si plated, satin finish $46.00
No. 1425 1/2 Br, Si plated, burnished $50.00
No. 1425 3/4 Br, Si plated, burnished, Go plated bell and mountings, very rich $64.00
CMV $50.00 - $200.00

Alto trombone in E flat, BF, PV, water key
No. 1422 Br $32.00
No. 1423 Br, Ni plated $37.30
No. 1422 1/2 Br, Si plated, satin finish $46.00
No. 1423 1/2 Br, Si plated, burnished $50.00
No. 1423 3/4 Br, Si plated, burnished, Go plated bell and mountings, very rich $64.00
CMV $150.00 - $300.00

Tenor trombone in B flat, BF, PV, water key
No. 1420 Br $36.25
No. 1421 Br, Ni plated $42.90
No. 1420 1/2 Br, Si plated, satin finish $54.00
No. 1421 1/2 Br, Si plated, burnished $57.75
No. 1421 3/4 Br, Si plated, burnished, Go plated bell and mountings, very rich $72.00
CMV $125.00 - $250.00

Baritone trombone in B flat, BF, PV, water key
No. 1426 Br $40.60
No. 1427 Br, Ni plated $50.00
No. 1426 1/2 Br, Si plated, satin finish $62.00
No. 1427 1/2 Br, Si plated, burnished $64.50
No. 1427 3/4 Br, Si plated, burnished, Go plated bell and mountings, very rich $85.00
CMV $125.00 - $250.00

[Tenor ?] trombone in [B flat], BF, slide model
No. 1466 Br $23.00
No. 1467 Br, Ni plated $26.90
No. 1466 1/2 Br, Si plated, satin finish $35.00
No. 1467 1/2 Br, Si plated, burnished $39.00
No. 1467 3/4 Br, Si plated, burnished, Go plated bell and mountings, very rich $50.00
CMV $50.00 - $100.00

Baritone horn in B flat, BU, PV, water key
No. 1408 Br $40.00
No. 1409 Br, Ni plated $50.00
No. 1408 1/2 Br, Si plated, satin finish $62.00
No. 1409 1/2 Br, Si plated, burnished $64.50
No. 1409 3/4 Br, Si plated, burnished, Go plated bell and mountings, very rich $85.00
CMV $125.00 - $200.00

Bass horn in B flat, BU, PV, water key
No. 1410 Br $48.45
No. 1411 Br, Ni plated $54.00
No. 1410 1/2 Br, Si plated, satin finish $67.00
No. 1411 1/2 Br, Si plated, burnished $75.00
No. 1411 3/4 Br, Si plated, burnished, Go plated bell and mountings, very rich $92.00
CMV $125.00 - $200.00

Bass horn in E flat, BU, PV, large size, water key
No. 1412 Br $62.75
No. 1413 Br, Ni plated $70.00
No. 1412 1/2 Br, Si plated, satin finish $86.90
No. 1413 1/2 Br, Si plated, burnished $100.00
No. 1413 3/4 Br, Si plated, burnished, Go plated bell and mountings, very rich $117.00
CMV $150.00 - $275.00

Bass horn in EE flat, BU, PV, water key
No. 1414 Br $69.00
No. 1415 Br, Ni plated $77.00
No. 1414 1/2 Br, Si plated, satin finish $95.00
No. 1415 1/2 Br, Si plated, burnished $105.00
No. 1415 3/4 Br, Si plated, burnished, Go plated bell and mountings, very rich $128.00
CMV $150.00 - $275.00

Cornet in B flat, BF, PV, Solo model, double water keys, extensively engraved, with C attachments, and an A shank
No. 961 Br $39.35
No. 963 Br, Si plated, satin finish $48.00
No. 964 Br, Si plated, finely burnished $51.00
No. 965 Br, Si plated, finely burnished, and Go tipped $55.00
CMV $75.00 - $300.00

Lyon & Healy Campaign edition. 1896.
Page 53. Instruments produced by various manufacturers.

Cornet in B flat, BF, light action PV, water key, with A shank. Instruments produced by unidentified manufacturer.
No. 302 Br $8.75
No. 303 Br, Ni plated $11.58
No. 302 1/2 Br, Si plated, satin finish $18.50
No. 351 Br, Si plated, finely burnished $20.50
CMV $50.00 - $300.00

Cornet in C, Gs PV, water key, with B flat crook, manufactured by F. Jaubert & Co.
No. 1250 Br $16.30
No. 1251 Br, Ni plated $18.90
No. 1250 1/2 Br, Si plated, satin finish $22.90
No. 1251 1/2 Br, Si plated, finely burnished $24.90
CMV $50.00 - $300.00

Flugelhorn in B flat, BF, PV, water key, manufactured by F. Jaubert & Co.
No. 1230 Br, $17.50
No. 1231 Br, Ni plated $22.50
No. 1230 1/2 Br, Si plated, satin finish $29.50
No. 1231 1/2 Br, Si plated, finely burnished $33.50
CMV $150.00 - $300.00

Flugelhorn in C, BF, Si PV, water key, with crook to B flat, possibly stamped Lyon & Healy
No. 430 Br $17.50
No. 431 Br, Ni plated, satin finish $22.50
No. 430 1/2 Br, Si plated, satin finish $29.50
No. 431 1/2 Br, Si plated, finely burnished $33.50
CMV $150.00 - $300.00
This instrument "is especially adapted for playing with piano or organ. No transposition of music being required. Plays much easier than a cornet."

Lyon & Healy Campaign edition. 1896.
Instruments produced by F. Jaubert & Co., Paris, with French piston valves, unless otherwise identified.

Tenor trombone in B flat, BF, slide model, water key
No. 1266 Br $11.65
No. 1267 Br, Ni plated $16.00
No. 1266 1/2 Br, Ni plated, satin finish $22.35
No. 1267 1/2 Br, Ni plated, finely burnished $25.35
CMV $25.00 - $75.00

Alto trombone in E flat, BF, slide model, water key (not shown)
No. 1268 Br $11.65
No. 1269 Br, Ni plated $16.00
No. 1268 1/2 Br, Ni plated, satin finish $22.35
No. 1269 1/2 Br, Ni plated, finely burnished $25.35
CMV $25.00 - $75.00

Baritone trombone in B flat, BF, slide model, water key (not shown)
No. 1270 Br $12.65
No. 1271 Br, Ni plated $16.45
No. 1270 1/2 Br, Ni plated, satin finish $22.80
No. 1271 1/2 Br, Ni plated, finely burnished $23.80
CMV $25.00 - $75.00

French horn [in F?], PV, unidentified crooks
No. 1280 Br $35.00
No. 1281 Br, Ni plated $41.00
No. 1282 Br, Si plated, satin finish $59.00
No. 1283 Br, Si plated, finely burnished $67.55
CMV $50.00 - $200.00

Ballad horn in C, PV, water key
No. 1284 Br $37.60
No. 1285 Br, Ni plated $42.00
No. 1286 Br, Si plated, satin finish $50.00
No. 1287 Br, Si plated, finely burnished $59.00
CMV $250.00 - $500.00

Lyon & Healy Campaign edition. 1896.
Manufactured by Joseph Higham. [Higham routinely placed a coin-shaped emblem on the bell of his instruments, suggestive of the British royal seal, instead of engraving his name.]

Cornet in E flat, BF, PV, patent clear bore model, water key
No. 0601 Br $58.35
No. 0602 Br, triple Si plated, satin finish $67.20
No. 0603 Br, triple Si plated and burnished $68.65
No. 0604 Br, triple Si plated, Go trimming and bell $73.00
CMV $125.00 - $400.00

Cornet in E flat, BF, PV, first class model, water key
No. 0701 Br $39.15
No. 0702 Br, triple Si plated, satin finish $49.00
No. 0703 Br, triple Si plated and burnished $50.65
No. 0704 Br, triple Si plated, Go trimming and bell $55.00
CMV $125.00 - $400.00

Cornet in B flat, BF, PV, patent clear bore, double water key
No. 0611 Br $58.35
No. 0612 Br, triple Si plated, satin finish $67.20
No. 0613 Br, triple Si plated and burnished $68.65
No. 0614 Br, triple Si plated, Go trimming and bell $73.00
CMV $75.00 - $350.00

Cornet in B flat, BF, PV, first class
No. 0711 Br $39.15
No. 0712 Br, triple Si plated, satin finish $49.00
No. 0713 Br, triple Si plated and burnished $50.65
No. 0714 Br, triple Si plated, Go trimming and bell $55.00
CMV $75.00 - $350.00

**Lyon & Healy Campaign edition. 1896.
Manufactured by Joseph Higham.**

**Cornet in B flat, BF, PV, Solo model, patent clear bore, double water key, and completely engraved. Advertised as being "... especially adapted for presentation or concert use."
No. 0616 Br $70.00
No. 0617 Br, triple Si plated, satin finish $78.50
No. 0618 Br, triple Si plated and burnished $80.60
No. 0619 Br, triple Si plated, Go trimming and bell $84.80
CMV $250.00 - $500.00**

**Cornet in B flat, [not shown, BF, PV], patent clear bore, echo attachment (shown)
No. 0611 1/2 Br $73.45
No. 0612 1/2 Br, triple Si plated, satin finish $83.80
No. 0613 1/2 Br, triple Si plated and burnished $85.30
No. 0614 1/2 Br, triple Si plated, Go trimming and bell $89.75
CMV $750.00 - $1500.00**

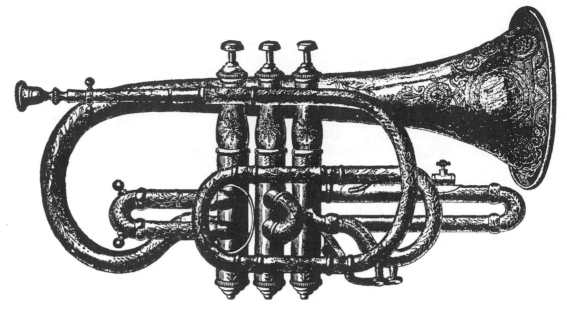

Cornet in B flat, BU, PV, Number 0616

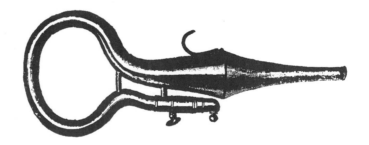

Echo attachment [for cornets]

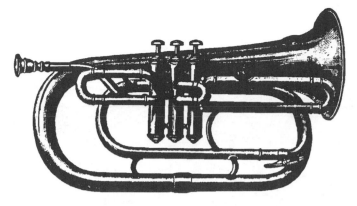

Alto in E flat, BF, PV, Number 0621

Alto in E flat, BU,
PV, Number 0626

Tenor in B flat, BU,
PV, Number 0641

**Lyon & Healy Campaign edition. 1896.
Manufactured by Joseph Higham.**

Alto horn in E flat, BF, PV, Solo model, patent clear bore, water key
No. 0621 Br $64.80
No. 0622 Br, triple Si plated, satin finish $76.00
No. 0623 Br, triple Si plated and burnished $80.00
No. 0624 Br, triple Si plated, Go trimming and bell $89.25
CMV $50.00 - $150.00

Alto horn in E flat, BF, PV, Solo model, first class, water key
No. 0721 Br $43.15
No. 0722 Br, triple Si plated, satin finish $55.00
No. 0723 Br, triple Si plated and burnished $60.00
No. 0724 Br, triple Si plated, Go trimming and bell $68.00
CMV $50.00 - $150.00

Alto horn in E flat, BU, PV, patent clear bore, water key
No. 0626 Br $61.55
No. 0627 Br, triple Si plated, satin finish $73.45
No. 0628 Br, triple Si plated and burnished $78.20
No. 0629 Br, triple Si plated, Go trimming and bell $87.20
CMV $50.00 - $150.00

Alto horn in E flat, BU, PV, first class, water key
No. 0726 Br $42.25
No. 0727 Br, triple Si plated, satin finish $54.45
No. 0728 Br, triple Si plated and burnished $58.90
No. 0729 Br, triple Si plated, Go trimming and bell $67.75
CMV $50.00 - $150.00

Tenor horn in B flat, BU, PV, patent clear bore, water key
No. 0641 Br $64.00
No. 0642 Br, triple Si plated, satin finish $77.35
No. 0643 Br, triple Si plated and burnished $82.90
No. 0644 Br, triple Si plated, Go trimming and bell $94.00
CMV $125.00 - $200.00

Euphonium in B flat, BU,
4 PV, Number 0691

Euphonium in B flat,
BU, PV, Number 0661

Bass in E flat, BU,
PV, Number 0671

Tenor horn in B flat, BU, PV, first class, water key
No. 0741 Br $47.90
No. 0742 Br, triple Si plated, satin finish $61.30
No. 0743 Br, triple Si plated and burnished $66.00
No. 0744 Br, triple Si plated, Go trimming and bell $78.00
CMV $125.00 - $200.00

Euphonium in B flat, BU, PV, patent clear bore, water key
No. 0661 Br $75.00
No. 0662 Br, triple Si plated, satin finish $91.00
No. 0663 Br, triple Si plated and burnished $98.00
No. 0664 Br, triple Si plated, Go trimming and $111.50
CMV $125.00 - $200.00

Euphonium in B flat, BU, PV, first class, water key
No. 0761 Br $57.70
No. 0762 Br, triple Si plated, satin finish $74.00
No. 0763 Br, triple Si plated and burnished $80.00
No. 0764 Br, triple Si plated, Go trimming and bell $92.80
CMV $125.00 - $200.00

Euphonium in B flat, BU, 3+1 PV, patent clear bore, water key
No. 0691 Br $89.75
No. 0692 Br, triple Si plated, satin finish $108.60
No. 0693 Br, triple Si plated and burnished $120.00
No. 0694 Br, triple Si plated, Go trimming and bell $134.00
CMV $250.00 - $400.00

Euphonium in B flat, BU, 3+1 PV, first class, water key
No. 0791 Br $68.15
No. 0792 Br, triple Si plated, satin finish $87.00
No. 0793 Br, triple Si plated and burnished $98.15
No. 0794 Br, triple Si plated, Go trimming and bell $112.50
CMV $250.00 - $400.00

Bass horn in EE flat HD, PV, patent clear bore, water key, identified as a bombardon
No. 0671 Br $89.75
No. 0672 Br, triple Si plated, satin finish $117.50
No. 0673 Br, triple Si plated and burnished $131.00
No. 0674 Br, triple Si plated, Go trimming and bell $144.00
CMV $300.00 - $500.00

Double bell euphonium in B flat, BU and BF, 4 PV, Number 0666

Contra bass in in E flat, Helicon shape, PV, Number 0671

Bass horn in E flat, BU, PV, first class, water key,
No. 0771 Br $80.50
No. 0772 Br, triple Si plated, satin finish $108.30
No. 0773 Br, triple Si plated and burnished $121.60
No. 0774 Br, triple Si plated, Go trimming and bell $135.00
CMV $125.00 - $300.00

Bass horn in EE flat, BU, PV, patent clear bore, water key,
No. 0676 1/2 Br $116.25
No. 0677 1/2 Br, triple Si plated, satin finish $146.25
No. 0678 1/2 Br, triple Si plated and burnished $160.00
No. 0679 1/2 Br, triple Si plated, Go trimming and bell $177.00
CMV $200.00 - $400.00

Double bell euphonium in B flat, BU and BF, 3+1 PV, water key
No. 0666 Br $116.40
No. 0667 Br, triple Si plated, satin finish $141.00
No. 0668 Br, triple Si plated and burnished $147.00
No. 0669 Br, triple Si plated, Go trimming and bell $160.00
CMV $750.00 - $1500.00

Bass horn in BB flat, HD, PV, clear bore pattern
No. 0681 Br $175.00
No. 0682 Br, triple Si plated, satin finish $211.00
No. 0683 Br, triple Si plated and burnished $224.00
No. 0684 Br, triple Si plated, Go trimming and bell $240.00
CMV $300.00 - $500.00

BB bass in B flat, BU, PV, Number 0681 1/2

Bass horn in BB flat, BU, PV, patent clear bore [bell diameter is 16 1/2 inches], water key
No. 0681 1/2 Br $151.95
No. 0682 1/2 Br, triple Si plated, satin finish $187.45
No. 0683 1/2 Br, triple Si plated and burnished $200.00
No. 0684 1/2 Br, triple Si plated, Go trimming and bell $212.45
CMV $350.00 - $600.00

Bass in BB flat, BU, PV, patent clear bore, monster model [bell diameter is 18 inches, not shown]
No. 0685 Br $188.00
No. 0686 Br, triple Si plated, satin finish $228.00
No. 0687 Br, triple Si plated and burnished $243.00
CMV $350.00 - $600.00

Alto trombone in E flat, BF, PV, patent clear bore
No. 0631 Br $65.65
No. 0632 Br, triple Si plated, satin finish $77.80
No. 0633 Br, triple Si plated and burnished $82.00
No. 0634 Br, triple Si plated, Go trimming and bell $90.00
CMV $250.00 - $400.00

Alto trombone in E flat, BF, PV, first class
No. 0731 Br $41.75
No. 0732 Br, triple Si plated, satin finish $54.00
No. 0733 Br, triple Si plated and burnished $58.45
No. 0734 Br, triple Si plated, Go trimming and bell $67.35
CMV $250.00 - $400.00

Tenor trombone in B flat, BF, PV, patent clear bore
No. 0646 Br $62.50
No. 0647 Br, triple Si plated, satin finish $75.90
No. 0648 Br, triple Si plated and burnished $81.45
No. 0649 Br, triple Si plated, Go trimming and bell $91.00
CMV $200.00 - $350.00

Tenor trombone in B flat, BF, PV, first class
No. 0746 Br $40.40
No. 0747 Br, triple Si plated, satin finish $55.40
No. 0748 Br, triple Si plated and burnished $59.30
No. 0749 Br, triple Si plated, Go trimming and bell $70.00
CMV $200.00 - $350.00

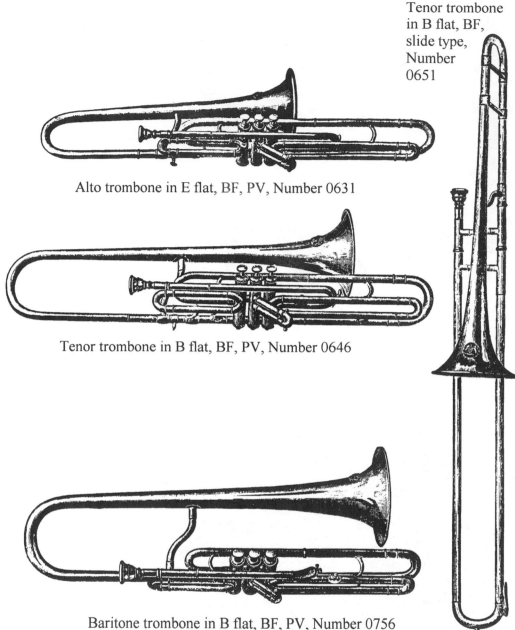

Alto trombone in E flat, BF, PV, Number 0631

Tenor trombone in B flat, BF, PV, Number 0646

Baritone trombone in B flat, BF, PV, Number 0756

Tenor trombone in B flat, BF, slide type, Number 0651

Baritone trombone in B flat, BF, PV, first class
No. 0756 Br $52.50
No. 0757 Br, triple Si plated, satin finish $68.50
No. 0758 Br, triple Si plated and burnished $76.00
No. 0759 Br, triple Si plated, Go trimming and bell $89.00
CMV $200.00 - $350.00

Tenor trombone in B flat, BF, slide model, patent clear bore, water key
No. 0651 Br $40.00
No. 0652 Br, triple Si plated, satin finish $50.00
No. 0653 Br, triple Si plated and burnished $51.50
No. 0654 Br, triple Si plated, Go trimming and bell $59.00
CMV $75.00 - $150.00

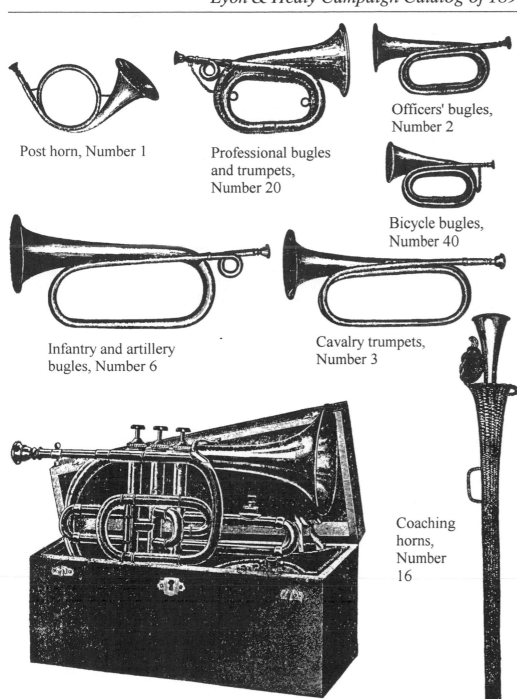

Post horn, Number 1

Professional bugles and trumpets, Number 20

Officers' bugles, Number 2

Bicycle bugles, Number 40

Infantry and artillery bugles, Number 6

Cavalry trumpets, Number 3

Coaching horns, Number 16

Cornet in B flat, BF, PV, Number 498 (shown with wood case)

Lyon & Healy Campaign edition. 1896. Instruments produced by unidentified manufacturer.
[Unless otherwise identified as such, no instruments here have valves.]
No CMVs were located for these instruments.

Post horn
No. 1 Br, one round (i.e. full loop of tubing) $1.00
No. 2 Br, two rounds $1.20
No. 3 Br, three rounds $1.60

No. 20 Officers' bugles, key of C, Co, 9 1/4 inches, with B flat crook $10.50, two rounds, and chain attached to mouthpiece
No. 25 Cavalry trumpet, key of F, Co 16 1/2 inches long $6.50
No. 30 infantry bugle, Co, key of C, 15 inches long, with B flat crook $10.50

Officers' bugle, two rounds
No. 2 Br, key of C $2.10
No. 5 Br, Ni plated, key of C $3.00
No. 7 Co key of C $3.15

Bicycle bugle, two rounds
No. 40 Br $1.85
No. 41 Br Ni plated $2.60

Infantry bugle, one round
No. 6 Br, key of C, with B flat crook $3.15
No. 8 Br, Ni plated, key of C, with B flat crook $4.20
No. 10 Co, key of C, with B flat crook $4.40

Artillery bugle (not shown)
No. 12 Br, key of G, with crook $4.35
No. 14 Br, Ni plated, key of G, with crook $5.35

Cavalry trumpet, two rounds
No. 3 Br, key of $2.90
No. 4 Br, Ni plated, key of F $4.20

Coaching horns, no rounds
No. 16 Co, Gs trimmed, superior quality, in basket $4.40
No. 17 Co, Ni plated, Gs trimmed, superior quality, in basket $6.00

Four-in-hand horns (not shown)
No. 18 Br, celebrated English maker, first quality $9.25

Tandem horns (not shown)
No. 20 Co, Br trimmed, celebrated English maker, first quality $13.80

Cornet in B flat, BF, PV, Amateur model. Instruments produced by unidentified French manufacturer.
No. 498 Br $8.75
No. 500 Br, Ni plated $11.75

Martin Brothers
Catalog of 1879

Little is known about Martin Brothers, except that this company is not related to Martin frères of Paris, France. Martin Brothers clearly was a U.S. manufacturer, beginning in 1879, and was based in New York City. The company also imported instruments from unidentified manufacturers in France and Germany, possibly even Martin frères. All instruments are equipped with three valves unless otherwise stated. Instruments marked with a * in this catalog were only made to order.

The quality of the artwork in this catalog was quite poor. To overcome the resulting vagaries, most of the illustrations have been heavily edited to make the artwork useable. In doing so, a number of examples were found to be identical. When so identified, such duplications have been eliminated here. Though the valve types suffered the worst from the artwork being so poor, enough information was clearly discernible to identify the types. Thus, some information was unavoidably lost, but the educated eye can clearly make out enough details to make the artwork useable. Also, the catalog reused numbers

The company is most often associated with other makers, notably Pollmann, but instruments simply marked Martin Brothers are rare.

Alto in E flat, BU, PV, Number 11

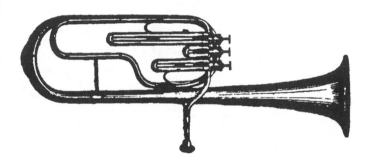

Tenor in B flat, BU, PV, Number 12

Martin Brothers "Band instruments, and celebrated guitars" 1879. Instruments produced by an unidentified German manufacturer. Not recommended highly in this catalog.

Alto horn in E flat, BU, BPV
Number 11 Gs trim $21.60
CMV $50.00 - $150.00

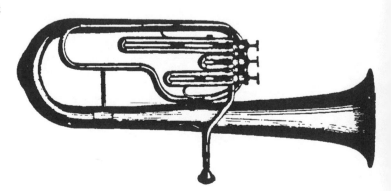

Baritone in B flat, BU, PV, Number 13

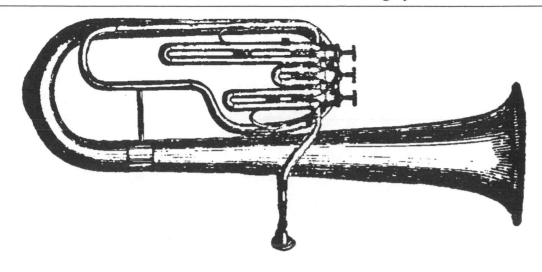

Tenor horn in B flat, BU, BPV
Number 12 Gs trim $25.20
CMV $100.00 - $300.00

Baritone horn in B flat, BU, BPV
Number 13 Gs trim $28.80
CMV $100.00 - $300.00

Bass horn in B flat, BU, BPV
Number 14 Gs trim $34.20
CMV $100.00 - $300.00

Bass horn in EE flat, BU, BPV
Number 15 Gs trim $41.50
CMV $100.00 - $300.00

Bass horn in EE flat, BU, BPV, largest size
Number 16 Gs trim $49.50
CMV $100.00 - $300.00

Bass in B flat, BU, PV, Number 14

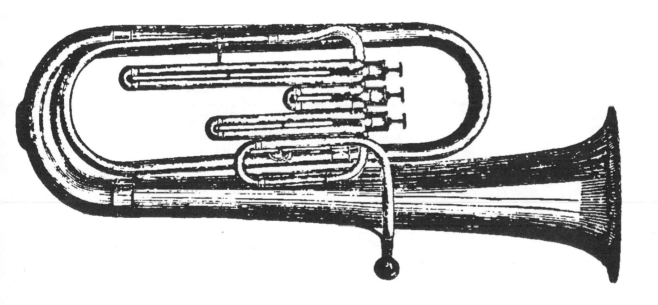

Contra bass in E flat, BU, PV, Number 15

Martin Brothers "Band instruments, and celebrated guitars" 1879.
Page 8. Instruments probably produced by Martin Brothers.

Cornet in E flat, OTS, TARV
Number 17 Br, Gs trim
$22.80
Number 41a Gs throughout
$30.00
CMV $2500.00 - $3000.00

Cornet in B flat, OTS, TARV
Number 18 Br, Gs trim
$25.00
Number 42 Gs throughout
$33.30
CMV $3000.00 - $4000.00

Alto horn in E flat, OTS, TARV
Number 19 Br, Gs trim
$29.00
Number 43 Gs throughout
$42.50
CMV $1700.00 - $2300.00

Tenor horn in B flat, OTS, TARV
Number 20 Br, Gs trim
$35.00
Number 44 Gs throughout
$51.50
CMV $1800.00 - $2400.00

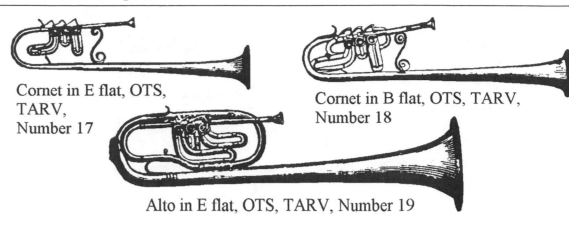

Cornet in E flat, OTS, TARV, Number 17

Cornet in B flat, OTS, TARV, Number 18

Alto in E flat, OTS, TARV, Number 19

Tenor in B flat, OTS, TARV, Number 20

Baritone in B flat, OTS, TARV, Number 21

Bass in B flat, OTS, TARV, Number 22

Contra bass in E flat, OTS, TARV, Number 23

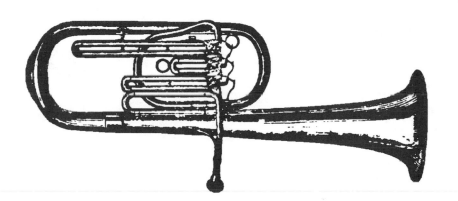

Baritone horn in B flat, OTS, TARV
Number 21 Br, Gs trim
$39.60
Number 45 Gs throughout
$57.60
CMV $1800.00 - $2400.00

Bass horn in B flat, OTS, TARV
Number 22 Br, Gs trim
$46.80
Number 46 Gs throughout
$64.80
CMV $1800.00 - $2400.00

Bass horn in EE flat, OTS, TARV
Number 23 Br, Gs trim
$54.00
Number 24 Br, Gs trim largest size $64.80
Number 47 Gs throughout
$84.60
Number 48 Gs throughout
largest size $90.00
CMV $1500.00 - $1900.00

Cornet in E flat, BU, TARV
Number 25 Br, Gs trim
$22.80
Number 49 Gs throughout
$30.40
CMV $2000.00 - $2800.00

Cornet in B flat, BU, TARV
Number 26 Br, Gs trim
$25.00
Number 50 Gs throughout
$33.30
CMV $2000.00 - $2800.00

Alto horn in E flat, BU, TARV
Number 27 Br, Gs trim
$29.00
Number 51 Gs throughout
$42.50
CMV $1200.00 - $1500.00

Tenor horn in B flat, BU, TARV
Number 28 Br, Gs trim
$35.00
Number 52 Gs throughout
$51.50
CMV $1200.00 - $1500.00

Baritone horn in B flat, BU, TARV
Number 29 Br, Gs trim
$39.60
Number 53 Gs throughout
$57.60
CMV $1100.00 - $1500.00

Bass horn in B flat, BU, TARV
Number 30 Br, Gs trim
$46.80
Number 54 Gs throughout
$64.80
CMV $1100.00 - $1500.00

Bass horn in EE flat, BU, TARV
Number 31 Br, Gs trim
$54.00
Number 55 Gs throughout
$84.60
CMV $1100.00 - $1400.00

Bass horn in EE flat, BU, TARV, largest size
Number 32 Br, Gs trim
$64.80
Number 56 Gs throughout
$90.00
CMV $1000.00 - $1400.00

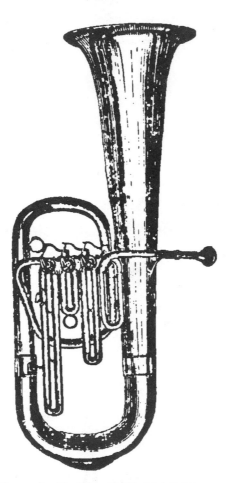

Bass in B flat, BU, TARV,
Number 30

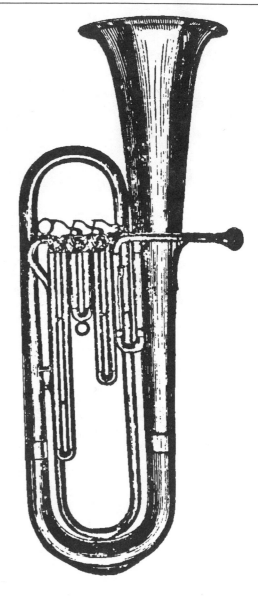

Contrabass in E flat, BU, TARV,
Number 31

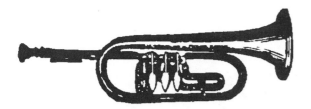

Cornet in E flat, BF, SARV, Number 33

Cornet in B flat, BF, SARV, Number 34

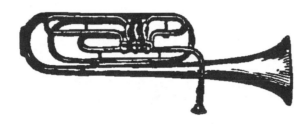

Alto in E flat, BF, SARV, Number 35

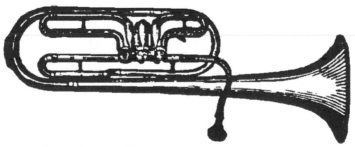

Tenor in B flat, BU, SARV, Number 36

Cornet in E flat, BF, SARV, tubes directly enter the valve cluster without bends
Number 33 Br, Gs trim $26.00
Number 57 Gs throughout $34.00
CMV $1000.00 - $1500.00

Cornet in B flat, BF, SARV
Number 34 Br, Gs trim, crooks to G $27.80
Number 58 Gs throughout, crooks to G $37.00
CMV $1000.00 - $1500.00

Alto horn in E flat, BU, SARV
Number 35 Br, Gs trim $34.20
Number 59 Gs throughout $44.50
CMV $900.00 - $1400.00

Tenor horn in B flat, BU, SARV
Number 36 Br, Gs trim $41.60
Number 60 Gs throughout $54.80
CMV $1000.00 - $1400.00

Baritone horn in B flat, BU, SARV
Number 37 Br, Gs trim
$47.50
Number 61 Gs throughout
$63.30
CMV $1000.00 - $1400.00

Bass horn in B flat, BU, SARV
Number 38 Br, Gs trim
$54.00
Number 62 Gs throughout
$70.20
CMV $1000.00 - $1400.00

Bass horn in EE flat, BU, SARV
Number 39 Br, Gs trim
$59.40
Number 63 Gs throughout
$93.60
CMV $1000.00-$1400.00

Bass horn in EE flat, BU, SARV, largest size
Number 40 Br, Gs trim
$68.40
Number 64 Gs throughout
$102.60
CMV $1000.00-$1400.00

Bass horn in EE flat, BU, 4 SARV, largest size
Number 41 Br, Gs trim
$86.00 *
Number 65 Gs throughout
$130.00 *
CMV $1200.00 - $1800.00

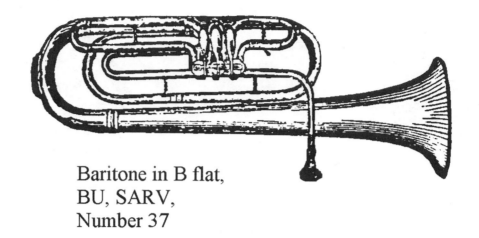

Baritone in B flat,
BU, SARV,
Number 37

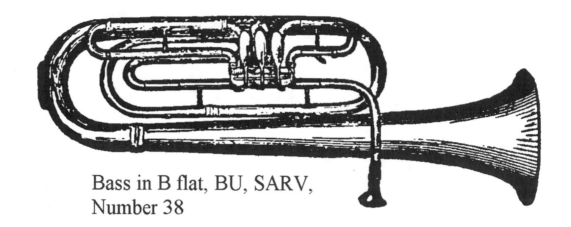

Bass in B flat, BU, SARV,
Number 38

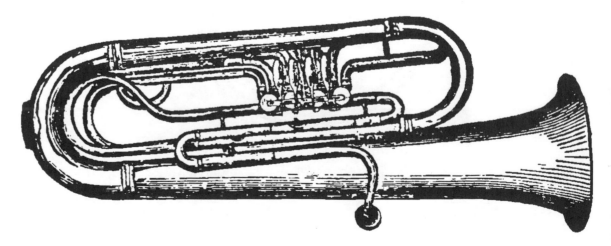

Contra bass in E flat, BU, SARV, Number 39

Cornet in E flat, HD, SARV
Number 72 Br, Gs trim
$26.50 *
Number 86 Gs throughout
$36.20 *
CMV $2500.00 - $3200.00

Cornet in B flat, HD, SARV
Number 73 Br, Gs trim,
crooks to G $29.20 *
Number 87 Gs throughout,
crooks to G $39.00
CMV $2500.00 - $3200.00

Alto horn in E flat, HD,
SARV
Number 74 Br, Gs trim
$89.40
Number 88 Gs throughout
$50.40
CMV $1100.00 - $1600.00

Cornet in E flat,
Helicon shape,
SARV, Number 72

Cornet in B flat,
Helicon shape,
SARV, Number 73

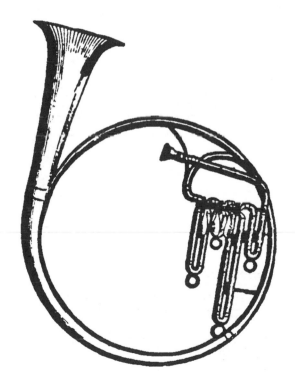

Alto in E flat, Helicon shape,
SARV, Number 74

Tenor horn in B flat, HD, SARV
Number 75 Br, Gs trim $42.90
Number 89 Gs throughout $59.40
CMV $1100.00 - $1600.00

Baritone horn in B flat, HD, SARV [Not shown]
Number 76 Br, Gs trim $48.90
Number 90 Gs throughout $66.60
CMV $1100.00 - $1600.00

Bass horn in B flat, HD, SARV
Number 77 Br, Gs trim $55.80
Number 91 Gs throughout $74.25
CMV $1000.00 - $1500.00

Alto horn in E flat, HD, PV, water key [Not shown]
Number 5060 Br $62.00 *
CMV $1200.00 - $1500.00

Tenor horn in B flat, HD, PV, water key [Not shown]
Number 5062 Br $68.00 *
CMV $1200.00 - $1700.00

Baritone horn in B flat, HD, PV, water key [Not shown]
Number 5064 Br $77.00 *
CMV $1200.00 - $1700.00

Bass horn in B flat, HD, PV, water key [Not shown]
Number 5066 Br $83.00 *
CMV $1200.00 - $1700.00

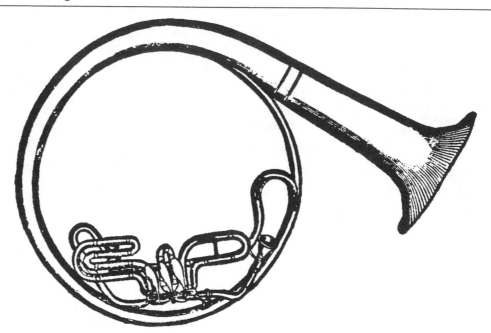

Tenor in B flat, Helicon shape, SARV, Number 75

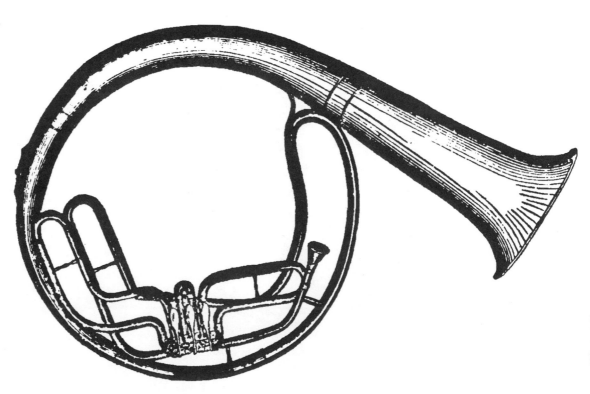

Bass in B flat, Helicon shape, SARV, Number 77

Cornet in E flat, BF,
PV, Number 5080

Tenor in B flat, BU, PV, Number 5083

Cornet in B flat, BF,
PV, Number 5081

Alto in E flat, BU,
PV, Number 5082

Baritone in B flat, BU, PV, Number 5084

Bass horn in EE flat, HD, SARV
Number 77 1/2 Br, Gs trim $66.60 *
Number 78 largest size, Br, Gs trim
$74.00
Number 91 1/2 Gs throughout $90.00*
Number 92 Gs throughout, largest size
$198.00
CMV $650.00-$1000.00

[The following instruments were only
listed on this page. No artwork was
included.]

Bass horn in EE flat, HD, PV, water
key
Number 5068 Br $94.00 *
Number 5070 Br largest size $105.00 *
CMV $300.00 - $500.00

Bass in BB flat, HD, PV, water key
Number 5072 Br largest size $150.00 *
CMV $500.00-$700.00

Martin Brothers "Band instruments,
and celebrated guitars" 1879.
Instruments produced by unidentified
manufacturer for Martin Brothers.

Cornet in E flat, BF, PV, water key
Number 5080 Br $44.80
Number 5090 Br, Si plated, satin fin-
ish $57.00 *
CMV $150.00 - $400.00

Cornet in B flat, BF, PV, water key
Number 5081 Br $50.20
Number 5091 Br, Si plated, satin fin-
ish $64.20 *
CMV $150.00 - $500.00

Alto horn in E flat, BU, PV, water key
Number 5082 Br $56.00
Number 5092 Br, Si plated, satin fin-
ish $80.00 *
CMV $50.00 - $175.00

Tenor horn in B flat, BU, PV, water key
[Not shown]
Number 5083 Br $62.00
Number 5093 Br, Si plated, satin fin-
ish $90.00 *
CMV $75.00 - $300.00

Baritone horn in B flat, BU, PV, water
key
Number 5084 Br $70.00
Number 5094 Br, Si plated, satin fin-
ish $104.00 *
CMV $75.00 - $300.00

Bass horn in B flat, BU, PV, water key
Number 5085 Br $75.00
Number 5095 Br, Si plated, satin finish $110.00 *
CMV $100.00-$300.00

Bass horn in EE flat, BU, PV, water key
Number 5086 Br $84.00
Number 5096 Br, Si plated, satin finish $135.00 *
CMV $100.00 - $300.00

Bass horn in EE flat, BU, PV, water key, largest size
Number 5087 Br $90.00
Number 5097 Br, Si plated, satin finish $146.00 *
CMV $100.00 - $300.00

Martin Brothers "Band instruments, and celebrated guitars" 1879.
Instruments probably produced by Martin Brothers.

Cornet in E flat, BF, TARV, 12 inch long model
Number 95 Br, Gs trim $22.80
Number 101 Gs throughout $30.40
CMV $1000.00 - $1500.00

Cornet in B flat, BF, TARV, 12 inch long model
Number 96 Br, Gs trim $25.00
Number 102 Gs throughout $33.30
CMV $1000.00 - $1500.00

Cornet in E flat, HD, TARV
Number 97 Br, Gs trim $27.00 *
Number 103 Gs throughout $36.00 *
CMV $2500.00 - $3000.00
"Also made in style like Bb cornet, Nos. 98 and 104."

Cornet in B flat, HD, TARV
Number 98 Br, Gs trim $29.00 *
Number 104 Gs throughout $38.00 *
CMV $2500.00 - $3000.00

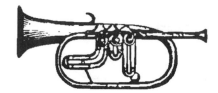

Cornet in E flat, BF, SARV, Number 95

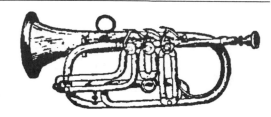

Cornet in B flat, BF, SARV, Number 96

Cornet in E flat, BF, SARV, Number 99

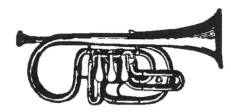

Cornet in B flat, BF, SARV, Number 100

Cornet in E flat, Helicon shape, TARV, Number 97

Cornet in B flat, Helicon shape, TARV, Number 98

Cornet in E flat, BF, SARV, 12 inch long model
Number 99 Br, Gs trim $25.00
Number 105 Gs throughout $34.00
CMV $1000.00 - $1500.00

Cornet in B flat, BF, SARV, 12 inch long model
Number 100 Br, Gs trim $27.80
Number 106 Gs throughout $37.00
CMV $1000.00 - $1500.00

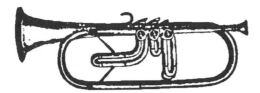

Cornet in B flat, BF, TARV,
Orchestra type, Number 107

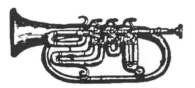

Cornet in E flat, BF, TARV,
Solo type, Number 138

Cornet in E flat, BF, SARV,
Solo type, Number 140

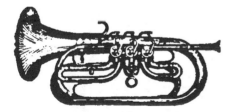

Alto in E flat, BF, TARV,
Solo type, Number 139

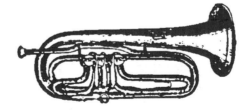

Alto in E flat, BF, SARV,
Solo type, Number 141

Cornet in C, BF, 12 inch long orchestra model (unless special ordered) [Not shown]
Number 111 3 TARV, Br, Gs trim $30.00 *
Number 112 4 SARV, Br, Gs trim $32.00 *
Number 117 3 TARV, Gs throughout $39.00*
Number 118 3 SARV, Gs throughout $42.00 *
CMV $1000.00 - $1500.00

G orchestra trumpets, with crooks to C made to order.

Cornet in E flat, BF, 10 inch, solo leader model
Number 138 TARV, Br, Gs trim $25.00
Number 140 SARV, Br, Gs trim $28.00
Number 142 TARV, Gs throughout $34.00
Number 144 SARV, Gs throughout $36.00
CMV $1000.00 - $1500.00

Numbers 140 and 144 could be had in 12 inch model

Alto horn in E flat, BF, solo model, 16 inch model (shorter if special ordered)
Number 139 TARV, Br, Gs trim $30.00
Number 141 SARV, Br, Gs trim $34.00
Number 143 TARV, Gs throughout $42.50
Number 145 SARV, Gs throughout $46.00
CMV $600.00 - $1200.00

Alto horn in E flat, BF, solo model
Number 5068 PV, Br $30.00
Number 5089 PV, Br $58.00
Number 5096 PV, Br, Si plated, satin finish $85.00 *
CMV $50.00 - $150.00

Cornet in B flat, BF, 12 inch long, orchestra model (unless special ordered)
Number 107 3 TARV, Br, Gs trim, crooks to G $26.00
Number 108 4 TARV, Br, Gs trim, crooks to G $38.00 *
Number 109 3 SARV, Br, Gs trim, crooks to G $28.80

Number 110 4 SARV, Br, Gs trim, crooks to G $40.00 *
Number 113 3 TARV, Gs throughout $34.50
Number 114 4 TARV, Gs throughout 48.00*
Number 115 3 SARV, Gs throughout $38.00
Number 116 4 SARV, Gs throughout $51.00*
CMV $1000.00-$1500.00

**Cornet in E flat, BF, PV, solo
model, water key**
Number 164 Br $24.80
Number 165 1/2 Br, Si plated,
satin finish $37.00 *
CMV $150.00 - $450.00

**Cornet in B flat, BF, PV, solo
model, water key, with
crooks to G**
Number 166 Br $25.50
Number 167 1/2 Br, Si plated,
satin finish $38.50 *
CMV $150.00 - $500.00

**Cornet in E flat, BF, pocket
model, either in 8 or 10 inch
long, water key [Not shown]**
Number 168 TARV, Br
$40.00 *
Number 169 SARV, Br
$42.00 *
CMV $2000.00+

**Cornet in B flat, BF, orches-
tra model, either in 8 or 10
inch long, water key, crooks
to G**
Number 170 TARV, Br
$42.00 *
Number 171 SARV, Br
$44.00 *
CMV $1000.00-$1500.00

**Cornet in B flat, BF, pocket
model, either in 8 or 10 inch
long, water key, crooks to G**
Number 174 TARV, Br
$50.00 *
Number 175 SARV, Br
$54.00 *
CMV $2000.00+

**Cornet in E flat, BF, artist model, 12 inches long, includes re-
pairing and repolishing implements, and extra fine case**
Number 176 Br bell, Gs TARV $60.00 *
Number 177 Br bell, Gs SARV $62.00 *
Number 181 TARV, Gs throughout $70.00 *
Number 182 SARV, Gs throughout $72.00 *
CMV $1000.00 - $1500.00

**Cornet in E flat, BF, solo model, 10 inches long, includes repair-
ing and repolishing implements, and extra fine case**
Number 178 Br bell, Gs TARV $64.00 *
Number 178a Br bell, Gs SARV $66.00 *
Number 183 TARV, Gs throughout $76.00 *
Number 184 TARV, Gs throughout $85.00 *
CMV $1000.00 - $1500.00

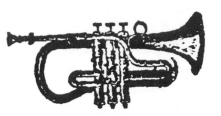

Cornet in E flat, BF, PV,
Solo type, Number 164

Cornet in B flat, BF, PV,
Orchestra type, Number 166

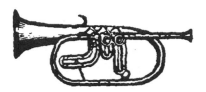

Cornet in E flat, BF, TARV,
Artist type, Number 176

Cornet in E flat, BF, SARV,
Artist type, Number 177

Cornet in E flat, BF, SARV,
Solo type, Number 178a

Cornet in E flat, BF, PV,
Number 179

Cornet in E flat, BF,
PV, Number 5080

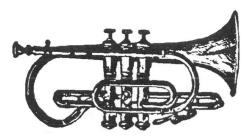

Cornet in B flat, BF, PV, Number 5081

Cornet in E flat, BF, TARV,
Miniature type, Number 179a

Cornet in E flat, BF, TARV,
Miniature type, Number 180

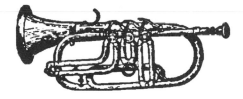

Cornet in B flat, BF,
TARV, Number 188

Cornet in B flat, BF,
SARV, Number 189

Cornet in E flat, BF, miniature model, 8 inches long, solid Br bell, includes repairing and repolishing implements, and extra fine case
Number 179a Gs TARV $72.00 *
Number 180 Gs SARV $74.00 *
CMV $2000.00 +

Cornet in E flat, miniature model, 8 inches long, includes repairing and repolishing implements, and extra fine case
Number 186 TARV, Gs throughout $82.00 *
Number 187 SARV, Gs throughout $84.00 *
Number 187 1/2 like Number 180, but Gs throughout, ornamental engravings along and around the bell, entirely and heavy Go plated, &c. excellent finish in case $110.00
CMV $2000.00 +

Cornet in B flat, orchestra model, 12 inches long, includes repairing and repolishing implements, and extra fine case
Number 188 Br bell, Gs TARV $64.00 *
Number 189 Br bell, Gs SARV $66.00 *
Number 193 TARV, Gs throughout $74.00 *
Number 194 SARV, Gs throughout $75.00 *
CMV $1000.00 - $1500.00

Cornet in B flat, miniature orchestra model, 10 inches long, includes repairing and repolishing implements, and extra fine case
Number 190 Br bell, Gs TARV $76.00 *
Number 191 Br bell, Gs SARV $78.00 *
Number 193 TARV, Gs throughout $86.00 *
Number 196 SARV, Gs throughout $88.00 *
Number 196 1/2 SARV, same as Number 191, but Gs throughout, ornamental engravings along and around the bell, entirely and heavy gold plated, &c., excellent finish, in case $130.00 *
CMV $850.00 - $1500.00

Alto trombone in E flat, BF slide model
Number 119 Br $22.00
Number 120 Br, Gs slide $30.00
Number 121 Gs throughout $40.00
CMV $250.00 - $500.00

Tenor trombone in B flat, BF, slide model [Not shown]
Number 122 Br $22.00
Number 123 Br, Gs slide $32.00
Number 124 Gs throughout $42.00
CMV $200.00 - $400.00

Tenor trombone in B flat, BF, artist slide model, solid bell, water key [Not shown]
Number 198a Br $45.00 *
Number 198b Go, Br $54.00*
Number 198c Gs $72.00 *
Number 199d Br [no price given] *
CMV $250.00 - $500.00

Alto trombone in E flat, BF, TARV
Number 126 Br $36.00
Number 127 Gs throughout $53.00
CMV $550.00 - $1000.00

Tenor trombone in B flat, BF
Number 129 TARV, Br $36.00 [Not shown]
Number 129 1/2 SARV, Gs throughout $42.00
Number 130 Br bell, Gs TARV $47.00
Number 131 TARV, Gs throughout $53.00
CMV $450.00 - $750.00

Tenor trombone in B flat, BF, SARV, artist model [Not shown]
Number 199b, Br, Gs trim $45.00 *
Number 199c, Gs throughout $72.00 *
CMV $450.00 - $850.00

Baritone trombone in B flat, BF, SARV, artist model [Not shown]
Number 199f, Br, Gs trim $64.00 *
CMV $450.00 - $850.00

Bass trombone in B flat, BF, SARV, artist model, [Not shown]
Number 199g Br, Gs trim $74.00 *
CMV $450.00 - $850.00

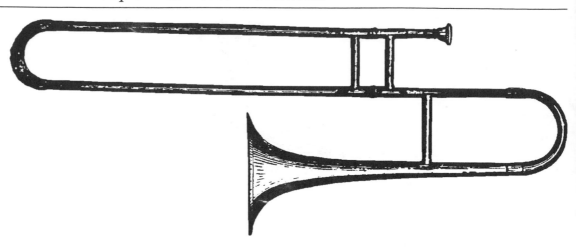

Alto trombone in E flat, BF, slide type, Number 119

Alto trombone in E flat, BF, SARV, Number 126

Tenor trombone in B flat, BF [Not shown]
Number 128 BPV, Br $31.50
Number 199a PV, Br $39.00
CMV $150.00 - $350.00

Tenor trombone in B flat, , BF, PV, artist model [Not shown]
Number 199e PV, Br, water key $70.00
CMV $150.00 - $350.00

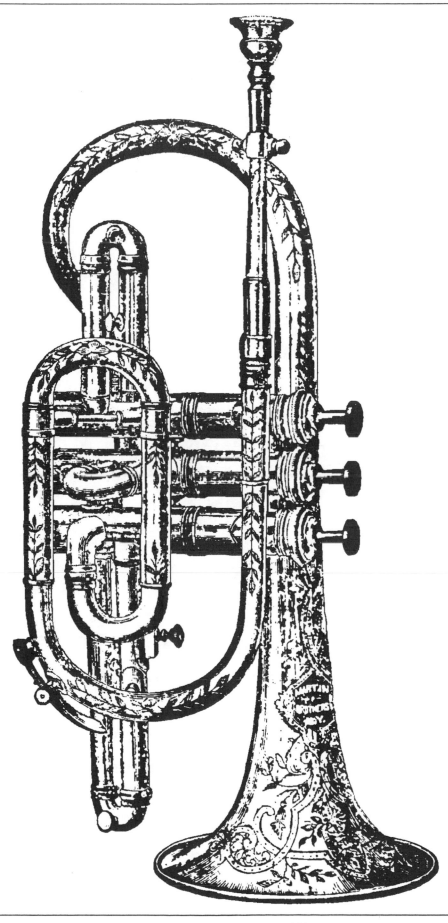

Cornet in B flat, BF, PV, Orchestra type, Number 6020

Cornet in E flat, BF, PV, solo model, 10 inch long, extension tubing slide to D, with 2 water keys, includes repairing and repolishing implements, and extra fine case
Number 179 Br, solid bell, Br pistons lined with Gs $75.00*
Number 185 like 179, except Gs throughout $85.00 *
CMV $450.00 - $750.00

Cornet in E flat, BF, PV, water key
Number 5080 Br $44.80
Number 5090 Br, Si plated, satin finish $57.00
CMV $150.00 - 450.00

Cornet in B flat, BF, PV
Number 5081 Br $50.20
Number 5091 Br, Si plated, satin finish $64.20
CMV $150.00 - $500.00

Martin Brothers "Band instruments, and celebrated guitars" 1879.
"Celebrated Artists model" instruments produced by Martin Brothers.

Cornet in E flat, BF, PV, water key [See number 6020]
Number 6000 Br $50.00
Number 6002 Br, Si plated, satin finish $64.00
Number 6004 Br, Si plated, burnished, gilt inside bell $72.00 *
Number 6006 Br, Si plated, burnished, almost entirely ornamentally engraved, heavy electroplate Go plated and gilt inside bell, complete in fine case $120.00 *
Number 6008 like number 6006, but with ornamental engravings inside bell, heavy electro Go plated, the finest instrument in existence, complete in fine case $145.00 *
CMV $150.00 - $550.00

Cornet in B flat, BF, PV, orchestra model, water key
Number 6020 Br $54.00
Number 6022 Br, Si plated, satin finish $69.00
Number 6024 Br, Si plated, burnished, gilt inside bell $76.00 *
Number 6026 Br, Si plated, burnished almost entirely ornamentally engraved, heavy electro Go plated and gilt inside complete in fine case $125.00 *
Number 6028 like number 6026, but with ornamental engravings inside bell, heavy electro Go plated, "the finest instruments in existence," complete in fine case $150.00 *
CMV $200.00 - $675.00

French horn [in F]
Number 133 SARV, Br, and crooks $80.00 *
Number 134 PV, Br, and crooks $100.00 *
Number 135 SARV, Gs, and crooks $120.00 *
CMV $150.00 - $450.00

Officer's bugle in C, 2 rounds, mouthpiece
Number 151 1/2 Br, best quality $4.50 to $8.00
Number 152 1/2 Gs, best quality $8.00 to $12.00
CMV $50.00 - $100.00

Infantry trumpet in C, one round, U.S. regulation pattern, mouthpiece
Number 154 Br $5.00
Number 155 Gs $9.00
Number 156 Co $9.00
Infantry trumpets in C, with B crooks made to order
CMV $50.00 - $100.00

Cavalry and artillery trumpets, two rounds, U.S. regulation pattern, mouthpiece
Number 158 in F, Br $6.00 to $12.00
Number 158 1/2 in G, with F crook, Br $10.00 to $14.00 *
Number 159 in F, Gs $12.00 to $16.00 *
Number 160 in F, Co $12.00 to $16.00 *
CMV $50.00 - $100.00

Boat, post or hunting horns, mouthpiece
Number 161 Br, one round $1.60
Number 162 Br, two rounds $2.00
Number 163 Br, 3 rounds $2.40
CMV $50.00 - $100.00

Martin Brothers "Band instruments, and celebrated guitars" 1879.
Page 31. Instruments produced by an unidentified French manufacturer.

Cornopean in B flat, BF, PV [Not shown]
Number 149a Br, with shanks $13.00
Number 150a Br, crooks to F $14.00 *
Number 150a Br, Ni plate, crooks to F $16.00 *
CMV $300.00 - $700.00

French horn [in F?], SARV, Number 133

Officer's bugle in C, BF, Number 151 1/2

Infantry trumpet in C, BF, Number 154

Cavalry and artillery trumpets, BF, Number 158

Fragment of an Undated J.W. Pepper Catalog Circa 1904?

James Welsch Pepper established his instrument manu-facturing company by 1882 in Philadelphia, having begun the company in 1876. According to the *NLI* (p. 298), Pepper employed a number of prominent people in the U.S. brass instrument industry, including Henry Distin, and Slater. Claims about Pepper's factory lead to controversy and al-most comical litigations with Conn. Another controversy still swirls around Pepper and Conn. Current thinking is that Pep-per produced the first true Sousaphone, having adapted Sousa's bell up bass instrument. Pepper's instruments range in quality from student grade to professional grade instru-ments. The *NLI* article lists the following trade names which Pepper used: American Climax; American Favorite; Excel-sior; Imperial; Premier; Special, Specialty, Surprise, Standard, and Twentieth Century. In 1910, the company ended produc-tion. No CMVs have been located for these instruments.

Two instruments that are offered in this catalog listed as being Sousaphones. Thus, the name Sousaphone predates that turning of the bell forward.

"We are the original makers of this most popular style of Eb and BBb Basses. The first BBb Sousaphone was made by us for Herman Conrad, and was used in Sousa's Famous Con-cert Band. The Eb Sousaphone Bass in entirely a new origi-nal brass instrument. ... Remember that we are the sole origi-nators of this style of brasses, and all others are imitations of these magnificent large proportioned monsters. ..."

Fragment of an undated J.W. Pepper catalog.
Instruments produced by J.W. Pepper, unless stated otherwise. Stan-dard trade name applied to all these instruments. All instruments equipped with silver plated mouthpiece and music lyre.

Alto horn in E flat [listed as B flat], BF, PV, water key
Br, highly polished $13.60
Ni plated, highly polished $16.15
Si plated, satin finish, inside of bell Go plated, neatly engraved on bell $21.20

Alto horn in E flat, circular design, bell down, PV, water key
Br, highly polished $15.30
Nickel plated, highly polished $18.50

Bass horn in E flat, HD, PV
Br, highly polished $42.35
Ni plated, highly polished $47.50
Si plated, satin finish, inside of bell and points burnished, handsomely engraved on bell $61.80

Bass horn in E flat, HD, PV, large design (diameter of bell 15 inches) [Same as above]
Br, highly polished $44.30
Ni plated, highly polished $49.00
Si plated, satin finish, inside of bell and points burnished, handsomely engraved on bell $63.90

Bass horn in E flat, BU, PV, short model, water key
Br, highly polished $28.65
Ni plated, highly polished $34.50
Si plated, satin finish, inside of bell and points burnished, handsomely engraved on bell $45.15

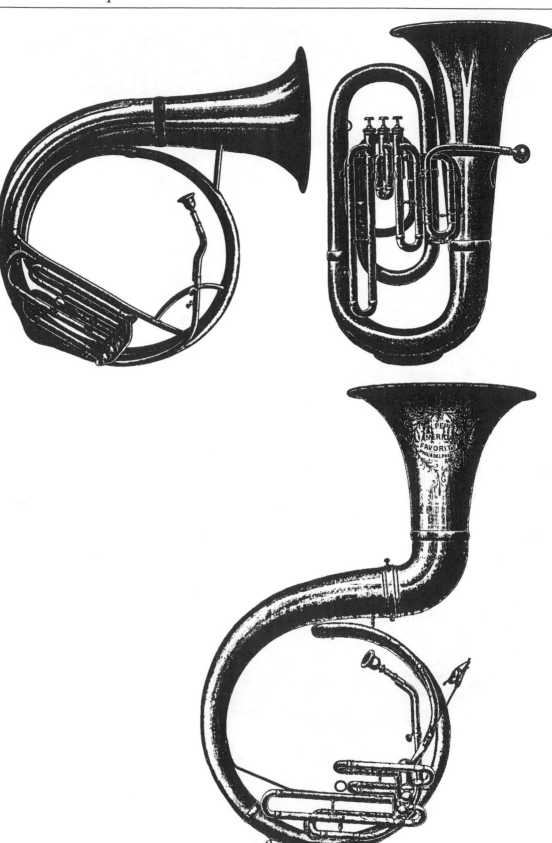

Bass in E flat, Rain catcher design, PV, with music lyra

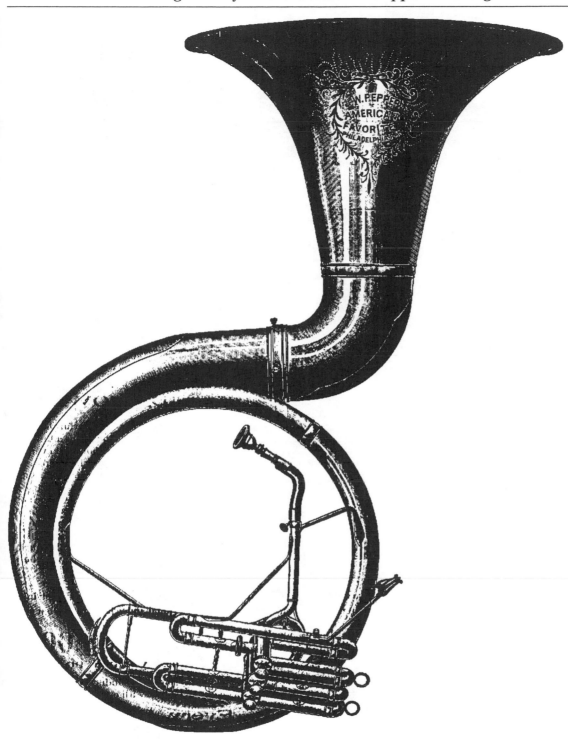

Bass in B flat, Rain catcher design, PV, with music lyre

Fragment of an undated J.W. Pepper catalog.
Pages not numbered. Instruments produced by J.W. Pepper, unless stated otherwise. American Favorite trade name applied to all these instruments. All instruments equipped with silver plated mouthpiece and music lyre.

Bass horn in E flat, BU Sousaphone, PV, water key (diameter of bell 17 3/4 inches, length 45 inches, width 24 inches, and weight 14 lbs.)
Br, highly polished, neatly engraved on bell $96.25
Ni plated, highly polished, neatly engraved on bell $100.90
Si plated, satin finish, inside of bell and points Go plated, neatly engraved on bell $119.25

Bass horn in B flat, BU Sousaphone, PV, water key (diameter of bell 28 inches, length 54 1/4 inches, width 27 1/2 inches, weight 22 1/2 lbs.)
Br, highly polished, neatly engraved on bell $119.35
Ni plated, highly polished, neatly engraved on bell $127.20
Si plated, satin finish, inside of bell and points burnished neatly engraved on bell $146.75
Si plated, satin finish, inside of bell and points Go plated, neatly engraved on bell $155.35

Cornet in B flat, BF, PV, double water key
Br, highly polished $10.85
Ni plated, highly polished $12.20
Si plate, satin finish, inside of bell Go plated, neatly engraved on bell $16.55

Cornet in B flat, BF, PV, water key
Br, highly polished $8.50
Ni plated, highly polished $10.00
Si plated, sating finish, inside of bell Go plated, neatly engraved on bell $14.20

Cornet in E flat, BF, PV, water key
Br, highly polished $8.00
Ni plated, highly polished $9.25
Si plated, satin finish, inside of bell Go plated, neatly engraved on bell $13.70

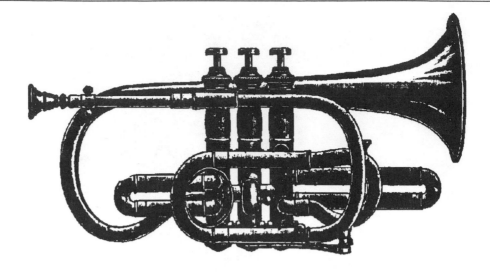

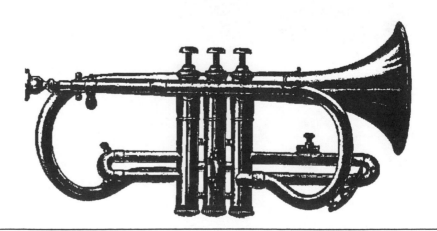

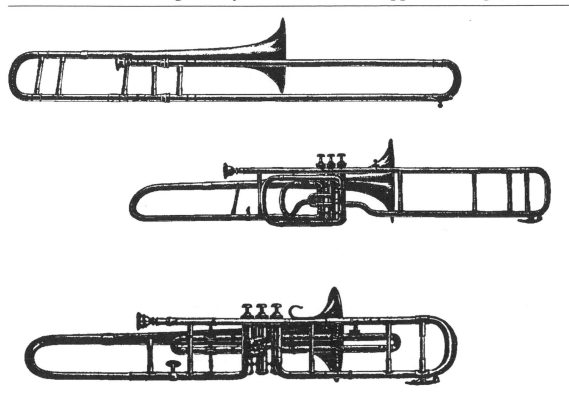

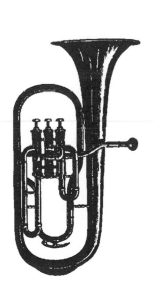

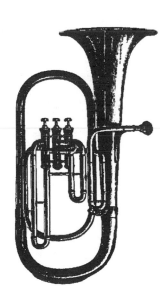

Tenor trombone in B flat, slide model, water key
Br, highly polished $10.20
Ni plated, highly polished $12.30
Si plated, satin finish, inside of bell Go plated, neatly engraved on bell $16.75

Tenor trombone in B flat, PV, water key
Br, highly polished $15.30
Ni plated, highly polished $19.25
Si plated, satin finish, inside of bell Go plated, neatly engraved on bell $27.75

Alto trombone in E flat, BF, PV, water key
Br, highly polished $13.70
Ni plated, highly polished $24.90
Si plate, satin finish, inside of bell Go plated, neatly engraved on bell $31.50

Alto horn in E flat, BU, PV, short model, water key
Br, highly polished $13.65
Ni plated, highly polished $16.20
Si plated, satin finish, inside of bell Go plated, neatly engraved on bell $21.25

Baritone horn in B flat, BU, PV, short model, water key
Br, highly polished $19.25
Ni plated, highly polished $27.75
Si plated, satin finish, inside of bell Go plated, neatly engraved on bell $29.45

Tenor horn in B flat, BU, PV, short model, water key
Br, highly polished $13.55
Ni plated, highly polished $19.25
Si plated, satin finish, inside of bell Go plated, neatly engraved on bell $24.75

Slater Catalog of 1874

Slater is one of many instrument manufacturers associated with another name, such as Martin, or Distin. These names helps to date an instrument, relying on the information in *NLI*. However, the 1874 catalog excerpted in this book gives the company's name as M. Slater, which is a year earlier than that given in *NLI*. The company made instruments that are quite collectible today. The company also imported instruments of varying quality. Though it is possible that the company stenciled its name on cheaper instruments, this supposition is rather unlikely. The catalog also states that OTS, BF, and BU designs were sold at the same price.

In this catalog, Slater points to his newly improved cornets, both E flat and B flat, as high quality instruments. Slater distinguishes between two types of B flat cornets, being an orchestral version and a street version, without defining these terms. He also offers upright E flat and B flat cornets. This design is almost never mentioned in any other brass wind catalog.

The following quote is found on page 7 of the catalog. "All side action instruments $5.00 more than top. Copper instruments same price as German Silver. In ordering instruments, please be very particular to state whether you wish over the shoulder, upright, or circular in shape, and whether they are to be used in orchestra or street band. Every description of brass or German Silver instruments made to order and the leading styles constantly on hand. Infantry bugles and cavalry trumpets, in brass, copper, or German Silver, all kinds. Each instrument is furnished complete with mouthpiece and bookrack."

This catalog offers items not regularly found in most musical instrument trade catalogs, including backgammon boards on p. 11, toy horns on p. 27 (not included in this book), piccolos made by Slater p. 26, and many other music-related items, such as harmonicas, violin strings, accordions. The important feature of this panoply of items is that most quality manufacturers such as Slater only sold brass wind instruments. Thus, one might encounter non-brass wind instruments stamped with Slater's name.

For this book, the Slater catalog's information has been reorganized. This was done, partly as the catalog scattered illustrations of the cornet types through the catalog. Also, the original catalog did not affix any numbers to the instruments, so the editor provided numbers for this book. Finally, the catalog was not always totally clear as to what metals were used to make an instrument.

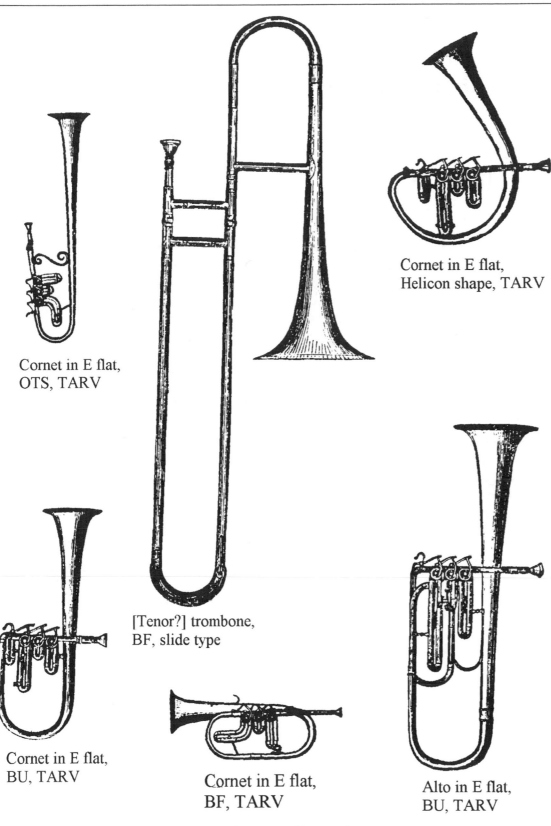

Cornet in E flat
Br, PV $19.00
Br, TARV $31.00
Gs, TARV $40.00
CMV BF, PV $750.00-
$1400.00
CMV BU, TARV $2500.00-
$3500.00
CMV HD, TARV $2500.00 -
$3500.00
CMV OTS $2500.00 -
$3500.00

[Tenor ?] trombone in B flat,
BF, slide model
Br $25.00
CMV $250.00 - $600.00

Alto horn in E flat, BU,
TARV
Br, PV $26.00
Br, TARV $43.00
Gs, TARV $53.00
CMV $1000.00 - $1400.00

Cornet in E flat,
Helicon shape, TARV

Cornet in E flat,
OTS, TARV

[Tenor?] trombone,
BF, slide type

Cornet in E flat,
BU, TARV

Cornet in E flat,
BF, TARV

Alto in E flat,
BU, TARV

Slater (formerly Slater & Martin) "Illustrated Catalogue of Brass and
German Silver Musical Instruments" [1874].
Instruments produced by Slater unless otherwise indicated. The instruments were offered in BF, BU, and OTS all for the same price. An
instrument with Gs SARV will probably sell for the most of these various models.

Cornet in B flat, BF
Br, PV $20.00
Br, TARV $33.00
Gs, TARV $43.00
CMV BF $750.00 - $1400.00
CMV BU $2500.00 - $3500.00
CMV HD $2500.00 - $3500.00
CMV OTS $2500.00 - $3500.00

Cornet in B flat, BF, with A and G crooks, short orchestra model
Br, TARV $35.00
Gs, TARV $46.00
Br, SARV $39.00
Gs, SARV $50.00
CMV $750.00 - $1400.00

Cornet in B flat, with A and G crooks, long orchestra model
[No metal given] BF, TARV (no price given)
CMV $650.00 - $1300.00

Officer's bugle, BF,
Br $5.00
Gs $8.00
CMV $50.00

Cornet in B flat,
Helicon shape,
TARV

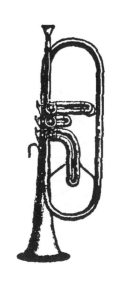

Cornet in B flat,
BU, TARV

Officer's bugle, BF

Cornet in B flat,
BF, SARV,
orchestra model,
short pattern

Cornet in B flat,
OTS, TARV

Cornet in B flat,
BF, TARV,
Orchestra model,
long pattern

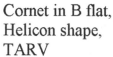

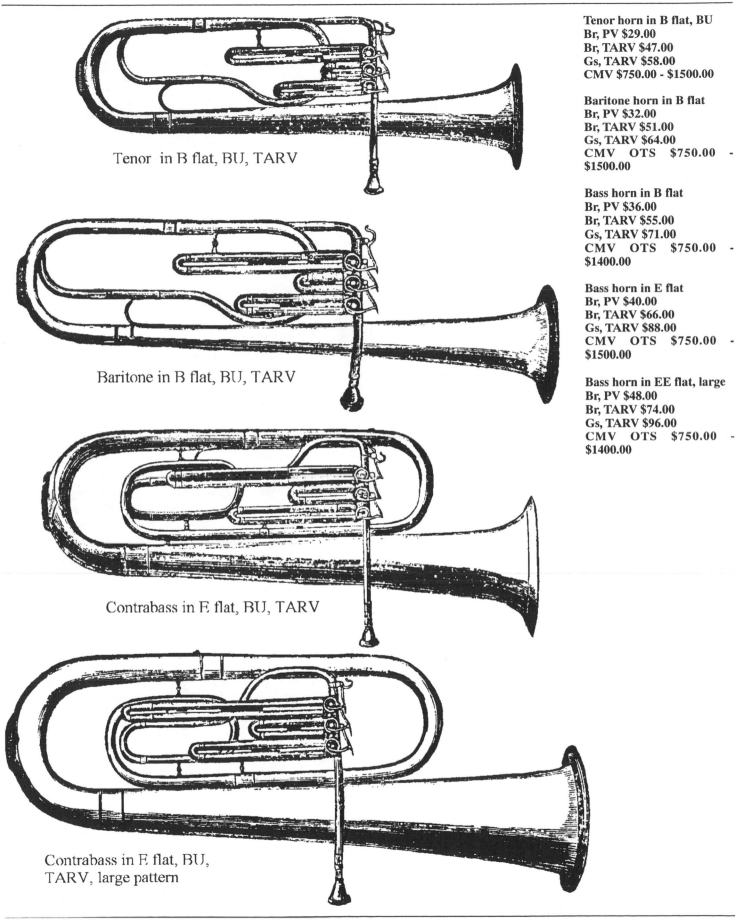

Tenor in B flat, BU, TARV

Baritone in B flat, BU, TARV

Contrabass in E flat, BU, TARV

Contrabass in E flat, BU,
TARV, large pattern

Tenor horn in B flat, BU
Br, PV $29.00
Br, TARV $47.00
Gs, TARV $58.00
CMV $750.00 - $1500.00

Baritone horn in B flat
Br, PV $32.00
Br, TARV $51.00
Gs, TARV $64.00
CMV OTS $750.00 -
$1500.00

Bass horn in B flat
Br, PV $36.00
Br, TARV $55.00
Gs, TARV $71.00
CMV OTS $750.00 -
$1400.00

Bass horn in E flat
Br, PV $40.00
Br, TARV $66.00
Gs, TARV $88.00
CMV OTS $750.00 -
$1500.00

Bass horn in EE flat, large
Br, PV $48.00
Br, TARV $74.00
Gs, TARV $96.00
CMV OTS $750.00 -
$1400.00

Alto horn in E flat, OTS,
Br, PV $26.00
Br, TARV $43.00
GS, TARV $53.00
CMV $1800.00-$2500.00

Tenor horn in B flat, OTS
Br, PV $29.00
Br, TARV $47.00
Gs, TARV $58.00
CMV $1800.00 - $2500.00

Baritone horn in B flat, OTS
Br, PV $32.00
Br, TARV $51.00
Gs, TARV $64.00
CMV $1800.00 - $2500.00

Bass horn in B flat, OTS
Br, PV $36.00
Br, TARV $55.00
Gs, TARV $71.00
CMV $1800.00 - $2500.00

Bass horn in EE flat, OTS
Br, PV $40.00
Br, TARV $66.00
Gs, TARV $88.00
CMV $1800.00 - $2500.00

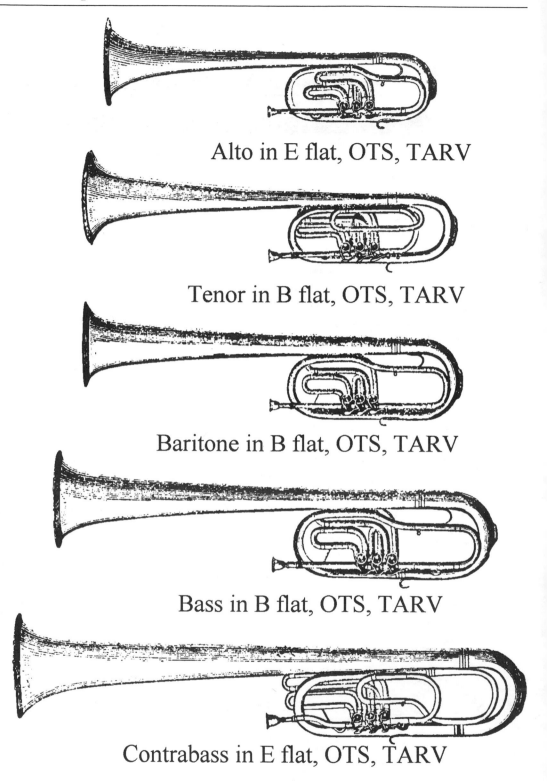

Alto in E flat, OTS, TARV

Tenor in B flat, OTS, TARV

Baritone in B flat, OTS, TARV

Bass in B flat, OTS, TARV

Contrabass in E flat, OTS, TARV

John F. Stratton & Son
Catalog of CA. 1893-1895

John Franklin Stratton was a maker and manufacturer of brasswind instruments, in both New York City, and Germany. He also imported brass and stringed instruments from Europe. *NLI* gives the working dates of his company as 1859-1912. This same article states that "he enjoyed the reputation of being able to make any part of every instrument he sold." At various times, he associated himself with J. Howard Foote (1864-1865), and later with Frank A. Stratton, his son (1898-1895). Instruments from this company are generally of good quality. Stratton imported instruments made by M. Goulet of France, for whom precious little information exists in *NLI*. Goulet's instruments, as can be seen from the catalog excerpted here, was a maker of medium-quality instruments.

The Stratton catalog excerpted here lists eight styles of instruments the company manufacturers on page 2.

1. Br, BU, PV
2. Br, BU, BPV
3. Br, OTS, RV
4. Br, BU, RV
5. Br, HD, RV
6. Gs, OTS, RV
7. Gs, BU, RV
8. Gs, HD, RV

On page 11, the catalog includes the following comments:

"At the present writing the great demand is for piston valves. For this reason we have discontinued the manufacturing of rotary valve instruments, and shall make no more until further notice. We wish to announce, however, that we have a small stock on hand which we will close out to parties preferring this style. We give below a list of styles and prices."

The catalog also provides the following information:

"Bell front cornets always go with upright instruments. The upright instruments with French Light Action Piston Valves are today the most popular style. We would remind bands, however, who desire to consult economy, that they can, if they wish, order the fine French Piston Valves for their *leading* instruments, and have the German Piston-valve instruments for second and third altos, second tenors, etc. The German Piston-Valve instruments are made in the same general style as the French Pistons, so that they will match perfectly in a set. The Helicon style is a nonsensical form of instrument, which we do not recommend. We make them because we are obliged to, but they are very little used."

John F. Stratton & Son catalog 1893 - 1895. Instruments made by various makers.

Cornet in B flat, BF, PV, double water key, A shank, instrument produced by Stratton
Br $11.00
Ni plated $13.00
Triple Si plated $20.00
Triple Si plated, and finely engraved bell $23.00
Triple Si plated, and fancy engraved throughout bell, crooks, slides, set pieces, &c. $25.00
Triple Si plated, and Go plated, and finely engraved bell $35.00
CMV $300.00 - $750.00

Cornet in B flat, BF, PV, water key, A shank instrument, produced by M. Goulet
Br $7.50
Ni $9.50
Triple Si plated $16.50
Triple Si plated, and finely engraved bell $19.50
Triple Si plated, and fancy engraved bell $21.50
Triple Si plated, Go plated, and finely engraved bell $31.50
Triple Si plated, Go plated, and fancy engraved bell $33.50
CMV $150.00 - $350.00

John F. Stratton & Son catalog 1893 - 1895. Instruments produced by Stratton & Son. [See page 137]

Cornet in B flat, BF, PV, Courtois model, double water key, A shank
Br $20.00
Ni plated $22.00
Triple Si plated, frosted or burnished $29.00
Triple Si plated, and finely engraved bell $32.00
Triple Si plated, and fancy engraved throughout bell, crooks, slides, set pieces, &c. $34.00
Triple Si plated, Go plated, and finely engraved bell $44.00
Triple Si plated, Go plated and fancy engraved throughout crooks, slides, set pieces, &c. $46.00
CMV $300.00 - $750.00

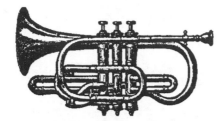

Cornet in B flat, BF, PV

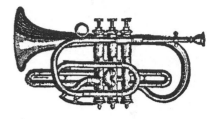

Cornet in B flat, BF, PV

Cornet in B flat, BF, PV

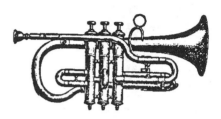

Cornet in E flat, BF, PV

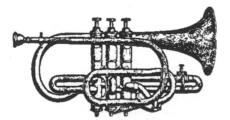

Cornet in B flat, BF, PV

Cornet in C, BF, PV

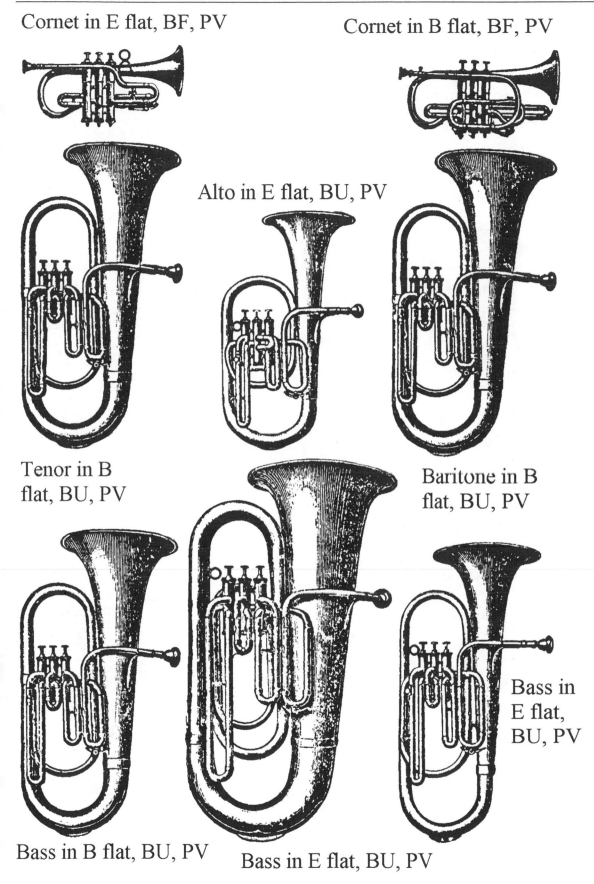

Cornet in E flat, BF, PV

Cornet in B flat, BF, PV

Alto in E flat, BU, PV

Tenor in B flat, BU, PV

Baritone in B flat, BU, PV

Bass in E flat, BU, PV

Bass in B flat, BU, PV

Bass in E flat, BU, PV

Cornet in B flat, BF, PV, double water key, same as top left p.136 but triple Si plated, and Go plated, and fancy engraved bell $37.00 CMV $500.00-$1000.00

Cornet in E flat, BF, PV, water key
Br $10.00
Ni plated $12.00
Triple Si plated $17.00
Triple Si plated, and finely engraved bell $20.00
Triple Si plated, and fancy engraved throughout bell, crooks, slides, set pieces, &c. $22.00
Triple Si plated, Go plated, and finely engraved bell $32.00
Triple Si plated, Go plated, and fancy engraved throughout bell, crooks, slides, set pieces, &c. $34.00
CMV $200.00-$600.00

Cornet in C, BF, PV, water key, B flat shank
Br $12.00
Ni plated $14.00
Triple Si plated $21.00
Triple Si plated, and finely engraved bell $24.00
Triple Si plated, and fancy engraved throughout bell, scrolls, slides, set pieces, &c. $26.00
Triple Si plated, Go plated, and finely engraved bell $36.00
Triple Si plated, Go plated and fancy engraved bell throughout bell, crooks, &c. $38.00
CMV $300.00 - $700.00

Alto horn in E flat, BU, PV, water key
Br $14.00
Ni plated $18.00
Triple Si plated $28.00
CMV $200.00 - $400.00

Alto horn in E flat, BF, PV, solo model, water key [Not shown]
Br $14.00
Ni plated $18.00
Triple Si plated $28.00
CMV $150.00 - $300.00

Tenor horn in B flat, BU, PV, water key
Br $16.00
Ni plated $22.00
Triple Si plated $31.00
CMV $200.00 - $400.00

Cornet in E flat, BF, PV

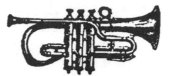

Cornet in B flat, BF, PV

Baritone in B flat, BU, PV

Contrabass in E flat, BU, PV

Alto in E flat, BU, PV

Bass in E flat, BU, PV

Tenor in B flat, BU, PV

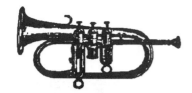

Cornet in E flat, BF, BPV

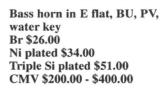

Cornet in B flat, BF, BPV

Baritone in B flat, BU BPV

Alto in E flat, BU, BPV

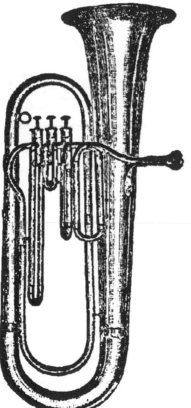

Bass in B flat, BU, BPV

Bass in E flat, BU, BPV

Tenor in B flat, BU, BPV

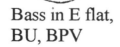

Bass horn in E flat, BU, PV, water key
Br $26.00
Ni plated $34.00
Triple Si plated $51.00
CMV $200.00 - $400.00

Bass horn in B flat, BU, PV, water key
Br $21.00
Ni plated $29.00
Triple Si plated $43.00
CMV $200.00 - $400.00

Bass horn in E flat, BU, PV, large size, water key
Br $30.00
Ni plated $40.00
Triple Si plated $58.00
CMV $175.00 - $400.00

John F. Stratton & Son catalog 1893 - 1895.
Instruments produced by M. Goulet, with water key, based upon Stratton's designs.

Cornet in E flat, BF, PV
Br $7.25
Ni $9.25
Si plated $14.20
CMV 75.00 - $300.00

Cornet in B flat, BF, PV
Br $7.50
Ni $9.50
Si plated $16.50
CMV $75.00 - $300.00

Alto horn in E flat, BU, PV
Br $10.50
Ni $14.50
Si plated $24.50
CMV $50.00 - $100.00

Baritone horn in B flat, BU, PV
Br $14.00
Ni $20.00
Si plated $34.00
CMV $75.00 - $250.00

Bass horn in B flat, BU, PV
[Not shown]
Br $16.50
Ni $24.50
Si plated $38.50
CMV $75.00 - $250.00

Bass horn in E flat, BU, PV
Br $21.0
Ni $29.00
Si plated $46.00
CMV $75.00 - $250.00

Bass horn in E flat, BU, PV, large size
Br $23.00
Ni $33.00
Si plated $51.00
CMV $75.00 - $250.00

John F. Stratton & Son catalog 1893 - 1895. Instruments surely produced by Stratton.

Cornet in E flat, BF, BPV
Br $5.25
Ni $7.25
Triple Si plated $12.25
CMV $400.00 - $850.00

Cornet in B flat, BF, BPV
Br $5.75
Ni $7.75
Triple Si plated $21.50
CMV $500.00 - $950.00

Alto horn in E flat BU, BPV
Br $7.50
Ni $11.50
Triple Si plated $21.50
CMV $150.00 - $400.00

Tenor horn in B flat, BU, BPV
Br $9.00
Ni $15.00
Triple Si plated $24.00
CMV $250.00 - $600.00

Baritone horn in B flat, BU, BPV
Br $10.75
Ni $16.75
Triple Si plated $30.75
CMV $250.00-$600.00

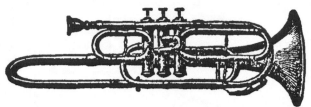

Alto trombone in E flat, BF, PV

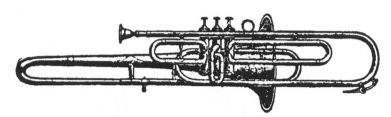

Tenor trombone in B flat, BF, PV

Baritone trombone in B flat, BF, PV

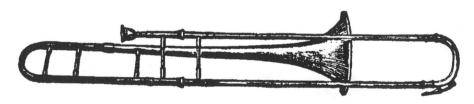

Tenor trombone in B flat, BF, slide model

Bass horn in B flat, BU, BPV
Br $12.00
Ni $20.00
Triple Si plated $34.00
CMV $250.00 - $600.00

Bass horn in E flat, BU, BPV
Br $15.50
Ni $23.50
Triple Si plated $40.50
CMV $250.00 - $600.00

Bass in E flat, HD, PV

John F. Stratton & Son catalog 1893 - 1895.
Instruments produced by Stratton. Instruments on this page were discontinued, reflected in the exceptionally low prices. Current market values for this can be inferred from Appendix C. See also the Boston Musical Instrument Manufactory catalog for CMV for comparable instruments. This is not to say that the prices for Stratton's instruments will have exactly the same CMV as the BMIM instruments. Yet, the BMIM instruments provide a guide to pricing Stratton's instruments. Instruments with catalog numbers are not discontinued instruments.

Cornet in E flat, Br, RV
BF $6.00
OTS $6.00
HD $6.00

Cornet in B flat, Br, RV
BF $6.50
OTS $8.50
HD $6.00

Cornet in C, Br, RV
BF $6.50

Alto horn in E flat, Br, RV
BU $8.50
OTS $8.50
HD $8.00

Tenor horn in B flat, Br, RV
BU $10.00
OTS $10.00
HD $9.00

Baritone horn in B flat, Br, RV
BU $11.00
OTS $11.00
HD $10.00

Bass horn in E flat, Br, RV
BU $15.00

Bass horn in B flat, Br, RV
OTS $12.00

Cornet in E flat, Gs, RV
BF $9.00
OTS $9.00
HD $9.00

Cornet in B flat, Gs, SARV
BF $10.00
OTS $10.00
HD $10.00

Cornet in C, Gs, RV
BF $10.00

Alto horn in E flat, Gs, RV
BU $12.00
OTS $12.00
HD $12.00

Tenor horn in B flat, Gs, RV
BU $13.00
OTS $13.00
HD $13.00

Tenor trombone in B flat, Gs, RV
BF $13.00

Baritone horn in B flat, Gs, RV
BU $14.00
OTS $14.00
HD $14.00

Bass horn in B flat, Gs, RV
BU $16.00
OTS $16.00
HD $16.00

Bass horn in E flat, Gs, RV
BU $20.00
OTS $20.00
HD $20.00

Bass horn in E flat, Gs, RV, large model
BU $23.00
OTS $23.00

Alto trombone in E flat, BF, Gs PV, water key. Produced by Stratton & Son.
Br $14.00
Ni $18.00
Si plated $28.00
CMV $150.00 - $300.00

Alto trombone in E flat, BF, Gs PV, water key. Produced by M. Goulet.
Br $10.50
Ni $14.50
Si plated $24.50
CMV $150.00 - $300.00

Tenor trombone in B flat, BF, Gs PV, water key. Produced by Stratton & Son.
Br $16.00
Ni $22.00

Si plated $31.00
CMV $150.00 - $300.00

Tenor trombone in B flat, BF, Gs PV, water key. Produced by M. Goulet.
Br $12.00
Ni $18.00
Si plated $27.00
CMV $150.00 - $300.00

Baritone trombone in B flat, BF, Gs PV, water key. Produced by Stratton & Son.
Br $19.00
Ni $25.00
Si plated $39.00
CMV $150.00 - $300.00

Baritone trombone in B flat, BF, Gs PV, water key. Produced by M. Goulet.
Br $14.00
Ni $20.00
Si plated $34.00
CMV $150.00 - $300.00

Tenor trombone in B flat, slide model, water key. Produced by Stratton & Son.
Br $15.00
Ni $19.00
Si plated $28.00
CMV $50.00 - $150.00

Tenor trombone in B flat, slide model, water key. Produced by M. Goulet.
Br $10.00
Ni $14.00
Si plated $23.00
CMV $50.00 - $150.00

Bass horn in E flat, HD, PV, water key Produced by M. Goulet
Br, small size $40.00
Br, large size $45.00
CMV $300.00 - $700.00

Appendix A:
Addresses of Museums & Other Resources

This list is designed to assist the reader in locating experts who can provide the best information about instruments. The following list is excerpted from the roster of the American Musical Instrument Society for 1996, and other resources. Specific names of curators have not been included to keep this list timely. Addresses for societies have not been included for the same reason. Many musical instrument museums also exist that are not included here, especially European museums. Museums tend to maintain the most timely list of experts.

The Library of Congress and any library, especially those associated with a large university music department, rarely maintain a list of experts. Even so, addresses for societies, and journals can be had here, along with other information. Also, the Library of Congress maintains a list of independent researchers who can research detailed questions within the library. These researchers will charge for their services, but will often provide answers quicker than the over-worked reference staff.

Clear photographs and concise questions will often elicit the quickest response. Vague questions will often be ignored. One must never expect an answer within a short time, due to staff shortages at all museums, and libraries. Most experts are self employed, and may or may not charge for their services, depending upon the assistance requested.

To locate an expert, write to any one of these museums and ask if they would send you a list of experts. Before allowing anyone to examine your instruments, first discuss that person's qualifications, and if that person also collects instruments. If you have only one instrument, the museum staff might be able to answer your question. If you have a number of instruments, first, document your collection. Take photographs of every instrument, including anything that seems important, even if the photographs are of poor quality. Any small objects should receive special attention. If time permits, create a list of the instruments, even if it is only the information copied from the bell. Write down everything that appears important, especially dimensions. Be careful not to scratch the instrument when you measure it. By doing this work, both parties will have little to question. Some experts, despite their reputations, have walked out with parts or entire items, such as mouthpieces, or valves. If, however, an expert is found by contacting a museum, that expert would be less likely to remove items.

No museum or library listed here will provide price lists for instruments. Most are legally prevented from doing so. Instead, the staff might describe an instrument as common, interesting, valuable, a museum specimen, or some such term to imply value. Only experts can give an idea of current market value. As with any collectibles, experts have been known to make mistakes. So, a second opinion for an especially valuable instrument is paramount.

Museums and libraries:

Department of Musical Instruments. Metropolitan Museum of Art. 1000 Fifth Ave. NY, NY 10028. Address letters to the curator of musical instruments. One of the most important collections in the U.S.
URL: www.metmuseum.org

Conservatoire Royal de Bruxelles. Rue de la Regence 30. B-1000 Brussels. Belgium. Simply the most important musical instrument collection in Europe.
URL: www.arkham.be

Kunsthistorisches Museum. Music department. Burgring 5. A-1010 Vienna, Austria. Address letters to the curator. This museum owns the oldest collection of instruments still existing.

Germanisches Museum. Kartäusergass 1. Postfach 9580. 90402 Nürnberg, Germany. Address letters to the curator.

Museum of Fine Arts, Boston. Collection of Musical Instruments, 465 Huntington Ave. Boston, MA 02115. Address letters to the curator of musical instruments.
E-mail: DKuron@mfa.org URL: www.mfa.org

Kenneth G. Fiske Museum of the Claremont Colleges. 450 N. College Way, Claremont, CA 91711-5253. Address letters to curator.
E-mail: arrice@rocketmail.com
URL: www.cuc.claremont.edu

Library of Congress. Music Division. Washington DC 20540. For general musical instrument questions, address letters to the Reference librarian. For questions about flutes, address letters to the curator of the Dayton C. Miller Flute collection.

Smithsonian institution. Division of Musical History. NMAH 4123, Smithsonian Institution. Washington DC 20560. Known for U.S. keyboard instruments. Some trade catalogs.
E-mail: HooverC@NMAIL.si.edu

Shrine to Music Museum USD. 414 East Clark St. Vermillion, SD 57069-2390. Address letters to the museum director. This museum owns arguably the largest collection of brass instruments in the U.S, especially American-made instruments. Reportedly it also owns 10,000 or more pieces of trade literature. However, staffing problems results in arbitrary decisions to answer questions; a problem not unique to this institution.

Yale University. Collection of Musical Instruments. 15 Hillhouse Ave., Box 208278. Address questions to the curator of musical instruments.
E-mail: musinst@Pantheon.yale.edu

Periodicals and Societies:

American Musical Instrument Society (address varies). The most important general society for the scholarly study of musical instruments in the U.S. The society prints a quarterly newsletter, a yearly journal, and a yearly roster of members that is quite a valuable resource.

Galpin Society (address varies). The first musical instrument society, quite excellent, and based in England.

The Historical Brass Society. (address varies) 2904 Hunter's Run. Greenview, NC 27858.

Addendum to Appendix A

This short list contains names and addresses that were not added to Appendix A, as information will no doubt change. This list consists of specialists, retail stores, and auction houses who provide musical instrument related services. Names found on this list, for the most part, are excerpted from the American Musical Instrument Society Roster for 1996. Inclusion of names here does not constitute an endorsement, rather as being known by this editor. Exclusion of names is not to be construed as a condemnation. The reader is strongly advised to obtain a more complete list of names from the resources listed in Appendix A of this book. Quality appraisals almost always cost money. So, ask for prices before sending documentation. Never send the item, until it has been requested by the appraiser. In most cases, a good-quality photograph will suffice. If the item is determined to be extremely important, take it to the appraiser, and sit with the appraiser while the item is being examined. This way, information unknown to the appraiser, such as history, can be provided. No question about loss, damage, or other actions can be questioned if this suggestion is followed.

Bein & Fuschi. Chicago, IL. Dealer in antique musical instruments, including Stradivari violins, etc.

Bingham, Tony. 11 Pond St. London, NW3 2PN England. Dealer in antique musical instruments, musical instrument reference material, and much more.

Center for Musical Antiquities. Lillian Caplin. 544 East 86th St. NY, NY 10028. Dealer in antique musical instruments, musical instrument reference material, and much more. Phone: 212-744-8168

Christie, Manson and Woods Ltd. 8 King Street, ST. Jame's. London SW1Y 6QT. England. Major auction house that regularly holds musical instrument auctions.

Craig, Gordon and Sandy. Craig's Antiques, 1119 Industrial Way. San Carlos, CA 94070. Phone 415-593-1300. Dealers in used wind instruments (mainly post-1920's instruments). Does not ship items for approval.

Dillon, Steven. Dillon Music, Inc. 325 Fulton St., Woodbridge, NJ 07095. Phone 908-634-3399. Appraiser and dealer of valuable brass instruments, both antique and recent.

Farrar, Lloyd. 14416 Marine Drive. Silver Spring, MD 20903-5922. Phone 301-384-7034. Repairer of civil war era drums, and researcher of American musical instrument history.

Lambert, Barbara. 201 Virginia Road. Concord MA 01742. Phone 508-369-9557. Professional appraiser.

Lark in the Morning. P.O. Box 1176. Mendocino, CA 95460. Phone 707-964-1979. Mainly sells ethnic instruments, and used musical instruments. Also does appraisals.

Oster, Frederick. 1529 Pine Street. Philadelphia, PA 19102. Phone 215-545-1100. Dealer who sells wide variety of old/antique musical instruments, specializing in stringed instruments, but also sells brass instruments.

Phillips. 101 New Bond Street. London W1Y 0AS. England. Major auction house that regularly offers auctions of musical instruments.

Rice, Albert R. 495 St. Augustine Ave. Claremont, CA 91711. Phone 909-625-7699. Appraiser of musical instruments, and current membership registrar for the American Musical Instru-ment Society.

Skinner Inc. Auctioneers and Appraisers of Antiques and Fine Arts. 63 Park Plaza. Boston, MA 02116. Phone 617-350-5400.
Also: 357 Main Street. Bolton, MA 01740. Phone 508-779-6241. Mainly auctions bowed stringed instruments. Often has some non-stringed instruments.

Sotheby's
34-35 New Bond St. London WIA 2AA England. Major auction house.

Stewart, Robb. 140 East Santa Clara Street, #18. Arcadia, CA 90027. Phone 818-447-1904. Dealer, and restorer of antique brass musical instruments. Also makes reproductions of historical brass instruments.

Wurlitzer-Bruck. 60 Riverside Drive. NY, NY 1024. Phone 212-787-6431 FAX 212-296-6525. Dealer in antique musical instruments, musical instrument reference material, and much more.

Appendix B:
A Selective List of Makers

Below is a selective list of manufacturers, makers, and importers of brass musical instruments who had an impact upon the U.S. musical instrument trade. This is to say, instruments bearing these names can be found. Some companies produced far more instruments than others. So, some names in this list might never come on the used instrument market.

This list is not intended to be complete in any aspect. It is simply intended to assist the reader in determining the quality of most of the prominent manufacturers and makers. Many rare makers are left to be documented in *NLI*. This list and all quotes found here are extracted from *NLI*.

One feature taken from *NLI* needs explanation. Dates when companies were active are rarely certain. The date p1950 means that the company was still active at that time. *NLI* does not concern itself with activities after 1950. As ever, wind instruments include brass and woodwind instruments. An * designates some of the prominent pre-1900 makers and manufacturers.

Alexander, Gebrüder. Mainz ca. 1802-p1950. Brass manufacturer of medium quality instruments and better.

Bach, Vincent. Germany, and later U.S. Known for his mouth pieces, and high-grade modern professional trumpets. Both are collected, especially by performers.

*Besson, Gustave Auguste. Paris, and London 1837-p1950. Made a wide range of very collectible instruments. Not to be confused with a myriad of other companies using the name Besson. Besson instruments from Paris are usually quite collectible. The Besson name is still in use, by Boosey & Hawkes, for student-grade instruments.

*Boosey. London 1851-1930. Primarily known as Boosey & Hawkes, manufacturer of quality woodwinds, and some brasswinds. The company also owned Distin & Co. between 1850 and 1890.

*Boston Musical Instrument Manufactory. Boston 1869-1919. Successor to E. G. Wright & Co. produced quality brass instruments. Best known for its Boston Three star cornet. Instruments are well collected. A large number of these instruments are still available. In 1913, the company changed its name to the Boston Musical Instrument Company.

Bruno, C. New York 1834-p1950. Importer of many kinds of musical instruments. Not believed to have manufactured. Some instruments were stamped with his name.

Cerveny, V.F. Königgrätz 1842-1946. Maker of a wide variety of wind instruments, not well known in the U.S. Especially important early maker of generally good-quality brass instruments. The company is now operating under the name Amati. Early instruments are often not in playing condition, and do not always sell well.

*Conn, C.G. 1879-p1950. One of the most prolific U.S. wind instrument manufacturers. Instruments range from professional to amateur instruments. Instruments from C.G. Conn are quite common today, with some varieties quite rare. Sadly, no listing of rare Conn instrument types presently seems to exist. Early Conn instruments are quite collectible, and some of the more recent instruments are sought by performers. Instruments marked Conn/Dupont are highly collectible, as are instruments marked Conn New York, and Conn Worcester. Instruments with very low serial numbers are also highly desirable (i.e. numbers less than 9999). Instruments marked with C.G. Conn Ltd. are not generally sought by collectors.

*Courtois. Paris ca. 1800-p1950. Family of makers, and manufacturers. Brass instruments are generally of very high quality. Foote was a prominent importer of this manufacturer. Instruments from this company are quite collectible, and appear in museums.

Couturier, Ernst Albert. Elkhorn, IN. Born 30, Sept. 1896. Died 28 February 1950. Inventor of the "Couturier Conoidal Bore." His design was incorporated into instruments produced by Holton (for whom he worked for a while), Lyon & Healy, J.W. York & Sons, and also E.A. Couturier of N.Y.C. The instruments are distinguished by having a conical bore, instead of a bore that increased by steps. Instruments sell well, but are not extremely rare.

Cundy-Bettoney Co. Boston 1907-p1950. Primarily known for medium grade wind instruments. Instruments not actively sought by collectors.

Deutsche Signal-instrumenten-Fabrik. Markneukirchen 1897-p1950. The company still markets an instrument called a signal horn, with multiple bells. Though it resembles a brass instrument with piston valves and a permanent or attached mouthpiece, it is in fact a free reed instrument (i.e. a relative of the harmonica). This instrument causes no end of confusion in its identification. Small examples of it are pictured in this book. It is known to have been manufactured with as many as nine bells, and was popular in Nazi Germany.

*Distin. London and U.S. 1800s. Family of makers and manufacturers. Instruments from this family range from scarce and quite collectible to cheap junk. Some collectors and most performers prefer Henry Distin instruments marked Williamsport. Other collectors prefer the New York or Philadelphia instruments. This company is not to be confused with the Ditson, a music retail company of about the same time. Henry Distin's history is quite complicated. See the Distin section of this book for more information.

Elkhart Band Instrument Co. Elkhart, IN. 1924-1928. Primarily manufacturer of student-grade wind instruments.

*Fiske, Isaac. Worcester, MA. 1842-1887. Manufacturer of all types of highly collectible brass instruments. Especially interesting for the various types of valve systems he used. The more unusual the valve system, the more collectible the instrument. He sold out to C. G. Conn, who continued the company until 1898. His instruments appear in many museums. His pre-civil war instruments tend to command the most attention by collectors.

*Foote, J. Howard. New York City 1833-1896. Importer, and dealer of high quality brass instruments, such as Courtois. Instruments stamped with Foote's name are occasionally found, even though he manufactured no instruments.

Franciolini, Leopoldo. Firenze 1875-c1925. Dealer in antique instruments, and forger of same. "Any musical instrument shown to have passed through his hands must be viewed with suspicion ..." *NLI* p. 121.

*Gautrot Aíné. Paris 1845-p1884. One of the largest Paris-based brass instrument manufacturers at the time. Instruments vary in quality. Yet are collectible and appear in many museum collections. Early valved instruments from this manufacturer are especially sought, though more collected outside the U.S.

Glier family. Poland and Russia after 1750-1930?. Family of makers of various types of instruments. Also known as dealers and importers. *NLI* reports no instruments from this family in U.S. collections. Quality uncertain.

*Graves & Co. New England (various cities) 1824-1869. One of few U.S. makers to use Vienna valves. Described as "the earliest large scale wind instrument manufacturer in America ..." Instruments will have various other names also engraved, such as Graves & Alexander. Instruments are highly collectible, with many examples in museums.

*Haas. Nürnberg 1600s-1700s. *NLI* (p. 153) describes this family as "the most illustrious and prolific of the Nürnberg brass instrument making family." All instruments are museum pieces.

*Hainlein. Nürnberg 1500s-1600s. "They pioneered the adoption of the Knauf (cast bell) and angle's head rim-decoration on the trumpet" *NLI* (p. 155). All instruments are museum pieces.

Haliday (Halliday), Joseph. Dublin. Invented the "Royal Kent Bugle," a keyed bugle. Not a maker.

Heckel. Biebrich 1800s-p1950. The family is better known for their woodwind instruments. Even so, the family produced brass instruments of quality. Instruments are not common in the U.S.

Holton, Frank. Chicago, later Elkhorn WI c1907-p1950. Manufacturer of brass instruments of some quality. Some collectors prefer instruments from specific times, which complicates valuing instruments from this company. No list of rare types seems to exist.

*Köhler. London ca. 1775-1900. Family of wind instrument makers producing highly collectible instruments, most noted for use of Shaw valves (and other early valve systems) during the early 19th century. See *NLI* (p. 210) for biographies of the three reported John Köhlers. Instruments from this family often appear at auction.

Kruspe. Leipzig 1800s-p1950. Family of wind instrument manufacturers producing medium and professional grade instruments. Not generally collected in the U.S. except for their French horns.

*Lehnert, Henry. Boston, later Philadelphia 1860-1916. "He vies with Fiske for innovative pre-eminence among earlier American makers ..." *NLI* (p. 231). His instruments are not plentiful, and are highly collectible, especially his very rare Centennial model instruments. This body type is designed so that the instrument wraps around the performer's head, resting on both shoulders. The bell points straight out, as can be seen in the illustration on page 30 of this book. Such examples are museum pieces. CMVs for his Centennial instruments are quite speculative. He also made instruments with Allen valves, which sell for substantially more than instruments with RV. His instruments with RVs seem to sell for more than instruments with PVs.

*Lyon & Healy. Chicago 1864-c1940. Mainly known as a retailer of all things related to brass bands. Due to loss of company's records, determining if this company was merely a retailer, relied on jobbers and assembled the parts, or actually manufactured instruments might never be known. Many medium-grade instruments are engraved with this company's name. Possibly the most common pre-1900 name to appear on U.S. brass instruments. The company still exists making professional-quality harps.

*Mahillon, C. Bruxelles 1836-1935. Manufacturer of wood wind instruments. Being the first curator of the Bruxelles Conservateur, and author of museum catalogs from this collection, Mahillon's instruments are sought for reasons beyond their own quality. Rare though not highly collectible.

Martin Frères. Paris 1840s-1927. Major French manufacturer of woodwind instruments. Imported by a number of U.S. companies. Not known for brass instruments. Evidently not associated with Martin Brothers of New York.

*Martin Brothers. New York 1879-1884. Family of manufacturers, whose early instruments are highly collectible. As sociated with Slater, Pollmann, and others at various times. Instruments with just the Martin Brothers name are quite rare. John Henry Martin worked in 1855 in New York, 1865 in Chicago, and in 1876 in Elkhart for C. G. Conn. Eventually he founded the Martin Band Instrument Company in Elkhart. After 1917, the two Martin companies merged.

Metzler. London 1833-p1936. Family of manufacturers, mainly known for collectible woodwind instruments. Many bassoons, clarinets, etc. exist, less common are serpents, and brass wind instruments. Instruments appear in most museum collections. Brasswinds by Metzler often command impressive amounts at auction, depending upon condition.

Olds, F.E. Los Angeles ca 1908-p1950. Mainly known for improvements to the trombone. One of the few west coast brass makers. Worked mainly outside the time frame of this book.

*Pace. England. Family of makers. Instruments from this family are generally very collectible, with many examples in museums. Generally worked before the advent of valves. Known for slide trumpets, and keyed bugles.

Pelitti. Milano ca 1828-1905. Major Italian manufacturer, though not well known in the U.S. Most Italian-made brass instruments found in the U.S. are not highly regarded by collectors.

*Pepper, J.W. Philadelphia 1876-1919. Brass manufacturer, who was in direct competition with C.G. Conn. One of the major importers during his time. Most of the instruments bearing his name were not made by him, simply sold by him, and are not of the quality of the instruments he made. Instruments range in quality from student to professional in quality. Instruments actually made by Pepper are well made, quite rare, and collectible.

Périnet, Francois. Paris 1834-p1950. Invented the cylindrical valve used on most brass instruments. Instruments made by Mr. Périnet surely are collectible, if not museum pieces.

Pollmann, Henry August. New York City, active from 1880-1905. Manufacturer of brass musical instruments, associated with Martin Brothers, Slater, and Distin. He never plated his instruments. Pollmann's instruments are comparable to Slater, or Stratton, and tend to sell for the same as Slater's instruments. Pollmann instruments can still be found in quantities. He also sold a wide variety of general musical merchandise, including violins, flutes, etc. Farrar states that no biographical information has yet been found for Pollmann.

Quinby. Boston. Family of brasswind manufacturers. Associated at various times with D.C. Hall, and E.G. Wright, which helps to date instruments. Not a prolific maker. Instruments are quite collectible.

Rampone. Milano. Family of woodwind and brass manufacturers. Instruments by Rampone are not very common in the U.S. See note under Pelitti.

*Sax. Paris and Bruxelles. Family of woodwind and brass makers. ca. 1815-ca. 1928. One of the most important families for brass instrument development. Includes father Charles-Joseph, several sons including Antoine Joseph (later Adolph). Adolph invented the Saxophone, and made (and claimed) improvements to brass instruments. Rather controversial person. Most instruments from this family are quite valuable, especially the earlier ones.

Selmer, H. & A. Boston 1904-1927. Mainly a woodwind manufacturer. Best known for quality student grade instruments. Not to be confused with Selmer of France.

Seefeldt, William F. Philadelphia 1858-1908. Probably associated with Klemm of Philadelphia. Maker of quality brasswind instruments. Not a prolific maker. Seefeldt Manufacturing Company instruments were production instruments of modest quality, after circa 1890. Instruments from before then sell for more.

*Slater, Moses. Successor to Slater & Martin. New York City 1865-ca 1920. Manufacturer of quality brass instruments. Known for his over the shoulder instruments. Instruments are collectible, and appear in museum collections.

Sousa, John Philip. Washington DC. Inventor of the bell up (rain catcher) bass, a helicon design with the bell pointing directly up, probably first constructed by J.W. Pepper. This instrument was later called the Sousaphone. Conn also claims to have made the first Sousaphone. Sousa used the Sousaphone for a while in his band, and later condemned it. Bell up basses persisted until about 1920, and are collectible mainly because of their novel appearance. Sousa is not the only composer to invent or suggest the invention of instruments. Both Verdi, and Wagner also are credited with instruments, such as the Aida trumpet, and the Wagner tuba.

Stölzel (Stoelzel), Johann Heinrich. Germany: inventor of the Stölzel valve ca. 1814. The valve was applied to instruments as late as circa 1916, generally on student grade instruments after 1860, made in France. The valve system is identified by having tubes enter from the side and bottom of the piston. Early examples are more valuable than later instruments.

*Stratton, John Franklin. New York City and Germany 1859-1912. Known for ordinary to moderately high-quality brass and other musical instruments. Manufactured over the shoulder instruments. Supplied many instruments used in the Civil War. His instruments are highly collectible.

Thibouville-Lamy. France, a1867-p1950. Family of wind instrument manufacturers. Mainly known for woodwind instruments. Sold brasswind instruments made by others.

*Uhlmann. Primarily in Wien (Vienna). Family of mainly woodwind manufacturers. Known for using Vienna valves, making these instruments quite collectible.

*Wright, Elbridge G. Massachusetts ca 1839-1859. One of this country's most important mid-19th century makers. His earliest instruments were equipped with Vienna valves. Later, he switched to rotary valves. Still later, he switched to Périnet-style valve. "Considered the foremost US maker of keyed brass instruments, 13 presentation silver key bugles being recorded" *NLI* (p. 436-437). Any unrecorded presentation keyed bugles would command the highest prices for collectors. Instruments equipped with Vienna valves are also rare. Instruments with rotary valves command a bit less, but are still very desirable. Instruments equipped with PVs command the least, which will still be more desirable than many other makers' instruments.

Wurlitzer. U.S. Family of importers, who later manufactured instruments. Instruments have been found with this name stamped on them. Rarely considered the best quality instruments, yet generally adequate, most likely having been made in Germany. Instruments do not generally command high prices.

York, J.W. Grand Rapids, MI 1882-1940. This company employed important persons to assist in construction. Trombones stamped with York & Holton (for example) might command more interest than other instruments from this company. Student grade bass instruments made by York are rather common. Yet, the company's tubas are now much in demand.

*Zoebisch, C.A. & Sons. New York City 1847-1904?. Comparable to Slater in quality. Zoebisch imported instruments from Germany. His instruments were conspicuously found in confederate bands, being one of the few companies supplying instruments before the Civil War. His instruments from 1850-1880 are most sought by collectors.

Appendix C:
A Subjective Price List for Instruments

All prices given in this list are in U.S. dollars. Prices originally given in British Pounds have been rounded up to the nearest U.S. dollars. All like instruments are grouped together. Thus, all trumpets, regardless of their pitch or subtype will be found in the same area of the list. At first this might present problems for someone looking for pocket trumpet. However, realizing that the instrument is primarily a trumpet, the reader should quickly find the instrument in question, assuming that a given instrument is indeed listed here. Any errors in this list are purely unintentional.

Because of the space limitations of this sort of list, the reader is directed to the body of this book for more detailed information about instruments. Otherwise the following comments apply. An instrument offered in only one metal is indicated with a Br or Si in the appropriate column. Gs/Br indicates that an instrument was offered only with German silver plate over Brass. An instrument that was offered with more than one metal finish is listed with the base metal described in the appropriate column. In the comments column, additional metals are indicated. Here, information is often truncated. Additionally, "Bass in BB flat" indicates that the instrument is a contra bass instrument pitched in B flat. Abbreviations for instrument and valve types, and metals are explained in the glossary of this book.

Before continuing further, please consider the following remarks, though they are somewhat a repeat of statements made throughout this book. Prices given for instruments are subjective. As a generality, instruments sold in California, or New York might sell for more that the prices listed here, while instruments sold in the Midwest might sell for less than the prices listed here. Even ignoring this fact, experts will never agree on prices. Therefore the prices given here are only suggestions. Even the prices found in auction catalogs are not without problems. All instruments listed here are assumed to be in working condition unless otherwise indicated, and requiring no significant repairs. Any important instrument should never ever be restored until examined by an expert, who should be able to recommend a competent restorer, if the expert determines that the instrument could be restored without harming the instrument.

Since this list was generated from various sources, including sales lists of dealers in old and antique musical instruments, and auction catalogs, some unavoidable, and frankly unsolvable problems exist with this list. First, a quick scan of the list shows that very important information was not always provided in the original lists, including serial numbers, condition, and bell direction. One could choose to exclude incomplete references. However, with care, this list is still a useable guide. As an example, instruments from such makers as Martin Brothers are quite rare, but appear throughout this list, giving the false sense that many of these instruments can be found. At the same time, instruments from companies such as Pollmann, and Stratton, are poorly represented in comparison to the number of instruments available today. In fact, no prices for Pollmann instruments were located while researching this book. This major flaw shows why no other list of this magnitude has appeared in print.

A second problem with this price list is that many instruments do not appear in dealers' lists or auction catalogs. Consider the following known situation. At various times, J.W. Pepper produced four grades of bass horns, ranging from student grade (a very inexpensive instrument even today) through a professional grade (which is quite collectible, considering the quality of this manufacturer's workmanship). However, in the accompanying list, only a price for the student grade instrument was located. Any competent brass player should be able to differentiate a student grade instrument from a professional grade instrument, even if the instrument is not in playing condition. The reader who finds a brass instrument with an important maker's name on it, but can not find a price for this instrument in the accompanying list is once again directed to a specialist, as found in Appendix A.

The current market prices given here are as accurate as possible for now. However, determining such prices is like shooting at a moving target. Experts will disagree, sometimes with themselves. Thus, prices followed by a + are inevitable, and are generally found associated with only important instruments here.

Instruments which were constructed by a maker of quality instruments will tend to command the highest prices. Instruments with interesting variations will command special attention, and often sell for higher prices than ordinary instruments. Instruments made solely of copper are rather scarce, and might command higher prices than one might otherwise expect (except for decorative, i.e. non-functional instruments currently made, mainly in or near India). Some makers and manufacturers working before circa 1880 even offered copper instruments for the same price as instruments plated with German silver. At the time, instruments made with German silver were then considered to be of a higher quality than those made only of brass. It is also worth noting that at least one manufacturer of the time complained that German silver was rather difficult to work, but performers preferred it, as it so completely hid the lap joint in the bell.

Placing a price on instruments with documented histories is beyond the scope of this book. However, all papers associated with an instrument will tend to increase the value of the instrument, possibly by ten per cent or more, depending upon the significance of the provable history.

Instruments made of non-traditional material, such as ceramic are not included here. Even so, some of these instruments command special attention, and often moderately high values.

This editor greatly wishes that all problems with pricing antique brass wind instruments did not exist. Sadly, this is currently the nature of this type of collectible. Not enough research has been conducted into this class of instruments, and virtually no standardization exists with regards to prices. The editor hopes that by publishing this modest list, some consensus will begin to emerge. In essence, this is the first detailed book of its kind for this class of collectible items.

ALTO HORN IN E FLAT

Maker	model	serial #	date	finish	condition	comments	price
[Anon.]			ca. 1879	Br		BU, PV, also offered in silver plate, satin finish, sold by Martin Bros.	$50-175
[Anon.]			ca. 1896	Br		BU, PV, water key, also offered in Ni or Si plate, sold by Lyon & Healy	75-150
[Anon.]	Beau ideal		ca. 1896	Br		BF, PV, water key, also offered in Ni or Si plate, and with Go plate bell and trim, heavily engraved, sold by Lyon & Healy	50-200
[Anon.]	Beau ideal		ca. 1896	Br		BF, PV, water key, solo model, also offered in Ni or Si plate, and with Go plate bell and trim, heavily engraved, sold by Lyon & Healy	50-150
[Anon.]	Beau ideal		ca. 1896	Br		BU, PV, water key, also offered in Ni or Si plate, and with Go plate bell and trim, heavily engraved, sold by Lyon & Healy	50-150
[Anon.]	short model		ca. 1896	Br		BU, BPV, water key, also offered in Ni plate, sold by Lyon & Healy	100-175
[Anon.]	solo model		ca. 1896	Br		BF, PV, water key, also offered in Si plate, sold by Lyon & Healy	75-250
[Anon. French]			ca. 1900	Ni/Br		PV	70
[Anon. German]			ca. 1879	Br		BU, PV, Gs trim, sold by Martin Bros.	50-150
BMIMC			1869-1874	Br		BF, PV, also offered in Gs	400-600
BMIMC			1869-1874	Br		BU, SARV, also offered in Gs	800-1100
BMIMC			1869-1874	Br		HD, SARV, also offered in Gs	800-1100
BMIMC			1869-1874	Br		OTS, TARV, also offered in Gs	2500
BMIMC	solo model		1869-1874	Br		BF, SARV, also offered in Gs	600-900
BMIMC			ca. 1870	Br		BU, RV	450-850
BMIMC		20XXX	1914	Si	very good	BU	150-300
C.G. Conn		70XXX		Br		BF	150
Couesnon				Br		BF	80
Isaac Fiske			ca. 1868	Br		BU, Push rod valves, mouthpiece to the right of the instrument, also offered in Gs	2200-2800
Issac Fiske			ca. 1868	Br		BU, SARV, mouthpiece to the left of the instrument, also offered in Gs	1200-1700
Issac Fiske			ca. 1868	Br		OTS, SARV, also offered in Gs	2200-2700
Grand Rapids	USA Line	16XXX	ca. 1930	Br	good		125
Goulet			ca. 1893	Br		BF, PV, water key, also offered in Ni, or Si plate, sold by Stratton	50-100
Goumat				Br			100
J. Higham	Clear bore		ca. 1896	Br		BF, PV, water key, solo model, also offered in Si, and with Go plate trim and bell	50-150
J. Higham	First class		ca. 1896	Br		BF, PV, water key, also offered in Si, and with Go plate trim and bell	50-150

J. Higham 1	Clear bore		ca. 1896	Br		BU, PV, water key, also offered in Si, and with Go plate trim and bell	$50-150
F. Jaubert			ca. 1896	Br		BU, PV, water key, also offered in Ni or Si plate	50-150
F. Jaubert	concert model		ca. 1896	Br		French horn shape, PV, water key, also offered in Ni or Si plate	125-200
F. Jaubert	solo alto		ca. 1896	Br		BF, PV, water key, also offered in Ni or Si plate	50-250
Fritz Horst			ca. 1890		dents in bell	RV	400
Holton					like new	BF	500
Jaubert	solo alto		ca. 1880	Ni/Br	good		225
Kalashen	The Yankee	P1XXXX	ca. 1920	Si	good+	made by C.G. Conn	225
Brua C. Keefer				Si/Br		PV	150
A. Lecomte			ca. 1879	Br		BU, inscribed "Made Especially for D.C. Hall, Boston"	325
A. Lecomte & Co.	Champion		ca. 1879	Br		large bore	50-150
H. Lehnert	solo alto		before 1900	Ni/Br		3 string SARV	1500
Mahillon							150
Martin Bros.			ca.1879	Br		BU, PV, water key, also offered in Si plate	50-174
Martin Bros.			ca. 1879	Br		BU, SARV, also offered in Gs trim or Gs throughout	900-1400
Martin Bros.			ca. 1879	Br		BU, TARV, also offered in Gs trim or Gs throughout	1200-1500
Martin Bros.			ca. 1879	Br		HD, PV	1200-1500
Martin Bros.			ca. 1879	Br		HD, SARV, also offered in Gs trim or Gs throughout	1100-1600
Martin Bros.			ca. 1879	Br		OTS, TARV, also offered in Gs trim or Gs throughout	1700-2300
Martin Bros.	solo alto		ca. 1879	Gs/Br		BF, SARV or TARV, also offered in Gs	600-1200
Martin Bros.			ca. 1879	Br		BU, PV, also offered in Si plate	50-150
Quinby Bros.			ca. 1879	Br		BF, SARV, also offered in Gs	200-600
Quinby Bros.			ca. 1879	Br		BU, SARV, also offered in Gs	1200-1500
Quinby Bros.			ca. 1879	Br		HD, SARV, also offered in Gs	800-1400
Prem Stab						RV	400
Jas. Sistek				Si/Br		3 PV	140
M. Slater			ca. 1880	Br	needs work	3 PV	200
M. Slater			ca. 1874	Br		BU, TARV	1000-1400
M. Slater			ca. 1874	Br		OTS, TARV	1800-2500
W. Stowasser				Br		Gs garland and trim, 3 RV	750
Stratton	solo alto		ca. 1893	Br		BF, PV, water key, also offered in Ni or triple Si plate	150-300
Stratton			ca. 1893	Br		BU, BPV, water key, also offered in Ni, or triple Si plate	150-400
Stratton			ca. 1893	Br		BU or BF, PV, water key, also offered in Ni or triple Si plate	150-300
York	solo alto	17XXX	ca. 1908	Si	good+		275

BALLAD HORN IN C

F. Jaubert			ca. 1896	Br		French horn design, PV, water key, also offered in Ni or Si plate	250-500

BARITONE HORN IN B FLAT

[Anon.]			ca. 1879	Br		BU, PV, also offered in Si plate, satin finish, sold by Martin Bros.	75-300
[Anon.]			ca. 1896	Br		BU, PV, water key, also offered in Ni or Si plate, sold by Lyon & Healy	125-275
[Anon.]	Beau ideal		ca. 1896	Br		BU, PV, water key, also offered in Ni or Si plate, and with Go plate bell and trim, heavily engraved, sold by Lyon & Healy	125-200
[Anon.]	short model		ca. 1896	Br		BU, BPV, water key, also offered in Ni plate, sold by Lyon & Healy	175-250
[Anon. French]			ca. 1885	Br		3 PV	150
[Anon. German]			ca. 1879	Br		BU, BPV, Gs trim, sold by Martin Bros.	100-300
Besson	2-20	39XXXX	1965	lacquer	good	BF euphonium	300
Besson & Co.				Si/Br		3 PV	350
BMIMC				Si/Br		3 PV	200
BMIMC			1869-1874	Br		BU, SARV, also offered in Gs	800-1100
BMIMC			1869-1874	Br		HD, SARV, also offered in Gs	800-1100
BMIMC			1869-1874	Br		OTS, TARV, also offered in Gs	2500
Continental							150
Elkhart Band Instrument Co.				Si/Br		3 PV	90
Isaac Fiske			ca. 1868	Br		BU, Push rod valves, mouthpiece to the right of the instrument, also offered in Gs	2200-2800

Maker	Model	Serial	Date	Material	Condition	Description	Price
Isaac Fiske			ca. 1868	Br		BU, SARV, mouthpiece to the left of the instrument, also offered in Gs	$1400-1800
Isaac Fiske			ca. 1868	Br		OTS, SARV, also offered in Gs	2200-2400
Getzen	Super Delux	82XXX	ca. 1958	lacquer	excellent	BF	375
Aug. Clem. Glier			ca. 1880	Ni		tenor or baritone	400
Goulet			ca. 1893	Br		BF, PV, water key, also offered in Ni, or Si plate, sold by Stratton	75-250
J. Higham				Br		4 PV	300
F. Jaubert			ca. 1896	Br		BU, PV, water key, also offered in Ni or Si plate	125-200
Brua C. Keefer				Si/Br	missing buttons	3 PV	200
King		42XXX					150
King		72XXXX	1985	lacquer	good	BF	300
Martin Bros.			ca. 1879	Br		BU, PV, water key, also offered in Si plate	75-300
Martin Bros.			ca. 1879	Br		BU, SARV, Gs trim or Gs throughout	1000-1400
Martin Bros.			ca. 1879	Br		BU, TARV, Gs trim or Gs throughout	1100-1500
Martin Bros.			ca. 1879	Br		HD, SARV, also offered in Gs trim or Gs throughout	1100-1600
Martin Bros.			ca. 1879	Br		HD, PV	1200-1700
Martin Bros.			ca. 1879	Br		OTS, TARV, also offered in Gs trim or Gs throughout	1100-1500
Martin Bros.			ca. 1879	Br		OTS, TARV, also offered in Gs trim or Gs throughout	1800-2400
Pan American							150
G.L. Penzel & Bro.				Si/Br		3 PV, heavily reliefed over all	350
Quinby Bros.			ca. 1879	Br		BU, SARV, also offered in Gs	1200-1500
Pierre Sartel (not listed in *NLI*)				Si/Br		3 PV	200
Carl Schubert						small	150
M. Slater			ca. 1874	Br		BU, TARV	750-1500
M. Slater			ca. 1874	Br		OTS, TARV	1800-2500
Stratton			ca. 1893	Br		BU, BPV, also offered in Ni, or triple Si plate	250-600
Stratton			ca. 1893	Br		BU, PV, water key, also offered in Ni or triple Si plate	200-400

BASS HORN [in ?]

Maker	Model	Serial	Date	Material	Condition	Description	Price
[Anon. German]	Saxhorn		ca. 1870	Br		3 BPV	350
John F. Stratton	Saxhorn		before 1900	Br	needs work	3 BPV	600

BASS HORN IN B FLAT

Maker	Model	Serial	Date	Material	Condition	Description	Price
[Anon.]			ca. 1879	Br		BU, PV, also offered in silver plate, satin finish, sold by Martin Bros.	75-300
[Anon.]			ca. 1896	Br		BU, PV, water key, also offered in Ni or Si plate, sold by Lyon & Healy	125-275
[Anon.]	Beau Ideal		ca. 1896	Br		BU, PV, water key, also offered in Ni or Si plate, and with Go plate bell and trim heavily engraved, sold by Lyon & Healy	125-200
[Anon.]	short model		ca. 1896	Br		BU, BPV, water key, also offered in Ni plate, sold by Lyon & Healy	175-250
[Anon. German]			ca. 1879	Br		BU, BPV, Gs trim, sold by Martin Bros.	100-300
Besson & Co.				Si/Br	minus 1 valve	PV	100
BMIMC			1869-1874	Br		BU, SARV, also offered in Gs	800-1100
BMIMC			1869-1874	Br		HD, SARV, also offered in Gs	800-1100
BMIMC			1869-1874	Br		OTS, TARV, also offered in Gs	2500
C.G. Conn			before 1900?			HD	950
Isaac Fiske			ca. 1868	Br		BU, Push rod valves, mouthpiece to the right of the instrument, also offered in Gs	2200-2800
Issac Fiske			ca. 1868	Br		BU, SARV, mouthpiece to the left of the instrument, also offered in Gs	1700-2400
Issac Fiske			ca. 1868	Br		OTS, SARV, also offered in Gs	1400-2400
Goulet			ca. 1893	Br		BF, PV, water key, also offered in Ni or Si plate, sold by Stratton	75-250
F. Jaubert			ca. 1896	Br		BU, PV, water key, also offered in Ni or Si plate	125-200
A. Lecomte & Co.	Champion		ca. 1879	Br		3 PV, 1 side PV, large bore	250-500
A. Lecomte & Co.	Champion		ca. 1879	Br		3 PV, large bore	50-150
Mahillion						4 TARV	1200
Martin Bros.			ca. 1879	Br		BF, PV, water key, also offered in Si plate	100-300
Martin Bros.			ca. 1879	Br		BU, SARV, also offered in Gs trim or Gs throughout	1000-1400
Martin Bros.			ca. 1879	Br		BU, TARV, also offered in Gs trim or Gs throughout	1100-1500
Martin Bros.			ca. 1879	Br		HD, PV	1200-1700

Martin Bros.			ca. 1879	Br		HD, SARV, also offered in Gs trim or Gs throughout	$1000-1500
Martin Bros.			ca. 1879	Br		OTS, TARV, also offered in Gs trim or Gs throughout	1800-2400
Quinby Bros.			ca. 1879	Br		BU, SARV, also offered in Gs	1200-1600
Quinby Bros.			ca. 1879	Br		HD, SARV, also offered in Gs	1000-1500
M. Slater			ca. 1874	Br		BU, TARV	750-1500
M. Slater			ca. 1874	Br		OTS, TARV	1800-2500
Stratton			ca. 1893	Br		BU, BPV, also offered in Ni, or triple Si plate	250-600
Stratton			ca. 1893	Br		BU, PV, water key, also offered in Ni or triple Si plate	200-400

BASS HORN IN BB FLAT

Besson		86XXX	ca. 1908	Si	fair+	4 valves, plays OK	575
C.G. Conn		18XXXX	1921	Si	very good	3 TARV	1500
L'Rae		87XX	ca. 1965	lacquer		4 RV	1300
A. Lecomte & Co.	Champion		ca. 1879	Br		large bore	100-300
J. Higham			ca. 1896	Br		BU, PV, water key, also offered in triple Si plate, and with Go trim and bell, offered in various sizes, same CMV	350-600
J. Higham			ca. 1896	Br		HD, PV, water key, also offered in triple Si plate, and with Go trim and bell	300-500
F. Jaubert			ca. 1896	Br		BU, PV, water key, also offered in Ni or Si plate	150-500
Martin Bros.	largest size		ca. 1879	Br		HD, PV, water key	500-700
Quinby Bros.			ca. 1879	Br		HD, SARV, also offered in Gs	1000-1500
Reynolds			1961	Si	very good	4 valves, recording bell	1900
Roth			ca. 1890	Br		RV	575
Schmidt						4 RV	1000
Yamaha	YBB-321	00XXXX		lacquer		includes case	2300

BASS HORN IN CC

Cerveny		XXX				4 RV	1700

BASS HORN IN C (valveless variety)

[Anon. European]			[before 1860?]			6 holes, 4 keys	4500

BASS HORN IN E FLAT

[Anon.]			ca. 1875	Br	needs work	BPV	450
[Anon.]			ca. 1896	Br		HD, PV, water key, also offered in Ni or Si plate, sold by Lyon & Healy	275-500
[Anon.]			ca. 1896	Br		BU, PV, water key, also offered in Ni or Si plate, sold by Lyon & Healy	125-300
[Anon.]	Beau ideal		ca. 1896	Br		BU, PV, water key, also offered in Ni or Si plate, and with Go plate bell and trim, heavily engraved, sold by Lyon & Healy	150-275
[Anon.]	short model		ca. 1896	Br		BU, BPV, water key, also offered in Ni plate, sold by Lyon & Healy	175-250
C. Bruno & Son				Si/Br	needs work		125
BMIMC			1869-1874	Br		BU, 3 SARV, also offered in Gs	600-1000
BMIMC			1869-1874	Br		BU, 4 SARV, also offered in Gs	1000-1600
BMIMC			1869-1874	Br		OTS, 1 SARV AND 3 TARV, also offered in Gs	2500+
C.G. Conn			before 1900?			HD	450
C.G. Conn	Army horn		ca. 1918	Si		HD	675
C.G. Conn		21XXX				HD	695
C.G. Conn-Dupont		15XX	1876-1879			early and rare instrument	1600
Courtois						4 RV	700
Isaac Fiske			ca. 1868	Br		BU, Push rod valves, mouthpiece to the right of the instrument, also offered in Gs	2200-2800
Issac Fiske			ca. 1868	Br		BU, SARV, mouthpiece to the left of the instrument, also offered in Gs	1500-2000
Isaac Fiske			ca. 1868	Br		OTS, SARV, also offered in Gs	1600-2200
Isaac Fiske			before 1887			HD, RV	1100+
Goulet			ca. 1893	Br		BF, PV, water key, also offered in Ni, or Si plate, sold by Stratton	75-250
Goulet			ca. 1893	Br		HD, PV, water key, offered in two sizes	300-700
Goulet			ca. 1893	Br		BU, PV, also offered in Ni, or Si plate	75-250
J. Higham	Clear bore		ca. 1896	Br		BU, PV, water key, also offered in Si plate, and with Go trim and bell	125-300
J. Higham	First class		ca. 1896	Br		BU, PV, water key, also offered in Si plate, and with Go trim and bell	125-300
F. Jaubert			ca. 1896	Br		BU, PV, water key, also offered in Ni or Si plate	125-300

Hall & Quinby			ca. 1865	Br?		HD, RV	$1100+
Hall & Quinby						Allen valves	1550+
Hall & Quinby				Ni/Br		HD, RV	850+
Hall & Quinby				Br		BU, SARV, also offered in Gs	1200-1600
Harry B. Jay			1910-1946			HD	550
Keefer						HD	600
Brua C. Keefer		11XXX	ca. 1920	Si	very good	enammeled buttons	650
King	recording	50XXX	ca. 1920	lacquer	very good	BF, TARV	550
A. Lecomte & Co.	Champion		ca. 1879	Br		large bore	100-300
H. Lehnert			ca. 1860	Ni/Br	needs work	HD, string RV	600
Missenharter				Br		HD, PV	475
J.W. Pepper	[student grade]			Br		high pitch, 3 PV	100
Quinby Bros.			ca. 1879	Br		BU, SARV, also offered in Gs	1200-1600
Quinby Bros.			ca. 1879	Br		HD, SARV, also offered in Gs	700-1000
M. Slater			ca. 1874	Br		BU, TARV	750-1400
M. Slater			before 1900	Br?	needs work	HD, RV	725
Stratton			ca. 1893	Br		BU, BPV, also offered in Ni, or triple Si plate	250-600
Stratton			ca. 1893	Br		BU, PV, water key, also offered in Ni, or triple Si plate	200-400
Stratton	largest size		ca. 1893	Br		offered in Ni plate, or triple Si plate	175-400
Stratton			ca. 1893	Br		HD, PV, water key, offered in 2 sizes	300-700

BASS HORN IN EE FLAT (contrabass)

[Anon.]			ca. 1896	Br		BU, PV, water key, also offered in Ni or or Si plate, sold by Lyon & Healy	125-300
[Anon.]	Beau Ideal		ca. 1896	Br		BU, PV, water key, also offered in Ni or Si plate, and with Go plate bell and trim, sold by Lyon & Healy	150-275
[Anon.]	short model		ca. 1896	Br		BU, BPV, water key, also offered in Ni plate, sold by Lyon & Healy	175-250
[Anon.]	largest size		ca. 1879	Br		BU, PV, also offered in silver plate, satin finish, sold by Martin Bros.	100-300
[Anon. German]			ca. 1879	Br		BU, BPV, Gs trim, sold by Martin Bros.	100-300
[Anon. German]			ca. 1879	Br		BU, PV, Gs trim, sold by Martin Bros.	100-300
BMIMC			1874	Br		HD, SARV, also offered in Gs	800
J. Higham			ca. 1896	Br		BU, PV, water key, also offered in triple Si plate, and with Go trim and bell	200-400
J. Higham			ca. 1896	Br		HD, PV, water key, also offered in triple Si plate, and with Go trim and bell	300-500
F. Jaubert			ca. 1896	Br		BU, PV, water key, also offered in Ni or Si plate	125-300
F. Jaubert			ca. 1896	Br		HD, PV, water key, also offered in Ni or Si plate	200-500
Martin Bros.			ca. 1879	Br		BU, PV, water key, also offered in Si plate	100-300
Martin Bros.	largest size		ca. 1879	Br		BU, PV, water key, also offered in Si plate	100-300
Martin Bros.			ca. 1879	Br		BU, SARV, Go trim or Gs throughout	1000-1400
Martin Bros.	largest size		ca. 1879	Br		BU, SARV, Gs trim or Gs throughout	1000-1400
Martin Bros.			ca. 1879	Br		BU, 4 SARV, Gs trim or Gs throughout	1200-1800
Martin Bros.			ca. 1879	Br		BU, TARV, Gs trim or Gs throughout	1100-1400
Martin Bros.	largest size		ca. 1879	Br		BU, TARV, Gs trim or Gs throughout	1000-1400
Martin Bros.			ca. 1879	Br		HD, PV, Br, water key, two sizes	300-500
Martin Bros.			ca. 1879	Br		HD, SARV, Gs trim or Gs throughout	650-1000
Martin Bros.	largest size		ca. 1879	Br		OTS, TARV, Gs trim or Gs throughout	1500-1900
Quinby Bros.			ca. 1879	Br		HD, SARV, also offered in Gs	700-1000
W.F. Seefeldt			[after 1900]			3 PV	350
M. Slater			ca. 1874	Br		OTS, TARV	1500-2200
M. Slater			ca. 1874	Br		BU, PV, water key, also offered in Si plate	100-300
M. Slater	largest size		ca. 1874	Br		BU, PV, water key, also offered in Si plate	100-300
M. Slater			ca. 1874	Br		OTS, SARV, also offered in Gs	1800-2500
M. Slater	largest size		ca. 1874	Br		OTS, SARV, also offered in Gs	1500-2200

BASS HORN IN F

F. Busch		ca. 1875-80	Br		3 PV	450
Eduard Riedl		ca. 1860	Gs	needs repairs	4 RV, oval bell	500
M. Slater		ca. 1874	Br		BU, TARV	750-1400
Ignaz Stowasser		ca. 1855	Gs	requires some restoration	3 RV	850

BUGLE (officer's, artillery, boat, bicycle, etc.)

[Anon. German]		ca. 1890	Br & Ni		set of 4	1200
Leedy				dents in bell, bent slide		20
Ludwig					one valve	60

Martin Bros.	Officer's		ca. 1879	Br		3 rounds, also offered in Gs	$50-100
M. Slater	Officer's		ca. 1874	Br		2 rounds	50

BUGLE, KEYED

[Anon.]				Co/Br		7 keys, in B flat	1200+
[Anon.]				Co/Br		7 keys, in B flat, odd design	1400+
[Anon.]	pocket			Co		6 keys, looks to be reproduction	600
John Bernhard Logier			ca. 1840	Co/Br		includes set pieces from another instrument	2127
Sax, Charles-Joseph			1842	Br		7 keys, very fine specimen	6808

CORNET in [?], RV

[Anon.]			ca. 1890	Br & Ni		abalone buttons	550
[Anon.]			ca. 1860	Si	poor condition	string action, crown insignia	300
[Anon.]			ca. 1878	Co&Ni		large RV, dummy 3rd bell	300
Hug				Ni			600

CORNET IN B FLAT

[Anon.]					minor dents	BF, PV, several crooks and bits, key change attachment to C	250
[Anon.]			ca. 1879	Br		BF, PV, also offered in Si plate, sold by Martin Bros.	150-500
[Anon.]			ca. 1896	Br		BF, BPV, water key, sold by Lyon & Healy	450-750
[Anon.]			ca. 1896	Si/Br		BF, PV, double water key, heavily engraved, triple Si plate, and with Go trim and bell, sold by Lyon & Healy	450-550
[Anon.]			ca. 1896	Br		BF, PV, double water key, C attachment, engraved mounts, also offered in Si plate, and with Go tipped, sold by Lyon & Healy	75-300
[Anon.]			ca. 1896	Br		BF, PV, water key, A shank, also offered in Ni or Si plate, sold by Lyon & Healy	50-150
[Anon.]	American Capitol			Br		long model	30
[Anon.]	Artists' model		ca. 1896	Br		BF, PV, water key, Bb and A set pieces, also offered in Si plate, and with Go plate bell and tips, sold by Lyon & Healy	95-300
[Anon.]	Artists' model		ca. 1896	Br		BF, PV, double water key, Bb and A set pieces, also offered in Si plate, and with Go plate bell, sold by Lyon & Healy	150-350
[Anon.]	Beau Ideal		ca. 1896	Br		BF, PV, double water key, also offered in Ni or Si plate, and with Go plate, heavily engraved, sold by Lyon & Healy	125-400
[Anon.]	Champion		ca. 1896	Br		BF, PV, water key, Bb and A set pieces, also offered in Si plate, and with Go plate bell, heavily engraved, sold by Lyon & Healy	150-350
[Anon.]	London model		ca. 1896	Br		BF, PV, water key, Bb and A set pieces, also offered in Si plate, and with Go plate bell and tips, sold by Lyon & Healy	95-300
[Anon.]	short model		ca. 1896	Br		BF, BPV, water key, also offered in Ni plate, sold by Lyon & Healy	450-750
[Anon.]	short model	18XXX	before 1900	Si/Br		BF, shepherd's crook, Pepper importer	200
[Anon.]	solo model		ca. 1896	Br		BF, PV, double water key, C attachment, heavily engraved, also offered in Si plate, and with Go plate tips, sold by Lyon & Healy	75-300
[Anon. German]	orchestra model		ca. 1879	Br		BF, PV, water key, crooks to G	150-350
Abbott Mgf. Co.			ca. 1935	Br	original Si pl.	3 PV	100
Blessing	Standard	52XXX	ca. 1955	lacquer	very good		110
Boosey & Hawkes	Oxford		ca. 1955	lacquer	good	tilted bell	125
Boosey & Hawkes	Oxford	25XXXX	1957	lacquer	very good		150
BMIMC			1869-1874	Br		BF, PV, also offered in Gs	600-1000
BMIMC			1869-1874	Br		BF, SARV, also offered in Gs	1000-1500
BMIMC			1869-1874	Br		BF, SARV, also offered in Gs, unusual body design	1200-1400
BMIMC			1869-1874	Br		HD, TARV, also offered in Gs	2500-3500
BMIMC			1869-1874	Br		3 PV, also offered in Gs	600-1000
BMIMC			1869-1874	Br		3 SARV, also offered in Gs	1200-1400
BMIMC			1869-1874	Br		3 SARV and 1 SARV, also offered in Gs	1200-1800
BMIMC			1869-1874	Br		TARV, also offered in Gs	1200-1400
BMIMC			1869-1874	Br		OTS, TARV, also offered in Gs	2500-3000
BMIMC	[echo model]		1879?	Br		BF, 3 PV, 1 SARV, also offered in Gs or Si plate	1200-1400+
Buescher	400	30XXXX	1942	lacquer	good+	shepherd's crook	250
Bundy				Br			30
C.G. Conn				Si	very worn,	odd slide, valve stuck	100

Maker	Model	Serial	Date	Finish	Condition	Description	Price
C.G. Conn			ca. 1899	Si/Br		3 PV	$250
C.G. Conn		50XXX				double water key	350
C.G. Conn	38A, Constellation	89XXXX	1961	lacquer	excellent		375
C.G. Conn	"The Conn-Querer"		c1907-08	Si/Br		3 PV, extra tuning slide, and case	170
C.G. Conn	[Crossover Model]		ca. 1905	Si/Br			200
C.G. Conn	Victor			Si	dents	unusual slide	150
C.G. Conn	Victor		ca. 1918	Br lacquer		3 PV	75
Couesnon				Br	worn finish		30
Couesnon				Br	worn finish		40
Couesnon				Br			80
Henry Distin				Si/Br		3 PV, engraved throughout, in case, with accessories	300+
Henry Distin				Si/Br		3 PV, key change attachment	300+
Henry Distin	Artist solo model			Si/Br		BF, PV, engraved, made in London	500-600
Henry Distin	London model			Br or Si			150
Henry Distin	solo model			Si/Br		BF, PV, equipped with echo attachment	900-2500
Carl Fischer				Br		3 PV	75
Isaac Fiske			ca. 1868	Br		OTS, SARV, also offered in Gs	3500+
Isaac Fiske			ca. 1868	Br		BF, Push rod valves, also offered in Gs	1600-2200
Isaac Fiske			ca. 1868	Br		BF, SARV, also offered in Gs	1400-1800
Goulet			ca. 1893	Br		BF, PV, water key, also offered in Ni, or Si plate, sold by Stratton	75-300
Goulet			ca. 1893	Br		BF, PV, water key, A shank, also offered in Ni, Si, or Go plate, and engraving, sold by Stratton	150-350
Goumat				Si		shepherd's crook	80
J. Higham	First class		ca. 1896	Br		BF, PV, water key, also offered in triple Si plate, and with Go plate trim and bell	75-350
J. Higham	Clear bore		ca. 1896	Br		BF, PV, double water key, also offered in triple Si plate, and with Go plate trim and bell	75-350
J. Higham	Clear bore		ca. 1896	Br		BF, PV, double water key, echo attachment, also offered in triple Si plate, and with Go plate trim and bell	750-1500
J. Higham	Clear bore		ca. 1896	Br		BF, PV, double water key, heavily engraved, also offered in triple Si plate, and with Go plate trim and bell	250-500
Holton				Si		shepherd's crook	200
Holton	29	14XXXX	1941	lacquer	good+		175
Holton	Collegiate			Br			20
Imperial			ca. 1890	Br		3 PV	60
F. Jaubert			ca. 1896	Br		BF, PV, water key, in Ni or Si plate	75-350
F. Jaubert	Artist model		ca. 1896	Br		BF, PV, double water key, also offered in Ni or Si plate, and Go plate bell	50-250
F. Jaubert	Artist model		ca. 1896	Br		BF, PV, double water key, engraved, also offered in Ni or Si plate, and with Go plate bell	150-400
F. Jaubert	Artist model		ca. 1896	Br		BF, PV, single or double water keys, C attachment, also offered in Si plate, and with Go plate bell	75-350
F. Jaubert	pocket model		ca. 1896	Br		BF, PV, single or double water keys, also offered in Si or Go plate	500-850
H.B. Jay	Columbia	89XX	ca. 1925	Si	very good	cornet mouthpipe only	425
Jenkins				Si			40
Kaempf	short model		1878-1911			RV, shepherd's crook	650
King		43XXX					50
King	Cleveland 602	33XXXX	1968	lacquer	very good		150
King	Master	17XXXX		Br		RV change	150
King	Silvertone			Br		Si bell	800
A. Lecomte & Co.			ca. 1879	Br		2 PV, and 1 "large valve"	200-400
A. Lecomte & Co.			ca. 1879	Br		3 "large valves"	200-400
A. Lecomte & Co.	oval bore		ca. 1879	Br		water key	200-400
A. Lecomte & Co.			ca. 1879	Br		Courtois, Arban, and Levy patterns	400
H. Lehnert			before 1900	Br		3 PV, two crooks	280
H. Lehnert			before 1900	Br		3 PV, two crooks, original mouthpiece, and case	375
H. Lehnert	short model		before 1900	Si/Br		shepherds crook	625
H. Lehnert (?)			before 1900	Br		Gs garland and trim, 3 string RV	750
Marceau				Si	valves stuck	shepards crook	200
Martin				Si			150
Martin	Committee	18XXXX	1952	lacquer	good+	lacquer worn	350
Martin Bros.			ca. 1879	Br		BF, SARV, Gs trim or Gs throughout	1000-1500
Martin Bros.			ca. 1879	Br		BU, TARV, Gs trim or Gs throughout	2000-2800
Martin Bros.			ca. 1879	Br		HD, SARV, Gs trim or Gs throughout	2500-3200

Maker	Model	Serial	Date	Material	Condition	Notes	Price
Martin Bros.			ca. 1879	Gs/Br		HD, TARV, also offered in Gs throughout	$2500-3000
Martin Bros.			ca. 1879	Br		OTS, TARV, Gs trim or Gs throughout	3000-4000
Martin Bros.	10 inch long		ca. 1879	Gs/Br		BF, SARV, also offered in Gs throughout, also offered with engraving, Go plate	850-1500
Martin Bros.	12 inch long		ca. 1879	Gs/Br		BF, SARV, also offered in Gs throughout	1000-1500
Martin Bros.	12 inch long		ca. 1879	Gs/Br		BF, Gs SARV or TARV, also offered in Gs throughout	1000-1500
Martin Bros.	12 inch long		ca. 1879	Gs/Br		BF, TARV, also offered in Gs throughout	1000-1500
Martin Bros.			ca. 1879	Br		BF, PV, also offered with Si plate	150-500
Martin Bros.	Artist		ca. 1879	Br		BF, PV, water key, heavily engraved, also offered in Gs or Go plate	200-675
Martin Bros.	orchestra		ca. 1879	Gs/Br		BF, SARV or TARV, crooks to G, also offered in Gs throughout	1000-1500
Martin Bros.	orchestra		ca. 1879	Br		BF, PV, water key, also offered with silver plate, satin finish, crooks to G	150-500
Martin Bros.	pocket		ca. 1874	Br		BF, RV, 8 or 10 inch, water key, crooks	2000+
Martin Bros.	pocket		ca. 1874	Gs		BF, RV, 10 inch orchestra model, also offered with Go plate, and heavily engraved	850-1500
[Mont.-Ward]	Concertone			Br		[unknown manufacturer]	40
Olds	Ambassador			Br	bottom cap missing		45
Olds	Ambassador	31XXXX	1959	lacquer	excellent		200
Olds	Super	68XXX	ca. 1950	lacquer	very good		300
Pan American				Br			150
J.W. Pepper			ca. 1910			heavily engraved	1000
J.W. Pepper	short model		before 1900	Si/Br		N.Y. and Philadelphia, shepherds crook	295
J.W. Pepper	short model	37XXX	before 1900	Ni/Br		shepherds crook	250
Henry Pourcelle				Si	dents	shepards crook	125
Quinby Bros.	short model		ca. 1879	Br		BF, SARV, also offered in Gs, rare tube arrangement	1500-2000+
Quinby Bros.	short model		ca. 1879	Br		Orchestra model, BF, TARV	1500-2200
Adolf Schmidt						shepards crook	150
M. Slater			ca. 1873	Gs	minor dents	3 string RV, circular crook	950
M. Slater			ca. 1874	Br		BF, PV, also offered with Gs valves	750-1400
M. Slater			ca. 1874	Br		BU, TARV, also offered with Gs valves	2500-3500
M. Slater			ca. 1874	Br		HD, TARV, also offered with Gs valves	2500-3500
M. Slater			ca. 1874	Br		OTS, TARV, also offered with Gs valves	2500-3500
M. Slater	short orchestra		ca. 1874	Br		BF, SARV, with crooks to A and G	750-1400
M. Slater	long orchestra		ca. 1874	Gs		BF, SARV, with crooks to A and G	650-1300
Stratton			ca. 1893	Br		BF, BPV, also offered in Ni, or triple Si plate	500-950
Stratton			ca. 1893	Br		BF, PV, double water keys, A shank, also offered in Ni, Si, or Go plate	300-750
Stratton			ca. 1893	Br		same as above, but heavily engraved	500-1000
Stratton	Courtois		ca. 1893	Br		BF, PV, double water keys, A shank, also offered in Ni, Si, or Go plate, and engraved	300-750
Thibouville						shepherd's crook	150
Georgi Vitock				Si		shepherd's crook	125
York		32XXX		Si	tarnished		80
York		22XXXX		Si	tarnished		40
York	Professional			Si	missing slide	shepards crook	100

CORNET IN B FLAT/A

Maker	Model	Serial	Date	Material	Condition	Notes	Price
[Anon.]			ca. 1890	Br	good		250
Besson, French	Concertiste	72XXX	ca. 1910	Si	good	crack near bell rim	550
Besson, French	Concertiste	75XXX	ca. 1920	Si	good		575
Besson, French	Dessideratum	58XXX	ca. 1895	Si	good+		575
Besson, French	Dessideratum	57XXX	ca. 1895	Si	very good		675
Besson, French	Francais	18XXX	ca. 1880	Br	good-		300
Besson, French	Francais	69XX	ca. 1865	Br	good		400
Boosey	Acme	10XXXX	1918	Si	very good	Distin pattern	400
C.G. Conn	Conn-Queror	93XXX	1905	Si	very good+	medium bore	500
C.G. Conn	New Wonder	14XXXX	1916	Si	good+	7A?, .465" bore	175
C.G. Conn	Perfected Wonder	94XXX	1906	Si	very good		425
C.G. Conn	Victor	36XXXX	1947	lacquer	very good		275
C.G. Conn	Victor, 80A	38XXXX	1949	Si	good	plays excellent	250
C.G. Conn	Victor, 80A	42XXXX	1954	lacquer	very good		225
C.G. Conn	Victor, 8A	32XXXX	1940	Si	very good+	long, thin Victor	325
C.G. Conn	Wonder	31XXX	1895	Si/Br	very excellent	newly restored	800
C.G. Conn	Wonder	88XXX	1905	Si	good	long bell	450
Couesnon			1924	Ni/Br	good		175
Couturier	short model	24XX	ca. 1920	Si	good+		350
Gautier	Virtuoso	44XXX	ca. 1920	Si	fair	Czech.	75
Gretsch	American Model	85XXXX	ca. 1915	Si	excelent	long shepherd's crook	175
Holton	Couturier	13XXX	1911	Go/Si	very good		250

Holton	Couturier	11XXX	1910	Si	very good	.482" bore	$250
Holton	New Proportion	16XX	1905	Go/Si	very good+	short model	425
[Holton ?]	Inspiration	30XX	ca. 1925	Si	good+		175
Keefer	short model	60XX		Si		highest grade, shepherd's crook	595
Keefer	short model	78XX				shepherd's crook	675
Kenny		52XX	ca. 1915	Si	good	made by Martin	125
King	Large Bore	92XX	ca. 1910	Si	good+		300
King	Large Bore	59XX	ca. 1905	Si	excellent		425
King	Silversonic	33XXXX	1954	lacquer	excellent		525
King	Silversonic	34XXXX	1955	lacquer	good+		350
King	Silvertone	19XXXX	1937	Go/Si	very good		700
King	Silvertone	20XXXX	1938	Go/Si	very good		525
King	Silvertone	21XXXX	ca. 1938	lacquer	very good+	original lacquer	525
King	Silvertone	33XXXX	1954	lacquer	excellent		525
Vimeux	short action		ca. 1880	Ni/Br	fair	probably Thibouville	450
Williams & Short			ca. 1905	Si	excellent		325
Wurlitzer	Symphony		ca. 1890	Ni/Br	very good		275
York	Monarch new mod	16XXX	ca. 1906	Go/Si	very good	short model	375
York	Professional	29XXX	ca. 1910	Go/Si	excellent		375

CORNET IN B FLAT/A/A FLAT

Gautrot			ca. 1860	Br	very excellent	2 Stoelzel and 1 PV, crooks to Eb	1400

CORNET IN C (basically same as below, no crooks or shanks)

[Anon.]				Br		3 PV	100
Martin Bros.	orchestra		ca. 1879	Gs/Br		BF, SARV or TARV, crooks to G, also offered in Gs throughout	1000-1500

CORNET IN C/B FLAT/A

C.G. Conn	Conn-queror	10XXXX	1907	Si	very good+		650
F. Jaubert			ca. 1896	Br		BF, PV, water key, also offered in Ni or Si plate	50-300
J.W. Pepper	American Favorite	68XXX	ca. 1920	Si	very good	BF, Couesnon, Bb slide missing	150
Quinby Bros.	short model		ca. 1879	Br		Orchestra model, BU, SARV, also offered in Gs	1400-1800
Stratton			ca. 1893	Br		BF, PV, water keys, also offered in Ni, Si, or Go plate and engraving	300-750

CORNET IN E FLAT

[Anon.]			ca. 1879	Br		BF, PV, also offered in Si plate, satin finish, sold by Martin Bros.	150-400
[Anon.]			ca. 1896	Br		BF, PV, water key, also offered in Si plate, sold by Lyon & Healy	150-450
[Anon.]	Artist model		ca. 1896	Br		BF, PV, water key, also offered in Si plate, and with Go plate trim and bell, sold by Lyon & Healy	150-500
[Anon.]	Beau Ideal		ca. 1896	Br		BF, PV, water key, also offered in Ni or Si plate, and with Go plate bell and trim, heavily engraved, sold by Lyon & Healy	150-400
[Anon.]	short model		ca. 1896	Si/Br		BF, BPV, water key, also offered in Ni plate, sold by Lyon & Healy	450-750
[Anon. German]	solo model		ca. 1879	Br		BF, PV, water key, sold by Martin Bros.	200-500
Besson		36XXX	1887	Si	good		300
BMIMC			1869-1874	Br		BF, SARV, also offered in Gs	1200
BMIMC			1869	Br		BF, 4 TARV, metal assumed, also offered in Gs	2000+
BMIMC	short model			Si/Br		BF, shepherd's crook	950
BMIMC	pocket	76XX	1869-1874	Br	very good+	BF, SARV, also offered in Gs, Si or Go plate	1500-2000+
BMIMC			1869-1874	Br		BF, SARV, or TARV	1200-1400
BMIMC	medium size		1869-1874	Br		BF, SARV or TARV	1200-1400
BMIMC			1869-1874	Br		HD, TARV, also offered in Gs	2500-3500
BMIMC			1869-1874	Br		OTS, TARV, also offered in Gs	2500-3000
Isaac Fiske			ca. 1868	Br		BF, SARV, also offered in Gs	1400-1700
Isaac Fiske			ca. 1868	Br		BF, Push rod valves, also offered in Gs	1800-2400
Isaac Fiske			ca. 1868	Br		OTS, SARV, also offered in Gs	2500-3500+
Goulet			ca. 1893	Br		BF, PV, water key, also offered in Ni, or Si plate, sold by Stratton	75-300
J. Higham	First class		ca. 1896	Br		BF, PV, water key, also offered in triple Si plate, and with Go plate trim and bell	125-400
J. Higham	Clear bore		ca. 1896	Br		BF, PV, double water key, also offered in triple Si plate, and with Go plate trim and bell	125-400

Maker	Model	Serial	Date	Material	Condition	Description	Price
F. Jaubert			ca. 1896	Br		BF, PV, water key, also offered in Ni or Si plate	$125-400
A. Lecomte & Co.			ca. 1879	Br		"best make"	300-600
A. Lecomte & Co.	Champion		ca. 1879	Br		"best make"	250-450
Martin Bros.			ca. 1879	Br		BF, SARV, Gs trim or Gs throughout	1000-1400
Martin Bros.			ca. 1879	Br		BF, PV, water key, also offered with Si plate, satin finish	150-450
Martin Bros.			ca. 1879	Br		BU, TARV, Gs trim or Gs throughout	2000-2800
Martin Bros.			ca. 1879	Br		OTS, TARV, Gs trim or Gs throughout	2500-3500
Martin Bros.			ca. 1879	Br		HD, SARV, Gs trim or Gs throughout	2500-3200
Martin Bros.			ca. 1879	Gs/Br		HD, TARV, also offered in Gs throughout	2500-3000
Martin Bros.	10 inch long, solo		ca. 1879	Gs/Br		BF, SARV or TARV, also offered in Gs throughout, also offered in Gs RV	1000-1500
Martin Bros.	12 inch long, artist		ca. 1879	Br		BF, SARV or TARV, also offered in Gs throughout, also offered in Gs RV	1000-1500
Martin Bros.	12 inch long		ca. 1879	Gs/Br		BF, SARV, also offered in Gs throughout	1000-1500
Martin Bros.	12 inch long		ca. 1879	Gs/Br		BF, TARV, also offered in Gs throughout	1000-1500
Martin Bros.	8 inch long, miniature		ca. 1879	Gs/Br		BF, Gs SARV or TARV, also offered in Gs throughout	2000+
Martin Bros.	Artist		ca. 1879	Br		BF, PV, water key, heavily engraved, also offered in Gs or Go plate	150-550
Quinby Bros.	short model		ca. 1879	Br		BF, SARV, also offered in Gs	1400-1800
Quinby Bros.	pocket		ca. 1879	Br		BF, SARV, also offered in Gs	1500-2200
M. Slater	long		ca. 1874	Br		BF, PV, orchestra model, also offered with Gs valves	650-1300
M. Slater	short		ca. 1874	Br		BF, PV, orchestra model, also offered with Gs valves	750-1400
M. Slater			ca. 1874	Br		BU, TARV, also offered with Gs valves	2500-3500
M. Slater			ca. 1874	Br		HD, TARV, also offered with Gs valves	2500-3500
M. Slater			ca. 1874	Br		OTS, TARV, also offered with Gs valves	2500-3500
Stratton			ca. 1893	Br		BF, BPV, water key, also offered in Ni, or triple Si plate	400-850
Stratton			ca. 1893	Br		BF, PV, water key, also offered in Ni or triple Si plate	300-750
Stratton			ca. 1893	Br		BF, PV, water key, also offered in Ni, Si, or Go plate	200-600

CORNO (variant of Cornet in Bb)

Maker	Model	Serial	Date	Material	Condition	Description	Price
BMIMC			1869			BF, TARV, bell below valves	2000-3500

CORNOPEAN

Maker	Model	Serial	Date	Material	Condition	Description	Price
[Anon. French]			ca. 1979	Br		BF, PV, crooks to F, sold by Martin Bros.	300-700
[Anon. French?]			1860-1890?	Si/Br		3 Stöelzel valves, 5 crooks, one bit	545
Durand	in Bb		ca. 1900?			comes with case and crooks	695
A. Lecomte & Co.			ca. 1879	Br		sold by D.C. Hall	400-800
John Koehler	3 Shaw valves		ca. 1850	Si/Br		shank for Bb, and crooks for F and Ab	6900

EUPHONIUM

Maker	Model	Serial	Date	Material	Condition	Description	Price
Besson	967	72XXXX	ca. 1994	Si	very excellent	compensating	2100
C.G. Conn	841	18XXXX	1921	Si	good	4 valve	325
J. Higham	Clear bore		ca. 1896	Br		BU, PV, water key, also offered in triple Si plate, and with Go trim and bell	125-200
J. Higham	First class		ca. 1896	Br		BU, PV, water key, also offered in triple Si plate, and with Go trim and bell	125-200
J. Higham	Clear bore		ca. 1896	Br		BU, 4 PV, water key, also offered in triple Si plate, and with Go trim and bell	250-400
J. Higham	First class		ca. 1896	Br		BU, 4 PV, water key, also offered in triple Si plate, and with Go trim and bell	250-400
Vox	4 valve	99X	ca. 1975	lacquer	very good	no case	450
Yamaha	YEP-321S	00XXXX		Si	very good,		825

EUPHONIUM, DOUBLE BELL

Maker	Model	Serial	Date	Material	Condition	Description	Price
C.G. Conn				Si		4 valves	1500
C.G. Conn	601 double bell	28XXXX	1932	Si	very good+	5 PV, Royal Hawaiian Band	1500
C.G. Conn	Wonderphone	79XXX	1903	Si	very good	4 PV, very large bore	850
C.G. Conn	Wonderphone	94XXX	1906	Si	very good	5 valves	1500
J. Higham			ca. 1896	Br		4 PV, water key, also offered in triple Si plate, and with Go bell and trim	750-1500
F. Jaubert			ca. 1896	Br		4 PV, water key, also offered in Ni or Si plate	500-1200
King		17XXXX				4 valves, added	1500
Lyon & Healy						4 valves	1500

FLUGELHORN IN B FLAT

Maker	Model	Serial	Date	Material	Condition	Notes	Price
Benge	FL5	38XXX	ca. 1985	lacquer			$500
Besson		72XXX	ca. 1907	Si	good	patch on bell	425
Besson	small bore	89XX	ca. 1868	Br	good	unusual valve design	600
Besson & Co.	French model			Si/Br		3 PV	200
Besson, French		52XXX	ca. 1893	Ni/Br	good	presentation	625
Besson, French		64XXX	ca. 1898	Br	very good		625
Blessing	Artist	36XXXX	1988	lacquer	very	good	350
Cerveny	rotary valves	14XXX	ca. 1925	Br	very	good	550
C.G. Conn	20A	M3XXXX	1969	lacquer	excellent		375
Couesnon		80XXX	ca. 1875	lacquer	very good	3rd slide trigger	650
Couesnon		79XXX	ca. 1975	Si	excellent		775
Couesnon	Elkhart	22XX	ca. 1975	lacquer	excellent		475
Gautrot Marquet		22XX	before 1900	Br		3 PV, pigtail crook	700
Goumat							250
F. Jaubert			ca. 1896	Br		BF, PV, water key, also offered in Ni or Si plate	150-300
Jupiter	JPH-746	00XXXX		lacquer	very excellent		325
Martin Mainer			ca. 1900	Br/Ni	good	RV	300
C.W. Moritz			before 1900	Gs	minus RV	garland and trim, 3 rotary	700

FLUGELHORN IN C

Maker	Model	Serial	Date	Material	Condition	Notes	Price
[Anon.]			ca. 1896	Br		BF, PV, water key, crooks to Bb, also offered in Ni or Si plate, sold by Lyon & Healy	150-300

FLUGELHORN IN E FLAT

Maker	Model	Serial	Date	Material	Condition	Notes	Price
P.E. Schmidt			ca. 1853-1872	Gs/Br		3 RV	750

FLUGEL HORN, RV

Maker	Model	Serial	Date	Material	Condition	Notes	Price
BMIMC			ca. 1860			in D, RV to E	1400
Arthur Peterson			ca. 1850	Br			500

FRENCH HORN

Maker	Model	Serial	Date	Material	Condition	Notes	Price
Boston	F	25XXX	ca. 1920	Si	good	Si worn	300
BMIMC	[in F?]		1869-1874	Br		SARV, also offered in Gs	200-400
C.G. Conn	4D	31XXXX	1936	lacquer	good+		250
C.G. Conn	natural Bb		ca. 1960	lacquer	very good		225
Courtois	single F	16X	ca. 1920	Si	very good	crooks to F, Eb & D	475
Getzen						double horn, mechanical action	250
A.K. Huttl				Gs		3 RV	350
F. Jaubert			ca. 1896	Br		PV, crooks, also offered in Ni or Si plate	50-200
King	single F	11XXXX	ca. 1928	lacquer	good		225
Martin Bros.	[in F?]		ca. 879	Br		PV, or RV, crooks, or Gs throughout	150-450
Quinby Bros.	F and C		ca. 1879	Br		SARV, crooks, also offered in Gs	300-700
Orse	double			Br	dents in bell	mechanical action	200
Viking	single F		ca. 1960	lacquer	good	no case	150

MELLOPHONE

Maker	Model	Serial	Date	Material	Condition	Notes	Price
Cerveny				Si	tarnished	RV	250
DEG	Dynasty	C4XXX		lacquer	good	BF	275
DEG	Dynasty	C4XXX		lacquer	good	BF	275
Elkhorn							75
Getzen							40
Grand Rapids Band				Si			35
Aug. Heinem							20
Imperial				Si	dents, broken braces		20
Lecomte							45
Pan American	Cavalier			Br	lead pipe crushed		30
Reynolds					dents		20
WHS Smith				Si	worn		35

NATURAL HORN

Maker	Model	Serial	Date	Material	Condition	Notes	Price
[Anon.]	in B flat			Br & Ni			200
John Harris			1725	Br		bell garland engraved "John Harris in Barwick Street, Old Soho, London Fecit 1725"	4000

OPHICLEIDE

Maker	Model	Serial	Date	Material	Condition	Notes	Price
[Anon.]	3 keys, 6 holes, in C						1275
[Anon.]	9 keys, in C						2500
[Anon. American?]	9 keys, in C					listed as "odd design"	1750
[Anon. French]	9 keys, in C		ca. 1850	Br		Br keys, and crook	2009
Gautrot	9 keys, in C	9XX	ca. 1850	Br	good	needs work	1800
Labbaye	9 keys, in C		before 1878				2700
J.B. Tabard	9 keys, in C		1812-1848				2500

POST HORN, VALVED

Maker	Model	Serial	Date	Material	Condition	Description	Price
Tomschik	in C		before 1914?				$1200

SERPENT

Maker	Model	Serial	Date	Material	Condition	Description	Price
Metzler			ca. 1825	wood	good	missing 4 ivory bushes	9600

SOUSAPHONE IN E FLAT

Maker	Model	Serial	Date	Material	Condition	Description	Price
Cleveland		XXXXXX	1935	Si	good		300
C.G. Conn		XXXXXX	1966	lacquer	very good		375
C.G. Conn	26K	82XXXX	1959	lacquer	good		300

TENOR HORN IN B FLAT

Maker	Model	Serial	Date	Material	Condition	Description	Price
[Anon.]			ca. 1879	Br		BU, PV, also offered in Si plate, satin finish, sold by Martin Bros.	75-300
[Anon.]			ca. 1896	Br		BU, PV, water key, also offered in Ni or Si plate, sold by Lyon & Healy	125-175
[Anon.]	Beau ideal		ca. 1896	Br		BU, PV, water key, also offered in Ni or Si plate, and with Go plate bell and trim heavily engraved, sold by Lyon & Healy	125-200
[Anon.]	short model		ca. 1896	Br		BU, BPV, water key, also offered in Ni plate, sold by Lyon & Healy	125-175
[Anon. German]				Br	needs repairs	Gs garland	300
[Anon. German]			ca. 1879	Br		BU, BPV, Gs trim, sold by Martin Bros.	100-300
BMIMC				Si/Br	needs work	3 PV	120
BMIMC			1869-1874	Br		BU, SARV, also offered in Gs	800-1100
BMIMC			1869-1874	Br		HD, SARV, also offered in Gs	800-1100
BMIMC			1869-1874	Br		OTS, TARV, also offered in Gs	2500
Isaac Fiske			ca. 1868	Br		BU, SARV, mouthpiece to the left of the instrument, also offered in Gs	1400-1800
Isaac Fiske			ca. 1868	Br		OTS, SARV, also offered in Gs	2200-2400+
Goulet			ca. 1893	Br		BF, PV, water key, also offered in Ni, or Si plate, sold by Stratton	75-300
J. Higham	Clear bore		ca. 1896	Br		BU, PV, water key, also offered in Si plate, and with Go plate trim and bell	125-200
J. Higham	First class		ca. 1896	Br		BU, PV, water key, also offered in Si plate, and with Go plate trim and bell	125-200
Holton	Collegiate	12XXXX	1939	Si	very good	BF	275
F. Jaubert			ca. 1896	Br		BU, PV, water key, also offered in Ni, or Si plate	125-200
Brua C. Keefer				Si/Br		3 PV	225
A. Lecomte	Champion		ca. 1879	Br		"best make"	150-300
H. Lehnert	Saxhorn		before 1900	Ni/Br		3 RV	1400
Martin Bros.			ca. 1879	Br		BU, PV, water key, also offered in Si plate	75-300
Martin Bros.			ca. 1879	Br		BU, TARV, Gs trim or Gs throughout	1200-1500
Martin Bros.			ca. 1879	Br		BU, SARV, Gs trim or Gs throughout	1000-1400
Martin Bros.			ca. 1879	Br		HD, PV	1200-1700
Martin Bros.			ca. 1879	Br		HD, SARV, Gs trim or Gs throughout	1100-1600
Martin Bros.			ca. 1879	Br		OTS, TARV, Gs trim or Gs throughout	1800-2400
Quinby Bros.			ca. 1879	Br		BU, SARV, also offered in Gs	1200-1500
Quinby Bros.			ca. 1879	Br		HD, SARV	900-1500
M. Slater			ca. 1874	Br		BU, TARV	750-1500
M. Slater			ca. 1874	Br		OTS, TARV	1800-2500
M. Slater	Tenor Saxhorn		before 1900	Br	needs repairs	3 PV	300
Stratton			ca. 1893	Br		BU, BPV, also offered in Ni, or triple Si plate	250-600
Stratton			ca. 1893	Br		BU, PV, water key, also offered in Ni or triple Si plate	200-400

TENOR HORN IN C

Maker	Model	Serial	Date	Material	Condition	Description	Price
Josef Lidl	bass trumpet		ca. 1895	Br/Ni	good	needs valve work	250
Wenzel	Oval model		ca. 1850	Br		Gs garland and 3 SARV, Bb crooks	750

TROMBONE, ALTO IN E FLAT (valve and slide models)

Maker	Model	Serial	Date	Material	Condition	Description	Price
[Anon.]	Beau Ideal		ca. 1896	Br		BF, PV, water key, also offered in Ni, or Si plate, and with Go plate bell and trim, sold by Lyon & Healy	150-300
[Anon.]			ca. 1897	Br		BF, PV, water key, also offered in Ni or Si plate, sold by Lyon & Healy	250-400
[Anon.]	short model		ca. 1896	Br		BF, BPV, water key, also offered in Ni plate, sold by Lyon & Healy	250-400
[Anon.]	short model		ca. 1896	Br		BF, PV, water key, also offered in Ni, or Si plate, sold by Lyon & Healy	250-400
Goulet	valve		ca. 1893	Br		BF, PV, water key, also offered in Ni, or Si plate, sold by Stratton	150-300

J. Higham	Clear bore		ca. 1896	Br		BF, PV, also offered in triple Si plate, and with Go trim and bell	$250-400
J. Higham	First class		ca. 1896	Br		BF, PV, also offered in triple Si plate, and with Go trim and bell	250-400
F. Jaubert			ca. 1896	Br		BF, PV, water key, also offered in Ni or Si plate	200-300
F. Jaubert			ca. 1896	Br		BF, slide model, water key, also offered in Ni or Si plate	25-75
Martin Bros.			ca. 1879	Br		BF, slide model, also offered in Gs slide, also offered in Gs throughout	250-500
Martin Bros.			ca. 1879	Gs/Br		BF, TARV, also offered in GS throughout	550-1000
Quinby Bros.	valve		ca. 1879	Br		BF, TARV, also offered in Gs	125-250
Stratton	valve		ca. 1893	Br		BF, PV, water key, also offered in Ni, or Si plate	150-300

TROMBONE, BARITONE (valve and slide models)

[Anon.]			ca. 1896	Br		BF, PV, water key, also offered in Ni or Si plate, sold by Lyon & Healy	150-300
[Anon.]	Beau Ideal		ca. 1896	Br		BF, PV, water key, also offered in Ni or Si plate, and with Go plate bell and trim, heavily engraved, sold by Lyon & Healy	125-250
Goulet			ca. 1896	Br		BF, PV, water key, also offered in Ni, or Si plate	150-300
J. Higham	Clear bore		ca. 1896	Br		BF, PV, also offered in triple Si plate, and with Go trim and bell	200-350
J. Higham	First class		ca. 1896	Br		BF, PV, also offered in triple Si plate, and with Go trim and bell	200-350
F. Jaubert			ca. 1896	Br		BF, PV, water key, also offered in Ni or Si plate	150-250
F. Jaubert			ca. 1896	Br		BF, slide model, water key, also offered in Ni plate	25-75
Martin Bros.			ca. 1896	Gs/Br		BF, SARV	450-850

TROMBONE, BASS

Bach	50B	39XXX	1979	Br	very good	BF, slide model, open wrap	1200
Bach	5OB3	50XXX	1981	lacquer	very good	BF, slide model, open wrap, etc.	1000
C.G. Conn	bass	B4XXX		lacquer	very good+	BF, 3 PV, 1 RV	850
John Green			ca. 1835	Br	no slide handle	BF, slide model	512
C.G. Conn	73H	H1XXXX	1966	lacquer	good+	BF, slide model, open wrap, etc.	1100
Jubilee	F bass	none	1971	lacquer	very excellent	BF, slide for G	600
R. Wunderlich	one valve	none	ca. 1900	lacquer	very good	BF, slide model, German style	475
Yamaha	YBL-612R	20XXXX		lacquer	very good+	BF, slide model	950

TROMBONE, SOPRANO

Joseph Higham	Superior class	31XXX	ca. 1870	Br		BF, slide model	936

TROMBONE, TENOR (valve and slide models)

[Anon.]				Br		[BF, PV]	120
[Anon.]			ca. 1896	Br		BF, PV, water key, also offered in Ni or Si plate, sold by Lyon & Healy	150-300
[Anon.]	Beau Ideal		ca. 1896	Br		BF, PV, water key, also offered in Ni or Si plate, and with Go plate bell and trim, heavily engraved, sold by Lyon & Healy	125-250
[Anon.]			ca. 1896	Br		BF, slide model, water key, also offered in Ni or Si plate, and with Go plate bell and trim, sold by Lyon & Healy	50-100
[Anon.]	Beau Ideal		ca. 1896	Br		BF, slide model, water key, also offered in Ni or Si plate, and with Go plate bell and trim, heavily engraved, sold by Lyon & Healy	50-100
[Anon.]	short model		ca. 1896	Br		BF, BPV, water key, also offered in Ni plate, sold by Lyon & Healy	200-400
[Anon.]	All Star			Silver	no spit valve	BF, slide model	35
[Anon.]	American triumph			Br	broken slide	BF, slide model	20
Bach	36B	10XXXX	1984	lacquer	near new	BF, slide model	950
Bach	36B	44XXX	1982	lacquer	very good	BF, slide model	700
Bach	8/12	62XX	ca. 1975	lacquer	very good	BF, slide model, .490" bore	575
F. Besson				Si/Br		BF, PV	200
BMIMC			1869-1874	Br		BF, SARV, also offered in Gs	600-900
BMIMC			1869-1874	Br		BF, slide model, also offered in Gs	200-400
[C. Bruno]	Kleartone			Si		BF, slide model	50
Cerveny		35XXX	ca. 1920	Br/Ni	excellent	tilted BF, RV	575
C.G. Conn		21XXX	1891	Si	valves leak	BF, PV	200
C.G. Conn				Br		BF, slide model	40

Maker	Model	Serial	Date	Material	Condition	Description	Price
C.G. Conn				Si		BF, slide model	$60
C.G. Conn				Si		BF, slide model	75
C.G. Conn	78H	383997	1949	lacquer	good	BF, slide model	350
C.G. Conn	8H	GL470006	1974	lacquer	very good+	BF, slide model	600
Courtois			ca. 1890	Br	fair	BF, slide model	150
Elkhart				Br		BF, slide model	25
Goulet			ca. 1893	Br		BF, PV, water key, also offered in Ni, or Si plate	150-300
Goulet			ca. 1893	Br		BF, slide model, water key, also offered in Ni, or Si plate	50-150
Harwood				Si		BF, slide model	40
J. Higham			ca. 1896	Br		BF, slide model, water key, also offered in triple Si, and with Go trim and bell	75-150
J. Higham	Clear bore		ca. 1896	Br		BF, PV, also offered in triple Si plate, and with Go trim and bell	200-350
J. Higham	First class		ca. 1896	Br		BF, PV, also offered in triple Si plate, and with Go trim and bell	200-350
Holton				Si	patch on slide	BF, slide model	75
Holton				Si	broken slide	BF, slide model	20
Holton				Si	tube loose	BF, slide model	20
Holton	Special			Br		BF, slide model	30
F. Jaubert			ca. 1896	Br		BF, PV, water key, also offered in Ni or Si plate	150-250
F. Jaubert			ca. 1896	Br		BF, slide model, water key, also offered in Ni or Si plate	25-75
King	2B	29XXXX	1948	lacquer	very good	BF, slide model	425
King	2B	37XXXX	1961	lacquer	good	BF, slide model	375
King	3B	70XXXX	1985	lacquer	very good	BF, slide model	475
King	Gardell Simons	20X	ca. 1935	lacquer	very good+	BF, slide model, "Cello-Tons"	250
Eugene La Seuer		11XXXXXXX	ca. 1900	lacquer	good+	[BF, slide model?]	125
Joe. Lidl	in C	12XXX	ca. 1925	Br/Ni	needs work	BF, 4 RV	200
King	flugabone	87XXXX	ca. 1990	Ni/Br	poor	[BF, slide model?]	150
Krumfansl			ca. 1920	Br	good	BF, RV	325
Lebrun	6 valves		ca. 1910	Si/Br		bent body design	5447
A. Lecomte & Co.	in C and B flat		ca. 1879	Br		BF, SARV	250
Mahillon				[Si]	tarnished	[BF, slide model?]	60
Marceau				Br	slide dents	BF, slide model	35
Marceau				Si		[BF, slide model?]	150
Marceau				Si	dents in slide	BF, slide model	25
Martin Bros.			ca. 1879	Br		BF, PV	150-350
Martin Bros.			ca. 1879	Br		BF, SARV or TARV, also offered with Gs throughout	450-750
Martin Bros.			ca. 1879	Gs/Br		BF, SARV, also offered in Gs throughout	450-850
Martin Bros.			ca. 1879	Br		BF, slide model, also offered in Gs throughout	200-400
Martin Bros.	Artist		ca. 1879	Br		BF, slide model, solid bell, water key, also offered with various plated metals	250-500
Martin Bros.	Artist		ca. 1879	Gs/Br		BF, PV or BPV, water key optional	150-350
Meinlschmidt	in C		ca. 1900	Br	very good	BF, RV	375
[Mont.-Ward]	Concertone			Si		BF, slide model	20
[Mont.-Ward]	Concertone			Si	bell dents	BF, slide model	50
[Mont.-Ward]	Sitone			Br	slide broken	BF, slide model	20
Olds	Ambassador			Br		BF, slide model	30
Olds	Golden Bear, M	24XX	ca. 1920	Go/Br	very good	BF, slide model	200+
Olds	Self Balancing	10XXXXXX	ca. 1935	lacquer	good	BF, slide model, 7 1/2 LM	150
Olds	Special	V4X	ca. 1955	lacquer	good+	BF, slide model	200
Olds	Standard	15XXX	ca. 1940	lacquer	good+	BF, slide model, "Tempered Bell"	200
Olds	Standard	16XXX	ca. 1940	Br	good	BF, slide model	150
Olds	Super	38XXXX	1958	Br	good	BF, slide model	225
Pan American				Br		BF, slide model	20
Pan American				Br		BF, slide model	35
Pan American	Cavalier			Br	slide dents	BF, slide model	20
J.W. Pepper				Br	needs clean up	BF, slide model	90
J.W. Pepper	"Surprise"		ca. 1905	Si/Br		BF, 3 PV, highly engraved	225
Prog. MIC	American Artist			Br		BF, slide model	25
Quinby Bros.			ca. 1879	Br		BF, slide model, also offered in Gs	150-400
Quinby Bros.			ca. 1879	Br		BF, TARV, also offered in Gs	400-600
Regent		76X	ca. 1920	Si	good	BF, slide model	95
Schmidt				Br		BF, slide model	20
Carl Schubert				Si	dents	BF, slide model	50
M. Slater			ca. 1874	Br		BF, slide model	250-600
Stratton			ca. 1893	Br		BF, slide model, water key, also offered in Ni or Si plate	50-150
Vega	Standard	22XXX	ca. 1920	Br	good+	BF, slide model	150
Whaley & Royce	1694		ca. 1900	lacquer	valves leak	[BF, slide model?]	225
H.N. White				Si		BF, slide model	30

[H.N. White]	American standard			Br	dented slide	BF, slide model		$20
H.N. White	King			Si		BF, slide model		35
H.N. White	King			Si	slide dents	BF, slide model		40
Windsor				Si		BF, slide model		30
Wurlitzer			ca. 1880	Br	good	BF, slide model, lacquer finish		225
Wurlitzer	lyric			Si		BF, slide model		30
York				Si		BF, slide model		50

TRUMPET IN B FLAT

[Anon.]	Commander			Si	needs work			20
[Anon.]	Supertone			Si				35
[Anon.]	Tone-Crest				slight leak			20
Alexander		48XX	ca. 1950	Br	good	not Gebr. Alex.		75
American Capitol				Br	valve stuck			20
American Diplom		98XXX	ca. 1980	lacquer	excellent			150
Bach	25L	47XXX	1969	Go/Br	very good	plating worn		500
Bach	37	42XXX	1968	lacquer	very good+			650
Benge	pocket	98XXXX	ca. 1990	Si	excellent			625
Besson	MEHA (Kanstul)	78X	ca. 1985	Si	good	crack in bell		350
Besson		88XXX	ca. 1935	Si	very good			750
Besson, French	.461" bore	84XXX	ca. 1930	lacquer	good+			750
Buescher				Si	slide loose			150
Calicchio	2 ML	18XX	1963	Si	very excellent			1100
Calicchio	pocket	17XX	ca. 1962	lacquer	excellent	1 bell		1200
Cantabile	pocket	11	ca. 1980	lacquer	very good+			300
C.G. Conn					valve missing			15
C.G. Conn		24XXXX		Si				45
C.G. Conn		28XXXX		Si				50
C.G. Conn		71XXXX		Br				80
C.G. Conn	18B director	S2XXXX		lacquer	very good			140
C.G. Conn	40A Vocabell	30XXXX	1936	lacquer	good+	plays excellent		375
C.G. Conn	40B Vocabell	29XXXX	1934	lacquer	very good	lacquer worn		350
W. Frank						narrow gauge		45
Getzen	Renaissance	POXXXX	1995	Go/Si	very excellent			600
H.B. Jay				Br				100
King	Super 20 Symph.	31XXXX	1952	lacquer	very good	.468 bore/sterling mouthpip		375
Otto Knoll				Br		RV		300
Martin	Committee	13XXXX	1940	lacquer	very good+			500
[Mont.-Ward]	Sitone, Artist			Si				20
Noblet		12XXX	ca. 1965	lacquer	good+	made by Courtois		250
Ohio Band Co.					missing valve			10
Olds	Recording	26XXXX	1958	lacquer	very good+	orig. lacquer		550
Olds	Recording	40XXXX	1962	lacquer	very good+			550
Olds	Recording	49XXX	ca. 1948	lacquer	very good	lacquer worn		550
Olds	Special	97XXXX	1976	Ni/Br	excellent			225
Olds	Standard	95XX	ca. 1937	lacquer	very good	"Tempered Bell"		275
Olds	Super	18XXX	1947	lacquer	good			325
Olds	Super	15XXX	ca. 1940	lacquer	excellent			475
Olds	Super	60XXX	1950	Br	good+			275
F.E. Olds & Son	Model S-10		ca. 1958			with original guarantee, and case		350
Pan American				Si	stuck valve	narrow gauge		15
Pan American	Cavalier							20
Pan American	Cavalier			Si				45
Schilke	B7	40XX	1969	Si	very good+			750
Karl Schubert				Si				20
Tone Craft				Si				30
[H.N. White]	American Standard			Si				25
[H.N. White]	American Standard			Br		embossed crown		50
R.W. Wunderlich								45
Yamaha	YTR-738	01XXXX	ca. 1980	Si	very excellent	large bore		525
York				Si		RV change		300

TRUMPET B FLAT/A

Beuscher		15XXXX	1923	Go/Si	good+	small bore		200
Beuscher		21XXXX	1927	Si	good	cracks in mouthpipe		150
Buescher	232	25XXXX	1929	lacquer	very good	long skinny		250
Cleveland		11XXXX	1928	Si	very good+			190
Cleveland	Superior	C4XXXX	1940	Si	good			95
C.G. Conn	26B	19XXXX	1922	Si	very good	.456" bore		300
C.G. Conn	22B	19XXXX	1923	Si	good+			275
C.G. Conn	22B	21XXXX	1924	Si	very good+			275
C.G. Conn	22B	21XXXX	1924	Si	good+			250
C.G. Conn	28B	21XXXX	1924	Go/Br	good	lady on bell, worn		350
C.G. Conn	28B	23XXXX	1926	Si	good+	.485" bore, Si worn		325

Maker	Model	Serial	Year	Finish	Condition	Notes	Price
C.G. Conn	22B	26XXXX	1929	lacquer	fair+	plays good	$150
C.G. Conn	22B	28XXXX	1931	Si	good		250
Holton	Collegiate	16XXXX		Si	excellent		175
J.W. Pepper	Imported	26XXX	ca. 1910	Ni/Br	good	shepherds crook	100
Keilwerth	Tone King	56XX	ca. 1950	Si	good+	German made	200
King	Liberty	32XXXX	1951	lacquer	very good		400
King	Liberty	34XXXX	1955	lacquer	good		175
Martin	Imperial	11XXXX	1935	Si	very excellent	orig condition	600
Martin	Imperial	12XXXX		lacquer		large bore, .468"	425
Martin	Committee	20XXXX	1956	Si	excellent		750
Martin	Superlative	86XXX	1927	Go/Br	good	worn	150
Selmer	20	30XX	1939	Br	good	worn, but plays excellent	400
Selmer	22	24XX	1939	lacquer	very good+		550
Selmer	Balanced, 19A	13XXX	1953	Si	very good	some Si wear	850
York	64	76XXX	ca. 1927	lacquer	good	.468" bore, RV change	225

TRUMPET IN C
Aubertin			ca. 1960	lacquer	very good	.452" bore	625
Bach		51XXX	1970	lacquer	very good+		700
Besson, French	MEHA	10XXXX	ca. 1958	Si	excellent		550
Holton	53	37XXXX	1964	lacquer	excellent		375
Thibouville-Lam			ca. 1950	Si	very good	Couesnon	300
Yamaha	YTR-6445HGS	33XXXX	ca. 1990	Si	very excellent		725

TRUMPET IN D
Yamaha	YTR-651	70XXX	ca. 1980	lacquer	excellent	475

TRUMPET IN E FLAT
Benge, Burbank		62XX	ca. 1965	lacquer	very good+		525
Getzen	Deluxe	10XXXX	ca. 1960	lacquer	very good		375
Schilke	E3L	56XX	1972	Si	very good+	Eb bell only	1200

TRUMPET IN E FLAT/D
Benge, Burbank		46XX	ca. 1960	lacquer	very good+	D slide only	475

TRUMPET, CAVALRY AND ARTILLERY
Martin Bros.	in F	ca. 1879	Br	Two rounds, also offered in Gs, and Co, also offered in G with F crooks	50-100

TRUMPET, HERALDIC
[Anon. Pakistan?]	natural	20th cent	Si,Br,Co	three examples, banners	409
C.G. Conn	in Bb	ca. 1960			350

TRUMPET, INFANTRY
Martin Bros.	in C	ca. 1879	Br	One round, also offered in Gs, and Co C trumpets with B crooks made to order	50-100

TRUMPET, KEYED
Charles Pace		ca. 1840	Co & Br	missing the Eb key	2 keys, brass mounts over Co	1362+
Janes Cowlan		ca. 1825	Br	one crook from another instrument	3 keys	3234

TRUMPET, NATURAL
[Anon.]	in Eb		Si	very excellent	425

TRUMPET, PICCOLO
Benge		41XXX	ca. 1983	Si	very excellent	4 valve	700
Getzen	Eterna	BPXXXX	1979	Si	very excellent		675
Getzen	Eterna	BPXXXX	1995	Si	new	4 valve	750
Yamaha	C/Bb	20XX	ca. 1980	Si	very excellent	long model	700

TRUMPET, SLIDE
DEG	Sporty	3x	ca. 1985	lacquer	very good	150
Getzen	delux					350

TRUMPET WITH ROTARY VALVES
[Anon.]		ca. 1890	Br & Ni	abalone buttons	400
[Anon.]		before 1900		string action, large size	1000

TRUMPET [IN ?]
John A. Koehler	2 Shaw valves	ca. 1845	Br	ornate bell garland, includes 4 set pieces	6128

TUBA IN B FLAT
see Bass horn in B flat

TUBA IN E FLAT
see Bass horn in E flat

Glossary

Allen valve: a relatively rare rotary valve invented by J. Lathrop Allen. The valve system is most often found on instruments made in Boston and possibly Philadelphia during the mid-1800s. The valve is easily identified by having a very flat appearance, which requires triangular pieces of tubing between the round pipes and the flatter valves. The valve system appears to be unique to the U.S.

Alto horn: a brasswind instrument most often pitched in E flat, but occasionally pitched in F. Some trade catalogs listed the instrument as a tenor in E flat. The instrument was produced in a number of shapes, including BU, BF, HD, and OTS. A large number of models were produced with the solo model being common. Manufacturers also produced special types of alto horns and marketed them under various names, including amateur voice horn, altophone, mellophone, orchestra horn, voice horn, vocal horn, and Vox horn. Each of these trade names connoted subtle differences that often interfere with identification.

Amateur voice horn: an alternate name for the ballad horn.

Antoniophone: a trade name for an exceptionally rare and uniquely-shaped brasswind family. It was produced under the name parlor horn by Thibouville-Lamy. The family is so rare that very few examples exist, and complete families are only known in collections in England. The Antoniophone was named for Antoine Courtois, its inventor. The distinguishing feature of the Antoniophone is the bell, which descends from the valve cluster in an "S" shape (i.e toward the player, then away). The bell therefore is placed below the valve cluster, but pointing slightly up. An example is found in the Foote section of this book. The CMV for examples of Antoniophones range from $2500 to $3500. Sometimes, examples are confused with the equally rare Königs horn.

Altophone: a trade name for a rare alto horn, pitched in either E flat or F with slide to E flat, invented by Distin. However, Distin called the instrument a melody horn. Others copying this instrument evidently called it an orchestra horn, as it was intended to replace the French horn. Farrar theorizes that Keefer created the name to complete with mellophone, which was used by Conn and also Buescher, for basically the same instrument. A Slater catalog of circa 1880 shows three body designs for the melody horn, being bell up with a circular body (not HD), bell down, and bell up. The instrument is otherwise shaped like a French horn with piston valves. Slides for E natural, D natural, and C could be had.

Back fire instruments: an alternate term for over the shoulder design for instruments (OTS).

Ballad horn: a trade name for a rare brasswind instrument invented by Henry Distin. The instrument is also called the amateur voice horn. The diameter of the bell was somewhere between 6 and 8 inches. The instrument, pitched in C, is pitched between the alto horn and the French horn. Amateur musicians could therefore play the top line of piano music without transposing. The instrument was most popular sometime between 1860 and 1900. It is shaped much like a small French horn (i.e. circular body), with the bell pointing either up, or down. An example appears in *NGDMM* Vol. 2, page 79. The instrument is not to be confused with the even rarer König's horn. As late as possibly the 1920's C.G. Conn Ltd. offered a ballad horn pitched in C with crooks to B flat.

Bass horn: a single term with two definitions. The first definition is for rare, obsolete brasswind instrument with a "V" shaped metal body, 6 finger holes, 3 or 4 keys, and pitched in C. It was invented around 1790, and was used in England before the invention of valve systems. The instrument is related to the serpent. The second, more generic definition for this term is the class of all brasswind instruments that are the lowest pitched members of this family. Instruments of this class include Sousaphones, tubas, etc.

BB: a means of identifying a contrabass horn in B flat.

Bell: the flaring end of a musical instrument from which sound emanates. The flare of the bell is very important, as it helps identify the type of instrument and its age. For example, early cornets tend to have a slow flare (producing a rather fat looking instrument), much like that found on keyed bugles. Later cornets tend to have a more pronounced flare (producing a slim looking instrument). Bells are generally where important information is often found. Multiple-belled instruments exist, and are uncommon, especially the double bell euphonium. Such instruments are quite collectible.

Bell back: see Over the shoulder design (OTS).

Berliner pumpen valve (BPV): a type of valve that is most common on instruments manufactured in Germany. It is characterized by a stubby piston, that might otherwise look like a Périnet valve. See illustration of valve types, p. 23.

Body length: the measurement from the bell straight back to the mouthpiece. Often, such a measurement is subjective. To prevent confusion, an explanation of what was measured is of value. This measurement is not be confused with the measurement of the entire windway. Measuring the windway is usually only important to scholars. The body length, however, helps in identifying the approximate size of the instrument.

BPV: Berliner pumpen valves

Bombardon: an obscure term found in this book only associated with bass horns in the Lyon & Healy catalog. Presumably this term means here a large bass horn. The term has a very complex history, and has been applied to a number of bass instruments.

Bore size: the diameter of the internal wind way of a brass instrument. Bore size will obviously increase the further away the wind way is from the mouthpiece. Specialists will often be very interested in the amount that the bore flares out and where. The bore can sometimes help to differentiate a cornet from a trumpet (after 1920). Different diameters impart different playing features. As a generality, smaller bores are found on an instrument that plays better in the upper register, but might lack volume. Larger bores are found on instruments that play better in the lower registers, and will have increased volume. Instruments with a bore between the two will generally have a mellower tone. Measuring bore size is generally only done by specialists who have the required tools and expertise. Experts should also look for oval bores on instruments equipped with rotary valves.

Brace: a small solid metal bar that connects adjacent tubes. Braces are protected from piercing the tubes by a mount that might be a circular piece of metal soldered onto the tubing. The purpose of braces is to add stability and strength to parts of brass instruments that might otherwise suffer damage.

Bugle: a brass instrument traditionally made without valves. The instrument might have one, two, or three rounds or bends in its tubing. The instrument is rarely offered in any specific pitch in the trade catalogs, as it is meant to be used in non-musical settings. Despite various body designs (see the Lyon & Healy catalog), these instruments today sell for about $50.00. The keyed bugle evolved from this instrument. Keyed bugles are described further in this glossary.

Burnished: a finishing technique characterized by a highly polished surface.

C attachment: see crooks.

CMV: an abbreviation for current market value (in U.S. dollars), as best as it can be determined. In this book, current market valves are given for instruments that require little or no repairs, and are otherwise complete, unless otherwise stated. Though condition is very important, brass instruments of a non-historical nature can often be repaired without altering their value. Historical instruments should never be repaired, without first consulting an expert. Repairing an historical instrument could destroy most of its value.

Composite instrument: an instrument assembled from parts made by various manufacturers. Often, these instruments are assembled by cannibalizing parts, especially from older, damaged instruments. Thus,

the bell could be French, the valve cluster could be German, and the braces, could be U.S. This instrument is often of little value to collectors, but might play quite well. The intention here is to create a playable instrument, not to defraud a potential buyer. The distinction is often rather arbitrary. See also copy and forgery. A second type of composite instrument also exists. Toward the end of the nineteenth century, people obtained parts from various sources, such as the manufacturer, and assembled instruments, which were then stamped with the jobber's name. These instruments are often a puzzlement to specialists, and are collectible, but do not regularly sell for high prices.

Contrabass: A term used inconsistently in the trade literature to indicate a bass instrument with an extra wide bore, or an overlarge bass instrument in general. For this book, such instruments are designated with double letters. Bass horn in BB flat here indicates a contrabass horn in B flat. This abbreviation is not uniformly used in current literature.

Copy: a faithful recreation of an original instrument, in which the person who made the new instrument provides his/her name. No deception is intended in the construction of that instrument. Altering a copy can constitute a forgery. See forgery, and fake.

Cornet: a 19th century predecessor of the trumpet, and more commonly used during the 1800s. In fact, the trumpet was disdained. Typically, the cornet is somewhat more compact, with a circular "shepherd's crook" tube below the mouthpiece. Later, the cornet was modified to look like the trumpet. Identifying these instruments will require an expert. However, after about 1940, cornets became obsolete, only to recently reappear.

Cornopean: an early type of brass instrument, generally pitched in B flat, and traditionally made with Stoelzel valves. Very few (if any?) U.S. makers produced this instrument. The cornopean began to disappear about 1850, during which time, the Périnet valve became popular. A few cornopeans were made with Shaw valves, especially in England. Because of the beauty of this valve type, these instruments tend to command higher prices than other cornopeans of similar quality, and condition.

Crook: a term often applied to curved, detachable tubing that can alter the key of a brass instrument. Crooks were invented before valves to alter key, and retained, especially for cornets, to transpose an instrument. Crooks are also found with concert horns (also called natural horns, resembling a French horn without valves). Concert horns with all its crooks are quite rare. For cornets, crooks (and shanks) existed that lowered or raised the pitch, depending upon the length of the crook. See also shank.

Echo attachment: an extra set of tubing usually applied to B flat cornets (often sold separately) that, according to the Foote catalog of 1893, "is capable of producing the most astonishing effects, from the softest pianissimo, hardly above a whisper, to any degree of power desired. The amateur and pupil have in this cornet one on which they can practice without disturbing sensitive neighbors." When the attachment is built into the instrument, depressing a fourth valve, found on the attachment, is required to produce the special effects described. Otherwise, simply inserting the attachment will be enough.

EE flat: a means of identifying a contrabass horn in E flat.

Euphonium: a term that has various historical uses. For the time period covered by this book, the term is used for baritone-range instruments with a conical bore, which produces a unique tone quality. The main bell of a double bell euphonium traditionally points up. The smaller bell might point forward, to the side, or even up. Both single and double bell instruments might have three or four valves. Some instruments have the fourth valve placed to the side of the instrument.

Fake: a musical instrument that has been altered or constructed to look like something else with the intention of selling it as an original. Brass instruments are rarely subjected to this indignity. See also composite instrument.

Fantasy instrument: a musical instrument that is much like a stage prop. It is usually designed to look fanciful or improbable, but might well be a playable instrument. Historic instruments of this type can be described as pageant instruments. At one time, the band that marched in the Disneyland parades included a trombone with seven bells, only one of which was functional.

Finger hole: see tone hole.

Forgery: an instrument either newly constructed or assembled from historic parts with the intention of deceiving someone into thinking the new instrument is something else. See composite, copy, and fake. See Franciolini.

Franciolini: one of the most famous musical instrument forger. During the 1800s, he sold legitimate antique musical instruments. However, he also ordered copies of instruments and altered them. He is best known, however, for taking fragments of antique instruments and combining them to create instruments that for the most part are quite unplayable. Virtually every musical instrument museum owns (or has owned) one of his forgeries, and will deny owning them.

French light action piston valve: an improvement of the Périnet-style valve, invented ca. 1870s. Most easily distinguished by its long profile, having two parts. One part is slightly bulbous above another section that is purely cylindrical, where the tubes enter the valves. This valve system was described as superior to all other valve systems when it was invented. For this book, abbreviated as PV.

German silver (Gs): a non-precious metal composed largely of nickel, but having an appearance of silver, if somewhat duller than silver. German silver has a tendency to produce a green surface after years of not being cared for. The metal contains no silver.

German piston valves: synonymous with Berliner pumpen valves (BPV).

HD: Helicon design.

Helicon: a term used mainly prior to the 1900s to designate a circular style of brass wind instrument design, not to be confused with a Sousaphone. The helicon style was especially useful in marching bands. The bells of helicon-style basses generally follows the curve of the instrument, pointing to the musician's left side. To the uneducated eye, the HD is suggestive of a Sousaphone. As late as circa 1920, Conn still offered E flat and BB flat helicon basses.

Hertz: the means of measuring pitch, such as inches can be used to measure distances. The higher the Hertz (often abbreviated Hz), the higher the pitch.

Horn: both a generic and a specific term. The term has ancient usage. Musicians might call any instrument a horn, as a slang term. More discerning persons might call just brasswind instruments a horn. Specifically, the term horn refers to all instruments that resemble a circular hunting horn, not just a French horn. In this book, the term is often joined with others to clearly identify an instrument; ex. Bass horn in B flat.

HP or high pitch: stamped on wind instruments to indicate high pitch. That is to say, approximating A=457 Hz. LP indicates low pitch approximating A=440 Hz. These designations were used between about 1880 and 1920. HP and LP are not makers marks.

Jobber: see Manufactured instruments.

Keefer valve system: a fictitious valve system. Farrar states that Keefer used Distin's valve design (which was a modified RV) rather than inventing a new valve system. As such, no Keefer valve system exists, despite statements to the contrary in some trade catalogs.

Key: not to be confused with the pitch of an instrument. A key (or touch key, or lever) is a mechanical device attached to an instrument, that, when touched, either closes or opens a pad over a tone hole. On brass instruments, touch keys are found mainly on keyed bugles and ophicleides. During the early 1800's some instruments were equipped with both valves, and keys. Such examples are quite rare.

Keyed bugle: a brass instrument without valves. Instead, the instrument, whose invention is credited to Joseph Haliday, has six to twelve keys. The instrument fell out of favor when valves were finally invented, and does not appear in trade catalogs of the time covered in this book, if ever. Keyed bugles are highly collected. Even unsigned instruments command interest, depending on condition. Many keyed bugles are museum pieces.

Königs horn: a trade name for an extremely rare brasswind instrument pitched in F, with PV. Courtois was the only one to make this instrument, and stamped "Königs horn" on each example. The Königs horn is a large ballad horn in use and structure. It was meant to be played by a soloist. The Königs horn is acoustically much like a French horn. The Königs horn came with many transposing crooks. Its CMV is at least $2000, depending upon condition, and the number of extant slides.

LP or Low pitch: stamped on wind instruments to indicate low pitch. That is to say, approximating A=440 Hz. HP indicates high pitch approximating A=457 Hz. These designations were used between about 1880 and 1920. HP and LP are not makers marks.

Maker: a loosely-used term to designate one who makes musical instruments either in his own shop or occasionally in a factory. However, the distinction blurs when discussing a factory owner, who might not know how to construct an instrument. The preferred term here would be a manufacturer. The only important distinction here is that a maker will rarely be able to produce as many instruments as a manufacturer. Though the maker will tend to be more flexible in the special features applied to an instrument, and quality will be more of an issue.

Manufactured instruments: an instrument constructed in a factory using standard parts, and molds. Manufactured instruments will look basically the same. Hand-made instruments are said to be "made" not manufactured. Manufactured instruments are generally not inferior to hand made instruments, just not unique. Often manufactured instruments are composed of parts constructed by other people, called jobbers or subcontractors. These jobbers often supplied parts from their own factories to many manufacturers, confusing identification.

Mellophone: a trade name for an alto brasswind instrument sold by Conn and Buescher. Today, the name is often used for marching alto horns, and is intended to be a substitute for the French horn. The bell generally points forward or occasionally points down, and has a diameter suggestive of a French horn. See alto horn.

Melody horn: a trade name for an alto brasswind instrument, pitched in E flat or F. Instruments pitched in F came with an E flat slide. This name was first used by Distin. The instrument substituted for the French horn, and is pitched an octave above the French horn. The bell is strongly suggestive of a French horn. The basic bell dimension of the melody is between 8 and 11 inches, while the alto Saxhorn is closer to 6 inches in diameter. The bell dimension of the ballad horn (pitched in C) is between the two instruments. Otherwise, the melody horn looks much like a circular alto horn. Besson and Courtois (both French manufacturers) produced this instrument with the bell pointing up. This variant is extremely rare. Occasionally this type of melody horn was called the voice horn, vocal horn, or Vox horn in the trade literature. This instrument is not to be confused with the Ballad horn. M. Slater, in a catalog of circa 1880 offered both of the above-mentioned types and a third type, which was a Saxhorn design, but with a very large bell.

Mount: a small piece of metal that reinforces or otherwise strengthens sections of an instrument. Braces often attach to mounts. Some makers heavily ornamented the mounts of the most expensive instruments, often applying a gold wash.

Mouthpiece: a metal bell or cup-shaped device, used on brasswind instruments, into which one places one's lips and produces a buzzing sound. Less often, a mouthpiece might be made of animal horn, ivory, wood, or ceramic. Experimental types have been made of virtually every hard substance. The mouthpiece has enjoyed considerable experimentation, resulting in people who only collect mouthpieces. The mouthpiece is manufactured so that it can be inserted and removed (or lost) from an instrument. Without a mouthpiece, brass instruments are quite unplayable.

NGDMM: New Grove Dictionary of Music and Musicians.

Orchestra horn: an altophone (Keefer's trade name for an alto horn), which came with slides for E flat, D, C, and B flat. The inclusion of the slides evidently differentiated this instrument from the altophone.

OTS: over the shoulder design.

Over the shoulder design (OTS): also called back fire, and American Military Band Style. A body design whereby the bell of the brass instrument in playing position rests over the shoulder of the player. This design appears to be unique to the U.S. and was most popular during the Civil War. Though such instruments were sold as late as the 1880's. The advantage of this design is that troops marching behind the band,

can hear the music. Because of the design, Périnet style valves are impractical. Either top action rotary valves (TARV) or side action rotary valves (SARV) are to be expected on these instruments.

Pad: generally a round piece of soft material (such as leather) that appears mainly on woodwind instruments, and forms a seal over a tone hole when a key is activated. Pads are also found on keyed bugles and ophicleides.

Périnet valve: the most common type of valve found on brass instruments. The valve looks like a piston with four tubes or pipes attached to it; abbreviated in this book as PV. Originally, the Périnet valve was longer and thinner than the Berliner valve, which it replaced. Around 1880, a second type of Périnet-style valve was invented, called the "Light action valve." Its most identifiable difference from the earlier valve style is that the light action valve is longer than the earlier style.

Pig tail shank: an extra piece of tubing inserted between the mouthpiece and the instrument, that lowers the instrument's key. The shank has a single round or turn of tubing, and is suggestive of a pig tail. Such shanks were often offered with B flat cornets.

Post horn: a small brass instrument dating from at least the Renaissance, with one or more turns of tubing. Traditionally, it did not have valves, and was only a signaling instrument, with limited musical uses. It was most often carried by a mail carrier, and used to indicate the delivery of a letter. The instrument was especially popular in the Germanic countries. In the 19th century, some instruments were made with valves.

Presentation instrument: a brass instrument either made specially for a specific event, or for a specific person. Presentation instruments are almost always highly engraved, with the name of the person receiving the instrument, and often the date of the presentation. These instruments often reflect the highest quality that a company can produce. Some of these instruments are even made of solid silver, with precious stones, or even more rarely made of solid gold. These are surely the most highly prized instruments from this time period.

Push-rod valve system: a rotary valve system that incorporates features of a piston valve system. In this system, a rod descends from the touch piece to a rotary valve. Isaac Fiske was a U.S. manufacturer who produced instruments with this valve system, as seen in this book. These instruments are quite collectible.

PV: Périnet-style valve system. See also French light action piston valve.

Rotary valve: a valve commonly found on French horns, and occasionally found on trombones. This valve is a relatively large, flat valve whereby the wind is diverted using a turning motion, instead of the normal up-and-down motion, as found in the Périnet valve.

SARV: side action rotary valve system.

Sackbut: a brasswind family dating from at least the end of the Renaissance. The instrument is characterized by having a narrow bore, narrow bell (which flares out only slightly), and no water key in historical instruments. Reproductions exist and are sought by performers. Praetorius, and others use the German "Posaun" when discussing members of this instrument family, ranging from an alto to a quart [bass].

Satin finish: an ornamental finish, suggestive of satin, easiest to see on the bell of instruments. The finish was created by sandblasting, and was cheaper than a burnished finish.

Saxhorn: a design for brass instruments created in 1844 by Adolphe Sax, that has become somewhat a standard in brass design today. The design is sometimes called bell up, with the largest members of this family generically called tubas. Valves are either Périnet, or rotary. The mouthpiece is placed to the side of the bell. The early design had a straight pipe across the top of the instrument, as found here in some of D.C. Hall's instruments.

Serial number: a number stamped into the instrument at the time of construction. Serial numbers help in dating instruments, with lower numbers occurring before larger numbers. Not all manufacturers used serial numbers. Smaller shops tended to put serial numbers on the bell of an instrument. Larger shops tended to put serial numbers on the valve cluster. Serial numbers will rarely consist of a single number. Single numbers found on valve clusters usually indicate the individual valve.

Serpent: the bass member of a wooden musical instrument family that dates from the Renaissance. Traditionally, the serpent is made of wood, covered with leather, and never had valves. The instrument has finger holes, some or all of which are covered by keys and levers. The instrument can be ascribed to the brass family, as it has a mouthpiece that looks much like present brass mouthpieces. Serpent mouthpieces, however, were often made of ivory or bone. The instrument's name is indicative of its general shape, being quite snake-like. This instrument was only one of a very few bass wind instruments to precede the invention of the valve. It was regularly used in marching bands, and concert music even after the invention of valve systems. Serpents are quite rare, and command extremely high prices at auction.

Set piece: a term found in trade catalogs that evidently describes the shank, and crooks (either or both). These tubes generally lower the pitch or key of an instrument.

Shank: a straight piece of tubing that was commonly used on cornets to lower the instruments' pitch. Shanks fit between the mouthpiece and the body of the instrument. Shanks can even be inserted into other shanks to further lower the instrument's pitch. Shanks are not rare, but are collectible, especially as they were often lost or damaged. See also crook.

Side action (SARV): the levers that activate the rotary valves are arranged so that the levers are placed sideways relative to the instrument's playing position, as opposed to top action.

Signal horn: a free reed instrument with Périnet-like valves, and is made with one or more bells. The mouthpiece may be a permanent part of the body. The instrument has been called a "Schalmei," which is a name for an older instrument. In 1988, Bleckblas-und Signal-Instrumenten-Fabrik was manufacturing 9 sizes of this instrument. It was previously made by Martin in Markneukirchen, Germany.

Solo alto: a term loosely applied to designate the E flat alto with its bell pointing forward. However, it appears to also indicates a finer quality of alto instruments.

Square valve: a rare valve system in use between circa 1816 to 1828. Johann Heinrich Stölzel is thought to have created a square valve ca. 1816. This system often leaked, and was subsequently replaced by piston valve systems. Several attempts were made at creating a square valve. However, none were totally successful, as they too leaked. Instruments made with square valves tend to be extremely valuable.

Sousaphone: a bass brass instrument whose invention is credited to John P. Sousa. His bass, also called the "rain catcher," has a bell that points directly up. This model, according to Farrar was first offered by Pepper circa 1892-3. Sousa's instrument was itself based upon a helicon design bass. The bell forward Sousaphone, the model that is currently in common use, has a bell that points forward. This model was first offered circa 1906-8? Sousa used the Bell forward bass for only a short while, and reportedly came to greatly dislike it, as he preferred the bass sound to come from above the band, not directly out from it. Both Pepper and Conn claimed to have made the first Sousaphone.

Stage instrument: a basically non-functional object that looks like a musical instrument, but was designed to be used during a theatrical production, such as an opera. See fantasy instrument.

Stencilled instrument: any type of musical instrument that bears a name intended to imply that it was made by a person or company, though the instrument was manufactured by someone else. Sometimes these instruments were intended to be sold by reputable music retailers, who wanted to offer a less expensive instrument, or offer instruments with their name on the instrument. Some specialists believe, with little proof, that Lyon & Healy's instruments are such instruments. However, stencil instruments are more commonly known as cheap imitations of quality instruments, often with names applied that imitate a famous name. Stencil instruments were especially known in the keyboard industry, where a jobber would order parts from various parts manufacturers, and then assemble the instrument. Eventually, the entire process became impossibly muddled, as reputable manufacturers stopped constructing every element in their factory. Lists of such brass instrument stencillers can be found in *NLI*, and similar books listed in the bibliography. See fake, and forgery.

Stölzel valve: invented by Johann Heinrich Stölzel. Though he invented (and co-invented) several valve systems, he is best known for a valve system that appears to be a piston, except that tubing passes in the side and out the bottom of the piston. Instruments that used this valve system were made between circa 1814 and 1916. This valve system persisted because it was inexpensive to make. Subsequently, toward the end of the 19th century, student grade instruments were made with this valve system. Instruments from the earlier part of the century are worth much more than the later instruments.

Subcontractor: see Manufactured instrument.

TARV: top action rotary valve system.

Tone hole: a hole in the body of a wind instrument. By either closing or opening such a hole, the instrument produces a different pitch. Often the tone hole is called a finger hole, and is not to be confused with an embouchure hole, which is found only on flutes.

Top action (TARV): a rotary valve system where the levers that activate the rotary valves are arranged above the valves relative to the instrument's playing position, as opposed to side action. See the section of this book that illustrates valve actions.

Trumpet: a term originally meaning a thin, straight brasswind instrument, with a mouthpiece, and no valves. Toward the end of the Middle Ages, various types of bends were added to shortened the instrument. The Herald trumpet dates from this time. Rare baroque examples might contain finger holes. During the early 1800s, instruments were fitted with keys, valves or both. Trumpets equipped with keys are rare. Trumpets with both keys and valves date from a very limited time period (circa 1850's) and are still rarer. The basic difference between the trumpet and the cornet is that the trumpet has a cylindrical bore, while the cornet has a conical bore resulting in a different tone color. Otherwise, the instruments are basically the same. After about 1920, the two instruments all but merged. Trumpets pitched in B flat are the most common types. Other pitches also exist, including bass trumpets in F, which are rare, and piccolo trumpets, with four valve versions preferred by many performers.

Tuba: a term not used here, as it was not used with any uniformity in the trade catalogs excerpted for this book. Bass horn is the preferred term here.

Tuning slide: a tube that can be pushed in or pulled out to adjust pitch. On modern brass instruments, one tuning slide is commonly found with each valve. These tuning slides appear where the tubing bends back toward a valve, i.e. where the tubing forms a U shape. A fourth tuning slide, not associated with the valves, is used to tune the entire instrument. Knobs, or some other device, are commonly attached to the tuning slide so it can be easily held in one's fingers. Lack of tuning slides or knobs on an instrument implies either an early construction date, or the instrument is of inferior quality.

Valve: a concept invented during the early 1800s that diverts the wind way of an instrument, either shortening or lengthening the wind way. Prior to its invention, brass instruments had tuning slides, occasionally finger holes, the performers' embouchure, and the hand placed in the bell to create different pitches. The valve might be singular or multiple, with three valves being most common. More than one valve assembled into a unit can be called a valve cluster. Many types of valves exist, with Périnet being the most common. Several types of rotary valves are also found. Less common are Berliner pumpen valves, and Vienna valves. Many other rare valve types also exist, such as Stölzel, and Shaw. Owing to the importance of valves, their condition is critical. Repairing or replacing valve clusters can exceed the cost of an inexpensive instrument. See pp. 23-24 of this book, and *NGDMM*, vol 19, p. 513 for illustrations of various valve systems.

Vienna valves: an elaborate type of valve that has double cylinders. Such valves are most often found on large brass instruments. Early instruments with Vienna valves are rare. Bates in *NGDMM* (page 514) states that this valve is still in limited production.

Vocal horn: an alternate name for an extremely rare form of the melody horn.

Voice horn: an alternate name for an extremely rare form of the melody horn.

Vox horn: an alternate name for an extremely rare form of the melody horn.

Water key: later called a spit valve. This is a small key that is only used to remove condensation from a brass instrument. Instruments without water keys tend to be a problem to play. Early brass instruments often did not have such keys. Toward the end of the 19th century, the better quality instruments had at least one water key.

Wind way: for wind instruments, this is the entire length of the tubing through which the wind would pass if no valves or other forms of diversion are considered. For instruments with multiple bends (such as trumpets), one measures from where the mouthpiece attaches to the instrument, through the valve cluster (but not including the tubing of the actual valves), and ending with the bell. Taking such a measurement is of value, but owning to the difficulty in doing this task accurately, the length of the wind way is only taken for very detailed scholarly work. Measuring the wind way should only be done with great care and a bendable measuring device that does not stretch, or scratch the instrument.

Zobophone: a family of wind instruments related to the kazoo. That is to say, any valves or slides are usually only decorative. Zobophones, and similar instruments are made either of cardboard or tin. Zobophones were sold mainly by Lyon & Healy. Similar instruments were sold by other companies under names like "Vocophone" or "Marxophone." Some companies manufactured these instruments to look roughly like Saxhorns, trombones, or cornets. Often these instruments are larger than similar toys made today. These kazoos were intended for use in burlesque and vaudeville productions. Examples of these instruments are not common, as they were rarely well made. Even so, few (if any) people collect these instruments. No scholarly information seems to exist for this ephemeral type of instrument.

Bibliography

Altman, Sylvia. *A Historical Study on the Horns and Trumpets.* 83, [3] l. Thesis (M.A.)—Columbia University, 1933. OCLC #4388314

Ayars, Christine Merrick. *Contributions to the art of music in America by the Music Industries of Boston, 1640-1936.* New York: H.W. Wilson Company, 1937. xv, 326 p. Discusses musical instrument manufacturers in Boston. LC CALL NUMBER: ML200.8.B7 A8. Microfilm: Ann Arbor, Mich.: University Microfilm International, [19—]. OCLC #22049162

Bahnert, Heinz, Theodor Herzberg, and Herbert Schramm. *Metallblasinstrumente.* Wilhelmshaven: Heinrichshofen, 1986. 250 p. ISBN 3-7959-0466-8.

Baines, Anthony. *Brass instruments, Their History and Development.* London: Faber & Faber, 1976. 302 p.

Baines, Anthony. *European and American Musical Instruments.* London: Batsford, 1966. x, 174 p. front., illus. (incl. music) 112 plates, diagrs. 30 1/2 cm. LC CALL NUMBER: ML460.B13

Baines, Anthony, ed. *Musical Instruments Through the Ages.* New ed. New York: Walker, 1976, c1961. 344 p., [16] leaves of plates: ill.; 24 cm. LC CALL NUMBER: ML460.B14 1976

Barbour, James Murry. *Trumpets, Horns and Music.* [East Lansing, Mich.]: Michigan State University, 1964. xii, 190 p. OCLC #564041

Barclay, R. L. *The Art of the Trumpet-Maker: the Materials, Tools, and Techniques of the Seventeenth and Eighteenth Centuries in Nuremberg.* Oxford [England]: Clarendon Press; New York: Oxford University Press, 1992. xi, 186 p.: ill., map; 26 cm. LC CALL NUMBER: ML961.B37 1992

Bate, Philip. *The Trumpet and Trombone: an Outline of their History, development and construction.* London: Benn, 1966. New York: Norton, 1966. xvi, 272 p. OCLC #907114

Berner, Alfred. *Preservation & Restoration of Musical Instruments: provisional recommendations.* London: Evelyn, Adams & Mackay, 1967. [6], 77 p. illus. 25 cm. LC CALL NUMBER: ML460.B33

Brussels. Conservatoire royal de musique. *Musee Instrumental. Catalogue Descriptif & Analytique du Musee Instrumental du Conservatoire Royal de Musique de Bruxelles.* Gand: A. Hoste, 1893-1900. 3 v. illus. 20 cm. LC CALL NUMBER: ML462.B91

Canadian Centre for Folk Culture Studies. *The CCFCS Collection of Musical Instruments.* Ottawa: National Museums of Canada, 1982-1984. 3 v.: ill.; 28 cm. LC CALL NUMBER: ML462.O85 C3 1982

The Collection of Musical Instruments. Tachikawa-shi, Tokyo, Japan: Kunitachi College of Music Research Institute, c1986. 319 p.: ill. (some col.); 27 cm. LC CALL NUMBER: ML462.T64 K82 1986

Coover, James. *Musical Instrument Collections: Catalogues and Cognate Literature.* Detroit: Information Coordinators, 1981. 464 p.; 24 cm. LC CALL NUMBER: ML155.C63 ALSO ML30.4b no. 2395 Miller

Crane, Frederick. *Extant Medieval Musical Instruments; a Provisional Catalogue by types.* Iowa City: University of Iowa Press [1972] xiv, 105 p. illus. 24 cm. LC CALL NUMBER: ML465.C72

Dahlquist, Reine. *The Keyed Trumpet and its Greatest Virtuoso, Anton Weidiger.* Nashville: Brass Press, [1975]. vi, 25 p. Brass research series; no. 1. OCLC #1418894

Diagram Group. *Musical Instruments of the World: an Illustrated encyclopedia.* New York: Paddington Press, c1976. 320 p.: ill.; 29 cm. LC CALL NUMBER: ML102.I5 D5

Dudgeon, Ralph Thomas. *The Keyed Bugle: Its History, Literature, and Technique.* Ph.D. dissertation. University of California, San Diego, 1980. (Xerox copy. Ann Arbor: University Microfilm International).

Dullat, Günther. *Blasinstrumente und Deutsche Patentschriften 1877-1970 Metallblasinstrument 1.* [Nauheim: the Author, 1985].

Dundas, Richard J. *Twentieth Century Brass Musical Instruments in the United States.* [Rutland, Vt.]: R.J. Dundas; Cincinnati, Ohio: Distributed by Queen City Brass Publications, c1986. x, 58 p.: ill.; 28 cm. LC CALL NUMBER: ML933.D86 1986

Eliason, Robert. *Early American Brass Makers. Brass Research Series: No. 10.* Stephen L. Glover, Editor. Nashville: Brass Press, 1979. 55 p.

Eliason, Robert. *Keyed Bugles in the United States. (Smithsonian Studies in History and Technology, 19.)* Washington, D.C.: Smithsonian Institution, 1972. 44 p.

Galpin, Francis William. *The Sackbut, its Evolution and History: Illustrated by an Instrument of the Sixteenth Century.* [London?: Musical Association, 1906.] 25 p., 3 leaves Extracted from: Proceedings of the Musical Association, thirty-third session, 1906-1907. Also discusses the trombone. OCLC #24102764

Garofalo, Robert Joseph and Mark Elrod. *A Pictorial History of Civil War Era Musical Instruments & Military Bands.* Charleston, W.Va.: Pictorial Histories Pub. Co., c1985. viii, 116 p.: ill. (some col.); 28 cm. + 1 sound disc (analog, 33 1/3 rpm, stereo.; 7 in.) LC CALL NUMBER: ML1311.4.G33 1985 <Phon Case>

Germanisches Nationalmuseum Nurnberg. *Instrumentenkataloge des Germanischen Nationalmuseums Nurnberg.* Wilhelmshaven; Hamburg; Locarno; Amsterdam: Heinrichshofen, 1979- v.: ill.; 30 cm. LC CALL NUMBER: ML462.N9 G45

Great Britain. *Patent Office. Patents for Inventions: Abridgements of Specifications Relating to Music and Musical Instruments, A.D. 1694-1866.* London: T. Bingham, 1984. xiv, 520 p. Facsim of second edition: London: Eyre and Spottiswoode, 1871. Includes index. OCLC #15223056

Griffith, Janet Entwise. *The Slide trumpet in the Early Renaissance.* 90 l. Thesis (Dr. of Musical Arts)—University of Cincinnati, 1992. OCLC #27926291

Heyde, Herbert. *Historische Musikinstrumente der Staatlichen Reka-Sammlung am Bezirksmuseum Viadrina Frankfurt (Oder).* 1. Aufl. Wiesbaden: Breitkopf & Härtel, 1989. 208 p., 96 p. of plates: ill. (some col.); 25 cm. LC CALL NUMBER: ML462.F83 B53 1989

Heyde, Herbert. *Musikinstrumentenbau: 15.-19. Jahrhundert: Kunst, Handwerk, Entwurf. 1. Aufl.* Wiesbaden: Breitkopf & Härtel, 1986. 305 p.: ill. (some col.); 28 cm. LC CALL NUMBER: ML460.H5 1986

Heyde, Herbert. *Das Ventilblasinstrument: seine Entwicklung im deutschsprachigen Raum von den Anfängen bis zur Gegenwart.* Leipzig: VEB Deutscher Verlag für Musik, 1987. 310 p. OCLC #18537752

Heyer, Wilhelm. *Musikhistorisches Museum Leipzig.* Kommissionsverlag von Breitkopf & Härtel, 1910- v. fronts., illus. (incl. music) plates, facsims. (part fold., incl. music) 25 cm. LC CALL NUMBER: ML138.M39

Holz- und Metallblasinstrumente : Zeitschrift für Instrumentenbau, 1881-1945. Edited by Günter Dullat. Siegburg: Verlag der Instrumentenbau-Zeitschrift, 1986. 256 p. [A collection of articles originally published in Instrumentenbau Zeitschrift between 1884 and 1940.] OCLC #17551870

Horniman Museum and Library, London. *The Adam Carse Collection of Old Musical Wind Instruments.* London: London County Council [1951] p. cm. LC CALL NUMBER: ML462.L6 H58

Instrumentenbau Zeitschrift. Konstanz a. B.: [n.d.] v. in illus. 31 cm. Periodical. LC CALL NUMBER: ML5.I57

International Directory of Musical Instrument Collections. Buren (Gld.), Netherlands: Frits Knuf for International Council of Museums (ICOM), 1977. ix, 166 p.; 23 cm. LC CALL NUMBER: ML12.I57

Keays, James Harvey. *An investigation into the Origins of the Wagner Tuba.* vii, 90 l. Thesis (D.M.A.)—University of Illinois at Urbana-Champaign, 1977. Microfilm: Ann Arbor, Mich.: Micro-films International, 1987. OCLC #26809431

Mahillon, Victor Charles. *Instruments á vent : le Trombone, son Historie, sa Théorie, sa Construction.* Bruxelles: Mahillon & Co., [1906]. 44 p. At head of title: Les instruments de musique au Musée du Conservatoire Royal de Musique de Bruxelles. OCLC #1939182

Marcuse, Sibyl. *Musical Instruments: a Comprehensive Dictionary. Corr. ed.* New York: Norton, 1975. xii, 608 p. 20 cm. LC CALL NUMBER: ML102.I5 M37 1975

Metropolitan Museum of Art (New York, N.Y.). *American Musical Instruments in the Metropolitan Museum of Art.* New York: The Museum: Norton, c1985. 224 p.: ill. (some col.); 29 cm. LC CALL NUMBER: ML476.M47 1985

Metropolitan Museum of Art (New York, N.Y.). Dept. of Musical Instruments. *A Checklist of American Musical Instruments.* New York: The Department, c1989. 48 p.: ill.; 22 cm. LC CALL NUMBER: ML462.N5 M48 1989

Meyers, Arnold. *Edinburgh University Collection of Historic Musical Instruments. Historic Musical Instruments in the Edinburgh University Collection : Catalogue of the Edinburgh University Collection of Historic Musical Instruments.* Edinburgh: the collection, [1990?]. 168 p. OCLC #24698522

Meyers, Arnold. *Historic Musical Instruments in the Edinburgh University Collection: Catalogue of the Edinburgh University Collection of Historic Musical Instruments.* Edinburgh: Edinburgh University Collection of Historic Musical Instruments, [n.d.]. 69 p. Vol. 2— Pt. H — Fascicle. iii. Trumpets and trombones. 1993. OCLC #30813709

Michigan. University. *Stearns Collection of Musical Instruments. Catalogue of the Stearns Collection of Musical Instruments, 2d ed.* Ann Arbor, MI.: The University of Michigan, 1921. 1 p. l., [5]-276 p., 1 l. front. (port.) plates, plan. 26 cm. LC CALL NUMBER: ML462.S81 1921

Moege, Gary Ray. *A Catalog of the Alto Brass Instruments in the Arne B. Larson Collection of Musical Instruments.* Unpublished master's thesis. University of Oklahoma, Norman, 1985.

Montague, Jeremy. *The French Horn.* [S.l.]: Shire, 1990. [32] p. Cataloging in progress record OCLC #21560466

Musik Instrumenten Zeitung. Berlin [1898?-1941?]. Microfilm: New York Publich Library, 1987. 20 reels. Periodical. OCLC #19222104

Musical Instrument Collections in the British Isles. Winchester: Piccolo Press, 1990. 127 p.: ill., 1 map; 21 cm. LC CALL NUMBER: ML461.M87 1990

The New Grove Dictionary of Music and Musicians. Stanley Sadie, editor. London: MacMillan Press, 1980. 20 vols.

The New Grove Dictionary of Musical Instruments. London: Macmillan Press; New York, NY: Grove's Dictionaries of Music, c1984. 3 v.: ill.; 26 cm. LC CALL NUMBER: ML102.I5 N48 1984

Presto music times. *Musical Instruments at the World's Columbian Exposition. A Review of Musical Instruments, Publications and Musical Instrument Supplies of all kinds Exhibited.* Chicago, IL: Presto Co., 1895. [328] p. illus., ports. 27 cm. LC CALL NUMBER: ML462.P93

Reed, Charles Vandeveer. *A History of Band Instrument Manufacturing in Elkhart, Indiana.* iv, 90 l. Thesis (M.S.)—Butler University, 1953. OCLC #16909879

Renouf, Nicholas. *Musical Instruments in the Viennese Tradition, 1750-1850 ...* New Haven, Conn.: The Collection, c1981. 32 p.: ill.; 23 cm. LC CALL NUMBER: ML462.N44 Y32 1981

Ripin, Edwin M. *The Instrument Catalogs of Leopoldo Franciolini.* Hackensack, N.J.: J. Boonin, [1974]. xix, 201 p. illus., facsims. 28 cm. LC CALL NUMBER: ML427.F68 R6

Romain, Lawrence B. *A Guide to American Trade Catalogs 1744-1900.* New York: R. R. Bowker Company, 1960. pp. 243-250 (Chapter 36).

Sachs, Curt. *Sammlung alter Musikinstrumente bei der Staatlichen Hochschule für musik zu Berlin.* Berlin: J. Bard, 1922. viii p., 384 col. Two columns to the page. OCLC #2010280

Solomonson, Glen Terrance. *The History of the Tuba to 1860: a Study of the Development of the Tuba Through its Ancestors.* vi, 38, [9] l. Thesis (M.M.Ed.)—University of Louisville. Microfilm: Ann Arbor, Mich.: University Microfilm International, 1978. OCLC #6548842

Stewart, Gary M. *Keyed Brass Instruments in the Arne B. Larson Collection.* Vermillion, SD: The Shrine to Music Museum, ca. 1980. 34 p.

United States. Bureau of the Census. *Census of Manufactures: 1905.* Washington, DC.: U.S. Govt. print. off., 1907. 34 p. 32 x 24 cm. LC CALL NUMBER: ML3790.U7 C3

United States. Bureau of the Census. *Census of Manufactures: 1914.* Washington, DC.: U.S. Govt. print. off., 1918. 21 p. incl. tables. 31 cm. LC CALL NUMBER: HD9999.M8 U5 1914

Victoria and Albert Museum. *Catalogue of Musical Instruments. 2d ed.* London: H.M. Stationery Off.; [Palo Alto, Calif.: obtainable from Pendragon House], 1978-1985. 2 v.: ill.; 25 cm. LC CALL NUMBER: ML462.L6 V53 1978

Vienna. Kunsthistorisches Museum. *Sammlung Alter Musikinstrumente. Katalog der Sammlung Alter Musikinstrumente.* Wien: Kunsthistorisches Museum, 1966- 1 v. illus. 21 cm. LC CALL NUMBER: ML462.V4 K84

Willcutt, J. Robert. *The Musical Instrument Collector.* New York: Bold Strummer, c1978. 136 p., [32] leaves of plates: ill.; 22 cm. LC CALL NUMBER: ML406.W54 1978

Winterthur Museum. *Musical Instruments and Supplies.* New York: Clearwater Pub. Co., [1984?]. 76 microfiches. Reproduces the trade catalogs at the museum. OCLC #17718074

Wit, Paul de. *Berlin aus der Instrumenten-Sammlung.* Leipzig: [s.n.], 1892. 14 p. The pref. and the descriptive notes in German, French, and English. OCLC #10213590

Wit, Paul de. *Katalog des Musikhistorischen Museums...* Leipzig: P. de Wit, 1903. 207, [1] p. illus. 23 cm. LC CALL NUMBER: ML462.W82

Wurlitzer Company. [Records 1860-1984. 53 linear feet.] Inventory available in repository. OCLC #14638928

Yale Collection of Musical Instruments. *Checklist.* New Haven, CN: Yale University, 1968. 43 p. 21 cm. LC CALL NUMBER: ML30.4b no. 2361

Young, Phillip T. *The Look of Music: Rare Musical Instruments, 1500-1900.* Vancouver: Vancouver Museums & Planetarium Association; Seattle, Wash.: Distributed in the U.S. by the University of Washington Press, c1980. 240 p.: ill. (some col.); 29 cm. LC CALL NUMBER: ML462.Y68

Zeitschrift für Instrumentenbau. Leipzig: Paul de Wit, 1880-1943? Periodical. OCLC #10325251

CORRECTIONS TO CAPTIONS

The following comments supplement "Antique Brass Wind Instruments." Font sizes are inconsistent. Also, water keys are not always visible in original illustrations resulting in inconsistent use of "water key" in book. HD and Helicon shape are used interchangeably.

Page 22:
Keyed bugle from: *Musical Instruments of the West*, p. 73
Mouthpiece not mouth piece
Shepherd's crook not Shephards crook
"Tuning slide" is the second U-shaped bend. Third valve slide is where "Tuning slide" is currently located
Cornet from Lyon & Healy's *Campaign Catalog* of 1896, p. 39

Page 23:
Stoelzel not Soelzel
Three views of European-style rotary valves
Artwork adapted from Curt Sach's *Sammlung alter Musikinstrumente*, p. 207

Page 24:
Inconsistent font sizes

Page 25:
Artwork from Robert E. Eliason's *Early American Brass Makers*, p. 45

Page 29:
Double and single French horns provided for comparison

Page 31:
Trombone provided for comparison

Page 33:
Suggestive not siggestive

Page 34:
[?] trombones are theater models

Page 35:
pseudo not psudo

Page 38:
Cornet in B flat, 3 + 1 SARV not 4 SARV
Cornet in B flat, BF, PV not SARV
Cornet in E flat, BF, 4 TARV not SARV

Page 39:
Both instruments are Tenor trombone in B flat ...
Page 41:
Bass in E flat, BU, 3 + 1 SARV not 4 SARV

Page 47:
[Tenor] trombone in [B flat], slide model
French horn in [F?], SARV
Bass in [EE flat], HD, SARV

Page 59:
Bass [in E flat], HD, PV, Highest grade, water key

Page 66:
Cornet in B flat, BF, PV, double water key, Number 5
Cornet in B flat, BF, Push rod rotary valves, water key, Number 6

Page 69:
Cornets Number 12, and 30 all have double water keys

Page 70:
All instruments appear to have water keys

Page 72:
Tenor trombone in B flat, BF, PV, water key, Number 658
Tenor trombone in B flat, BF, slide model, water key, Number 667

Page 74:
Bass in EE flat, BU, TARV, Number 5028

Page 75:
All instruments on page have water keys

Page 76:
Instruments Number 5067, 5124, 5127, 5133 all have water keys

Page 79:
Tenor trombone not [Tenor?] trombone

Page 80:
Bass in BB flat, BU, PV, Number 100
Bass in B flat, BU, 3 + 1 PV, Number 104

Page 81:
Cornet in B flat, BF, SARV, Number 47

Page 82:
Bass trombone in B flat, BF, slide model, Number 34
French horn in F, SARV, Number 35

Page 83:
Bass in E flat, HD, SARV, Number 42 not Bass in B flat ...

Page 84
Bass in EE flat, HD, SARV, Number 43 not Contrabass in E flat ...

Page 87:
Cornet in B flat, BF, PV, double water key, Number 903
Cornet in E flat, BF, BPV, water key, Number 50
Cornet in B flat, BF, BPV, water key, Number 51

Page 88 through 95:
All instruments have water keys
Cornet in B flat, BF, PV, double water key, Number 460
Cornet in B flat, PV, PV, double water key, Number 475

Page 95:
Missing caption.
Cornet in B flat, BF, PV, water key, Number 375